James Kendall Hosmer

The Jews

In ancient, mediaeval and modern Times

James Kendall Hosmer

The Jews
In ancient, mediaeval and modern Times

ISBN/EAN: 9783337138073

Printed in Europe, USA, Canada, Australia, Japan

Cover: Foto ©ninafisch / pixelio.de

More available books at **www.hansebooks.com**

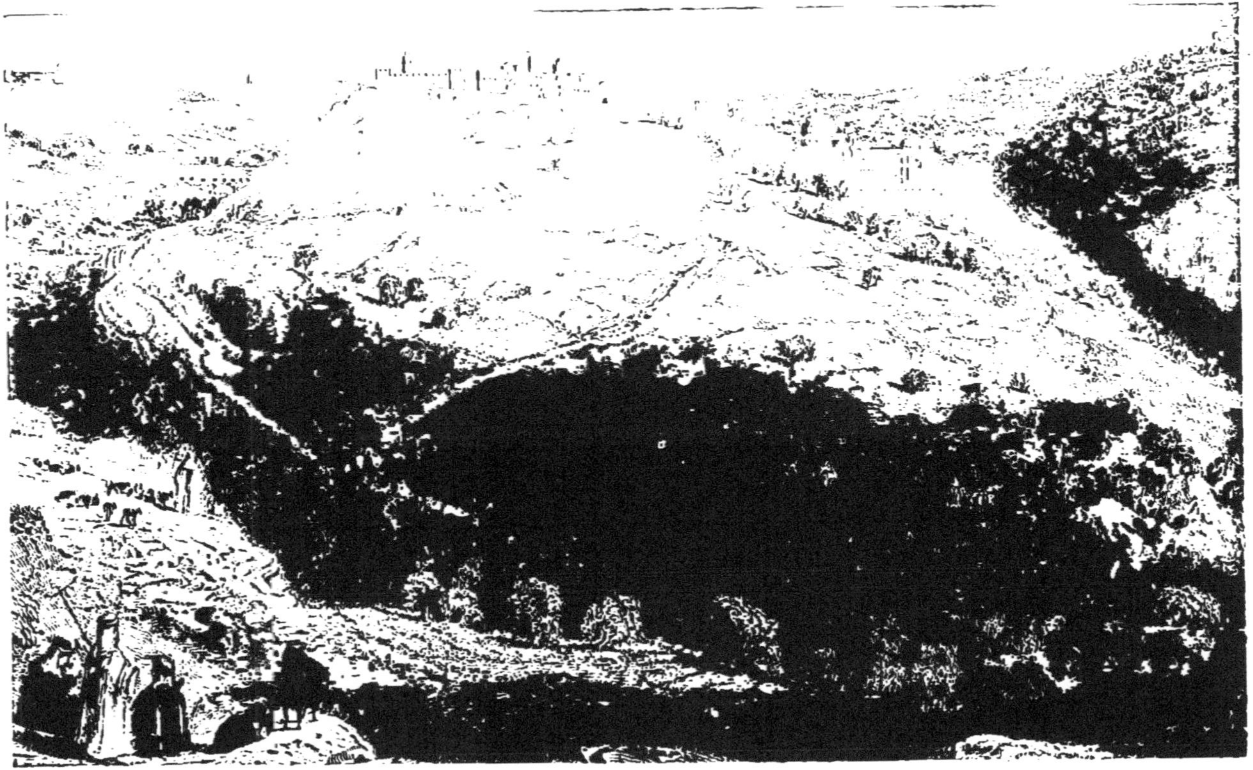

Frontispiece. JERUSALEM FROM THE HILL OF EVIL COUNSEL.

THE JEWS

IN ANCIENT, MEDIÆVAL AND
MODERN TIMES

BY

JAMES K. HOSMER

PROFESSOR IN WASHINGTON UNIVERSITY; AUTHOR OF "A SHORT HISTORY OF
GERMAN LITERATURE," ETC.

London
T FISHER UNWIN
26 PATERNOSTER SQUARE
MDCCCLXXXVI

PREFACE.

To write "The Story of the Jews" for the series in which it is to appear has been a task beset with certain special embarrassments.

In the first place, it may reasonably be doubted whether a faithfully related story of the Jews is suitable reading for immature minds. The prudent parent shrinks from putting into the hands of his child Hamlet, or Lear, or Othello. In the first, the terrible soul agony,—in the second, the ruthless exercise of the most savage passions,—in the third, the malignant, snake-like craft crushing in its folds unsuspecting manly worth and womanly loveliness,—this tragedy of the deepest requires full maturity in order that its lessons may be intelligently received and its power fully realized. Such literature is meat for men, not milk for babes; and it is quite premature to undertake it, until experience has thoroughly settled the character. Has not history as well as poetry its tragedies quite too sombre for childhood,—and among its tragedies is there any quite so dark as the story of the Jews? Where else are problems presented which so defy satisfactory solution? Where else is it necessary to contemplate the play of spiritual forces so tremendous? Where else is there anguish so deep and long-continued?

A second embarrassment arises from the fact that in the story of the Jews many points are presented with regard to which the feelings of men are so keen and at the same time so conflicting. To-day, throughout the civilized world, many regard the Hebrews with dislike, perhaps aversion, as an unattractive, indeed a dangerous element in society. Certainly this story cannot be written without demonstrating to how large an extent this prejudice is cruel and unjust, however inveterate and explicable,—an effort which is certain, in some quarters, to be ill taken. As regards the ancient period, can the account be given without some attempt to separate fact from myth,—to circumscribe within just limits the natural and the supernatural; and can such discriminations be attempted without giving offence in one quarter or another? Protestant, Catholic, Rationalist, Jew, have, each one, his peculiar point of view,—and each one, if he is at all earnest, regards the matters in dispute as things by no means far off, but of vital, present importance.

The writer of this volume has dealt with these embarrassments as well as he could. As to the first, interpreting in a liberal way his commission "to write a story for the young," he has tried to adapt his chapters to those in the later stages of youth,— to those, indeed, already standing upon the threshold of maturity. Prominence has been given to the more picturesque and dramatic features of the record. The profundities are only touched upon; the mysteries of the Cabala, and the inspiration that may lie within the fantastic rhapsodizing of the Talmudists, no attempt has been made to fathom. At the same time, there has been no effort to dwarf and emasculate the absorbing account into the dimensions of a proper "juvenile." Here are details of exterminating warfare, of sharpest torture, of bitterest cursing. Here are presented sages as they study the darkest problems,—poets, as they thrill the human heart-strings with marvellous, subtle power;— characters shining in the very beauty of holiness,— characters, too, black with malignity most appalling. All this stands in the record: to present Israel faithfully, these traits must be given, and the attempt has been made to present Israel faithfully. A tale, it is, full of thrilling fascination and fruitful in instruction; a tale, however, that sobers and that requires soberness in its readers,—the ripeness which comes when childhood has been left behind.

As regards the second embarrassment, it will be at once apparent to the reader that the writer feels that Israel, among the nations, should be regarded with reverence, even with awe, in times modern as well as ancient. In what sense the Hebrews are the chosen people of God,—whether the special protection of Heaven supposed to be extended in ancient times has lasted to the present hour,— whether the sufferings of the race for eighteen centuries are due to the crime committed upon Calvary,—these are questions to which an answer has not been attempted. Among the ancient traditions—whether Heliodorus was driven away from the Temple treasures by Heaven-

sent messengers; whether David heard the voice of
God in the rustling of the balsam-trees; whether the
sun and moon stood still at Joshua's command, or the
angel of the Lord really smote the host of Sennacherib,—such legends as these are given as they
stand, with no effort to separate the nucleus of
reality from the accretions of fable. The writer
cannot hope to escape the condemnation of some
critics, perhaps of all. The Supernaturalist will
probably find him too indifferent to the miraculous;
the Rationalist, too lenient toward ancient superstitions; the Jew, not sufficiently cognizant of the
divine mission of Israel upon the earth. The writer
can only trust that while dealing with subjects in
which the feelings of multitudes are so deeply en-
listed and on such opposite sides, he may at least
escape the charge of flippancy and irreverence. While
the account in the case of many a comparatively insignificant figure is given with considerable detail,
the narrative of the Gospels is presented only in outline. That tale, the possession as it is of every
memory, it has been thought unnecessary to give
with fulness. At the same time it will be evident, it
is hoped, that the figure of Jesus has been regarded
as possessing sublime, overshadowing importance
among those who have come forth from Israel.

As to authorities, the foot-notes must be consulted.
The effort has been made to become acquainted with
every thing of value contained in our tongue, but the
French and the Germans have worked this mine far
more thoroughly. In particular, use has been made
of the great work of Graetz, "Geschichte des Juden-

thums," and of the work of Reinach, "Histoire des Israélites depuis leur Dispersion jusqu' à nos Jours," which appeared in Paris just in time to be made available for this book. Many a picturesque passage has been derived from Heinrich Heine, an apostate from Israel, whose soul, however, always yearned toward the mother whom he had spurned. The vivid portrayal of the circumstances of mediæval Jewish life, given in chapter XI., is an adaptation from his incomplete novel, "The Rabbi of Bacharach," combined with facts derived from Graetz. It enters with profound sympathy and thorough learning into the atmosphere that surrounded the persecuted Hebrews of that sombre time.

In conclusion, while acknowledging obligation to many helpers, the writer desires in a special way to thank Rabbi S. H. Sonnenschein, of St. Louis, and Dr. Abraham S. Isaacs, of the *Jewish Messenger*, of New York, for suggestions and books, which have been of great value to him in his work.

J. K. H.

St. Louis, *November*, 1885.

CLASSIFIED CONTENTS.

PART I.

THE ANCIENT PRIDE.

I.

WHY THE STORY OF THE JEWS IS PICTURESQUE . 1–8

Hebrew assertions of the greatness of their race, 1—The Christian view, 2—The Rationalist's view, 3—Remarkable character of Hebrew literature, 3—Tenacity of Hebrew national life, 4—Purity and solidarity of the race, 5—Their spiritual force as shown in love and hate, 6—Intensity of Hebrew piety, 7—Position of the Jews unique among races of men, 8.

II.

THE MORNING-TIME IN PALESTINE . . . 9–28

Physical characteristics of Palestine, 9—The Jordan, Sea of Galilee, Dead Sea, 10—The fertility of the land, 10—Antiquity of the Jewish stock, 12—The Patriarchs, 12—Moses leads Israel out of Egypt, 14—Worship of one God, 16—The ark of the covenant, 16—The Canaanites, 18—Career of the Judges, 18—Saul and David, 20—Solomon, 22—Building of the Temple, 23—Its dedication, 24—Decline of Hebrew vigor, 25—The two kingdoms, Judah and Israel, 26—The Assyrians, 27.

III.

ISRAEL AT NINEVEH 29–45

Legend of Semiramis, 29—Assyrian sculptures in the British Museum, 30—Authorities for Assyrian study, 32—Cities as

x   THE STORY OF THE JEWS.

PAGE

libraries, 33, 34—Antiquities of Mesopotamia, 35—Niebuhr, Botta, Layard, 36—The Cuneiform, 36—Nature of Assyrian dominion, 37—Palestine overcome, 38—Accession of Sennacherib, 39—His splendor and power, 40, 41, 42—An Assyrian palace, 43, 44—Refinement at Nineveh, 45.

IV.

THE DESTRUCTION OF SENNACHERIB . . 46–56

State of the Assyrian kings, 46—The Medes and Phœnicians subjected, 47—Judah overwhelmed, 48—The battle-order, 49, 50—Hebrew defiance, 52—Isaiah's prophecy, 53—Its fulfilment, 53—Fall of Assyria, 54—Permanence of its memorials, 55—Its cruel sway, 56.

V.

JUDAS MACCABÆUS, THE HEBREW WILLIAM TELL, 57–73

The captivity at Babylon, 57—The return from the Babylonian exile, 58—Alexander the Great at Jerusalem, 60—The Jew meets the Aryan, 61—Who the Aryans were, 62, 63—Palestine under the Seleucidæ, 64—The revolt of Mattathias, 65—First victories of Judas Maccabæus, 66, 67—The Temple purified and restored, 68—Judas subdues the Idumæans and Ammonites, 68—Heroism of his brethren, 68—Death of Eleazar, 69—Judas defeated and slain by Bacchides, 69—Alliance with Rome, 70—The later Asmonæans, 71—Heliodorus tries to rob the Temple, 72—The coming of the Romans, 73.

VI.

THE BEAUTY OF HOLINESS 74–93

Condition of the Jews after the time of the Maccabees, 74—Ezra establishes the Canon, 75, 76—The Septuagint and Targums, 76—The oral Law, 77—Sadducees and Pharisees, 78, 79—The Essenes, 80—Hillel and his followers, 81—The Samaritans, 82—Jewish religious observances, 83—Feasts and fasts, 84—Expectations of a Messiah, 85—Birth of Jesus, 86—His life and work, 87, 88, 89—The disciples go forth, 90—Conversion of Saul, 90—The beauty of Christian holiness, 92, 93.

VII.

VESPASIAN AND JOSEPHUS 94–107

Gessius Florus marches against Jerusalem, 94—His failure, 95—Josephus defends Galilee against Vespasian, 95—The siege of Jotapata, 96, 97, 98—Jotapata captured, 99—Josephus a captive, 100—Vespasian emperor, 100—Description of Jerusalem, 102—The Temple, 103—The Antonia, 104—The walls, 106—Portents of ill omen, 106.

VIII.

TITUS ON THE RUINS OF ZION . . . 108–129

Titus marches against Jerusalem, 108—His formidable host, 109—Factions among the Jews, 109—John of Giscala and the Zealots, 110—Simon, son of Gioras, 111—Narrow escape of Titus, 111—The tenth legion in danger, 112—The "Conqueror" makes a breach, 114—Capture of the outer walls, 114—Appalling condition of the defenders, 115—John and Simon undismayed, 116—Destruction of the Antonia, 117—Capture of the Temple and of the upper city, 118—Death of John of Giscala, imprisonment of Simon, and sufferings of the Jews, 119—Incidents of the siege, 120—Return of Titus to Rome, 121—His magnificent triumph, 122—Death of Simon Gioras, 123—Arch of Titus, 124—Spiritual conquest of the Aryan by the Jew, 126, 127, 128—The apotheosis of Jesus of Nazareth, 129.

PART II.

THE MEDIÆVAL HUMILIATION.

IX.

HOW THE RABBIS WROUGHT THE TALMUD 133–151

The revolt of Bar Cocheba, 133—Ælia Capitolina and the Jewish dispersion, 133—Gentile persecution and Hebrew scorn, 134—How the Jews became traders, 136—Their services and high character in commerce, 137—Jew and Moslem, 138—Charlemagne, 139—Famous persecutors, 140

—Deserts of the Hebrews, 140—Origin of the Talmud, 141
—Mischna and Gemara, 142—Value of the Talmud, 143—
Difficulty of understanding it, 144—Its wisdom and beauty,
145, 146—Sandalphon, 146, 147—The Karaites, 148—
Hygienic value of Talmud and Torah, 148—Maimonides,
149, 150.

X.

THE HOLOCAUSTS IN SPAIN 152–164

The "Sephardim," 152—Insincere conversions, 153—A
Jewish shrine, 154—The Inquisition, 155—Torture chambers, 156—Sufferings of Hebrews, 157—Ferdinand and Isabella resolve upon expulsion, 158—The departure of the
exiles, 159—Dreadful hardships, 160—Lamentations, 161—
An *auto-da-fé*, 162, 163.

XI.

THE BLOODY HAND IN GERMANY . . . 165–188

A synagogue on the Rhine, 165—The Juden-gasse at Frankfort, 166—The Black Death and the Flagellants, 167—Jews
on the Rhine, 168—Story of Rabbi Abraham and Sarah,
169, etc.—A passover celebration, 170, 171—The plot to
destroy, 172, 173—Flight of Abraham and Sarah, 174—
Down the Rhine, 176, 177—A mediæval city, 179, 180—
The Jewish quarter, 181—The synagogue, 182—The service,
183—The roll of the Law, 184—The massacre, 186—The
flight to Turkey, 188.

XII.

THE FROWN AND THE CURSE IN ENGLAND,
ITALY, AND FRANCE 189–202

Persecution in England, 189—Protection extended by early
Plantagenets, 189—Suffering in time of Richard Cœur de
Lion, 190—Tragedy of York, 191—Banishment by Edward
I. and restoration by Cromwell, 192—The drowning in the
Thames, 192—Comparative mildness of Italian powers, 193
—Antiquity of Jewish colony in Rome, 194—Varying treatment of the popes, 195—The Jews in Southern Italy and

Sicily, 195, 196—Persecution in France, 197—Philip Augustus and Saint Louis, 197—Philip the Fair and the Pastoureaux, 198—A burning in France, 199—The cry "Hep! hep!" 200—Jewish badges, 201—Protestant narrowness, Luther, and the Puritans, 201—Gibbon, Voltaire, and Buckle, 202.

XIII.

SHYLOCK—THE WANDERING JEW . . . 203–214

Jewish retaliation, 203—What Shylock might have heard on the Rialto, 204, 205—Palliation for his cruelty, 206—Heine's idea of Shylock, 207—The Wandering Jew, different forms of the legend, 208, 209—Combined with the Wild Huntsman, 210, 211, 212—The Wandering Jew before the Matterhorn, 213.

XIV.

THE CASTING OUT OF A PROPHET . . . 215–231

The bitterness of Hebrew scorn, 215—False Messiahs, 216—Career of Sabbatäi Zevi, 217—Sabbatäi becomes a Mohammedan, 218—Holland as a refuge for the oppressed, 219—Birth and childhood of Spinoza, 220—He revolts at the Cabala, 222—His excommunication, 223—The curse, 224—His magnanimity, 226—His philosophy, 226, 227, 228—His fame, 229—His position in the history of modern thought, 230—Tributes to his greatness, 231.

PART III.

THE BREAKING OF THE CHAIN.

XV.

ISRAEL'S NEW MOSES 235–253

Number and distribution of the Jews at the present time, 235—Their eminence, 235—Their small achievement as soldiers, farmers, and handicraftsmen, 236—Prominence in trade and in music, 237—Wagner's hostility, 238—Prominence as scientists, philosophers, and writers, 238—Especial

xiv   THE STORY OF THE JEWS.

PAGE

narrowness of Germany toward the Jews, 239, 240—Birth and early career of Moses Mendelssohn, 242—Introduced to fame by Lessing, 243—" Phædo," 243—" Jerusalem," 244—Tribute of Kant, 245—Mendelssohn embarrassed by Lavater, 245—Letter to Lavater, 246, 247, 248—Mendelssohn's death, 248—His wooing, 249, 250—" Nathan the Wise," 251, 252, 253.

XVI.

THE MONEY KINGS 254–272

Business ability of Jews, 254—Cicero's condemnation of trade, 254—Ill-repute of Jews undeserved, 255, 256—They break a path for themselves, 258—Meyer Anselm Rothschild and the Landgrave of Hesse Cassel, 259—A great house founded, 260—Heine and Börne at the Hanoukhah in the Judengasse, 261—The mother of the Rothschilds and her five sons, 262—Nathan Meyer founds the London house, 263—How ten millions were made out of Waterloo, 263, 264, 265—Alleged rapacity of the Rothschilds, 266—Nathan Meyer's death, 267—Baron Lionel, 268—Baron James at Paris, 269—His brusque manners, 270—His fear of Heine, 271—Baron Alphonse, 272.

XVII.

SIR MOSES MONTEFIORE . . . 273–294

Were the Rothschilds honorable ? 273—Cicero on the morals of trade, 274—American rapacity, 275—The brothers Pereire, 276, 277—Sir Moses Montefiore as a typical Jew, 278—His origin and early career, 280—His philanthropic journeys, 281—Persecutions at Damascus and Rhodes in 1840, 282—Montefiore at Damascus, 282—Judith Montefiore, 283—Her diary, 284—Montefiore at Jerusalem, 286, 288—At Morocco, 288—Lands at Tangier, 289—Last visit to Jerusalem, 290—His practical good sense and breadth of mind, 292—His widespread fame and personal appearance, 293—An orthodox Jew, 293—Belief in the restoration of the Jews to Palestine, 294.

XVIII.

HEBREW STATESMEN 295–311

Eminence of Jews as Statesmen, 295—Castelar, Lasker, 295—Leads the national-liberty party in the German Parliament, 296—Achille Fould, Crémieux, Gambetta, 298—Gambetta's origin 298—Puts out an eye, becomes famous, 300—In the Corps Législatif, 301—His energy in 1870, 302—His oratory, 303, 304—Origin of Beaconsfield, 305—Beards Daniel O'Connell in Parliament, 306—Rises to fame, 308—His wife's devotion, 308—His enthusiasm for his race, 310, 311.

XIX.

A SWEET SINGER IN ISRAEL 312–329

Heine as the voice of the Jewish spirit, 312—His birth, 312—At Frankfort, Göttingen, and Berlin, 313—His apostasy and scoffing, 314—Becomes famous in prose and poetry, 316 The "mattress-grave," his death, 317—His descriptive power illustrated, 318—Picture of Napoleon, 319—His wit, 320—Scoffs at Germany, 321—His bitterness and want of earnestness, 322—His tenderness, 323—"Ilse," 324—Lines to his wife, 325—"Lorelei," 326—He utters the Hebrew soul, 327—Heine and the Venus of Milo, 328, 329.

XX.

SOME HARMONIOUS LIVES 330–354

Felix Mendelssohn Bartholdy, the type of the Hebrew artist, 330—The descendants of Moses Mendelssohn, 330—Career of Dorothea, 331—of Joseph and Abraham, 332—Abraham and Leah, the parents of Felix, 333—The father's idea of religious education, 334—Fanny Mendelssohn, 335—The mother's letter to her daughter's lover, 336—The Mendelssohn home, 337, etc.—Distinguished visitors, 339—Professors at fault, 340—Music of Mendelssohn, 342—His appearance, 342—Description in "Charles Auchester," 343, etc.—Fanny's concerts, 346—Beautiful family life, 347—Sojourn in Rome, 348, 349—The father in death, 349—Felix with Victoria and Prince Albert, 350, etc—Death of Felix and Fanny, 352—Ideal lives, 353.

XXI.

OUR HEBREW CONTEMPORARIES . . 355-370

Israelites feared, 355—Anti-Semitism in Germany, 356—Hebrew bitterness, 357—Attachment to old traditions and usages, 358—" The Jewish Cemetery at Newport," 359, 360—Jews in Poland, 361—" Measuring the bounds," 362—Story of Leah Rendar, 363—The apostate Jewess, 364, 365—Jews and Yankees, 366—Felix Adler on his countrymen, 367—The orthodox nucleus of Judaism, 368—The Reformers, 369.

LIST OF ILLUSTRATIONS.

	PAGE
MAP, COUNTRIES CONNECTED WITH EARLY JEWISH HISTORY	*Front lining*
MAP, CANAAN, AS DIVIDED AMONG THE TWELVE TRIBES	*Back lining*
JERUSALEM FROM THE HILL OF EVIL COUNSEL,	*Frontispiece*
MOUNT OF OLIVES FROM THE WALL	xx
JACOB AND RACHEL	11
JOSEPH INTERPRETING PHARAOH'S DREAM	13
MOSES IN BULRUSHES	15
PROBABLE ARRANGEMENT AND FORM OF THE TABERNACLE CAMP	17
THE SETTING UP OF THE TABERNACLE	19
THE RETURN OF THE ARK	21
JONAH CALLING NINEVEH TO REPENTANCE	31
JERICHO	51
THE REBUILDING OF THE TEMPLE	59
BETHLEHEM	87
THE SITE OF THE ANCIENT TEMPLE	91
THE SEA OF GALILEE	97
PLAN OF ANCIENT JERUSALEM	101
GRADUAL FORMATION OF JERUSALEM	105
JERUSALEM BESIEGED BY TITUS	113
ARCH OF TITUS	125
ROMAN MASONRY, JERUSALEM	135
JEWS' PLACE OF WAILING, JERUSALEM	187

xviii *THE STORY OF THE JEWS.*

	PAGE
THE WANDERING JEW	211
SPINOZA	211
MOSES MENDELSSOHN	241
IN THE FRANKFORT JUDEN-GASSE	257
NATHAN MEYER ROTHSCHILD	265
SIR MOSES MONTEFIORE	279
JERUSALEM FROM THE MOUNT OF OLIVES	285
VALLEY OF JEHOSHAPHAT OR KIDRON	287
THE GOLDEN GATE	291
LASKER	297
GAMBETTA	299
ISAAC DISRAELI	307
LORD BEACONSFIELD	309
HEINRICH HEINE	315
FELIX MENDELSSOHN	341

MOUNT OF OLIVES FROM THE WALL.

PART I.

THE ANCIENT PRIDE.

"If any reference is made to the Jews, some hearer is sure to state that she, for her part, is not fond of them, having known a Mr. Jacobson who was very unpleasant ; or that he, for his part, thinks meanly of them as a race, though, on inquiry, you find he is little acquainted with their characteristics. A people with Oriental sunlight in their blood, they have a force which enables them to carry off the best prizes. A significant indication of their natural rank is seen in the fact that, at this moment, the leader of the Liberal party in Germany is a Jew, the leader of the Republican party in France is a Jew, and the head of the Conservative ministry in England is a Jew. Tortured, flogged, spit upon,—their name flung at them as an opprobrium by superstition, hatred, and contempt,—how proud they have remained !" — GEORGE ELIOT ("Impressions of Theophrastus Such").

THE STORY OF THE JEWS.

CHAPTER I.

WHY THE STORY OF THE JEWS IS PICTURESQUE.

IN the fiftieth Psalm stands the passage: "Out of Zion, the perfection of beauty, God hath shined." If we understand the word Zion in this sentence to mean, as it is often explained, the Hebrew nation, we find here an enthusiastic utterance by a Jewish poet of his sense of pride in his race: the Hebrew people is chosen out from among the nations of the earth to exhibit the perfection of beauty,—is, in fact, an outshining of God himself upon the world.

What is to be said of such a declaration? If it were made concerning any other race than the Jewish, it would be scouted and ridiculed as arrogance pushed into impiety, a claim not to be tolerated even in the most impassioned poetry. Can the world bear the assertion any better when it is made concerning the Jews? Such claims, at any rate, the Jews have always made. Declarations of Israelitish greatness scarcely less strong than that of the Psalmist, can be found in the writings of our cotemporaries. Says a rabbi of Cincinnati in a book published within a few years: "Had the Hebrews not been disturbed in their progress a thousand and more years ago, they would have solved all the great problems of civilization which are being solved now." The Earl of Beaconsfield, glorying in his Jewish blood, was accustomed to maintain, without qualification, the indomitable superiority of the Hebrews over the most powerful modern races, and alleged that in an intellectual sense they had conquered modern Europe. In the immense extent of time which stretches from the singer of the Psalms to the Cincinnati rabbi and the marvellous Jew who, a few years ago, superintended the management of the greatest empire of the earth, there is no age in which Israelites have not uttered just as confidently their conviction of Jewish supremacy.

In what way are we who are without trace of Semitic blood to treat these claims of our Hebrew neighbors? In the Christian world it has been customary, as far as the assertions of superiority relate to antiquity, to concede every thing. It is part of the Christian faith, in fact, to believe that the Jews were the chosen people of God, selected from among the races of the earth to be the subjects of a special covenant, guided through ages by successive supernatural revelations from Heaven, their history set with miracles, their poets inspired prophets, the royal house of David at length giving birth to a child in whom the Deity himself became flesh and dwelt with men. Here, however, the Christian pauses. The incarnate God was rejected by the very people among whom he chose to appear. They should have adored ; they preferred to crucify. In penalty for this they have undergone for eighteen centuries the most unexampled punishment,—suffering and humiliation not less extreme than their previous exaltation. Such is the sentence imposed upon them by inexorable justice as a penalty for the worst of crimes.

But not all are Christian believers, even in countries nominally Christian. We find, besides, a class whom for convenience' sake we may designate as rationalists, and what treatment will Jewish assertions of supremacy receive from these? Even though we should deny all the supernatural claims made in behalf of the Hebrews, there is still much reason for holding them to be an extraordinary people. Not for numbers certainly, for at no time have they been numerous; not for the extent of their territorial dominion, for their empire, even in the days of its greatest extension, covered only a tract which afterwards formed but a small part of the successive empires of Macedonian, Roman, and Turk. But how wonderful in words—how wonderful in deeds! Even if we should reject the idea of divine inspiration, how extraordinary is the ancient literature of the race! In originality, poetic strength, and religious importance, it surpasses that of all other nations. The old Hebrew writers seldom employ their genius upon any trifling matter, but occupy themselves with the most momentous questions of life; as if, persuaded that God himself had dignified the characters of their language by tracing them with his finger upon tablets of stone, they dared not employ an alphabet so consecrated upon any frivolous theme.

Give a comprehensive glance at the career of the Jews. It is the marvel of history that this little people, beset and despised by all the earth for ages, maintains its solidarity unimpaired. Unique among all the peoples of the earth, it has come undoubtedly to the present day from the most distant antiquity. Forty, perhaps fifty, centuries rest upon this venerable cotemporary of Egypt, Chaldea, and Troy. The Hebrew defied the Pharaohs; with the sword of Gideon he smote the Midianite; in Jephthah, the children of Ammon. The purple chariot-bands of Assyria went back from his gates humbled and diminished. Babylon, indeed, tore him from his ancient seats and led him captive by strange waters, but not long. He had fastened his love upon the heights of Zion, and like an elastic cord, that love broke not, but only drew with the more force as the distance became great. When the grasp of the captor weakened, that cord, uninjured from its long tension, drew back the Hebrew to his former home. He saw the Hellenic flower bud, bloom, and wither upon the soil of Greece. He saw the wolf of Rome suckled on the banks of the Tiber, then prowl, ravenous for dominion, to the ends of the earth, until paralysis and death laid hold upon its savage sinews. At last Israel was scattered over the length and breadth of the earth. In every kingdom of the modern world there has been a Jewish element. There are Hebrew clans in China, on the steppes of Central Asia, in the desert heart of Africa. The most powerful races have not been able to assimilate them,—the bitterest persecution, so far from exterminating them, has not eradicated a single characteristic. In mental and moral traits, in form and feature, even, the Jew to-day is the same as when Jerusalem was the peer of Tyre and Babylon. In the greedy energy of the Jewish trader smoulders something of the old fire of the Maccabees. Abraham and Mordecai stand out upon the sculptures of Nineveh marked by the same eye and beard, the same nose and jaw by which we just now recognized their descendants. Language, literature, customs, traditions, traits of character, —these, too, have all survived. The Jew of New York, Chicago, St. Louis, is, in body and soul, the Jew of London, of St. Petersburg, of Constantinople, of the fenced cities of Judah in the days of David. There is no other case of a nation dispersed in all parts of the world and yet remaining a nation. Says Mr. E. A. Freeman: "They are very nearly, if not absolutely, a pure race in a sense in which no other human race is pure. Their blood has been untouched by conversion, even by intermarriage." It is an asbestos, which no fire of hate or love has been hot enough to consume. Many a Jew still looks to the old home of his race with affection abated by no single particle, and anticipates a joyful time when the throne of Jacob shall again be established upon Zion. They cling with startling tenacity to every element of nationality. Their history is like a great bear-baiting, in which every nation has figured among the bull-dogs, but with bite after bite of outrage and contumely, all have not been able to drive the life out of their Judæan prey.

Who will deny to the Jews pre-eminent force of passion and intellect in the most various directions? The skilful writer of fiction to-day, who depicts a Jewish personage, feels that at any rate the character must be made intense. A weak Jew would be the greatest contradiction of probability. Whether he loves or hates, he must go to extremes. We instinctively feel that no object is so cherished as that toward which the affection of the Jew is turned, whether it be parent or child, wife or friend. How Isaac of York in "Ivanhoe" defies the torturers as he thinks of Rebecca! How burning the charity of Nathan in the masterpiece of Lessing! What strange persistent ardor in Mordecai pouring inspiration into the soul of Daniel Deronda!

Nor does the world see elsewhere perhaps such capacity for malevolence. What scorn and scowl has the Hebrew had for the rest of the earth! The land which fell especially under his malediction, like Samaria, if human maledictions could blast, would have found the grass withering in its fields, and the water in its bosom. Perhaps avarice never wears its most hideous aspect except in the soul of the Jew. The pursuit to which oppression for ages restricted him, has exposed him peculiarly to be the prey of this vice. In the popular idea, the Jew is the embodiment of covetousness, and perhaps into no other soul does the love of gain eat with such bitter and deep corrosion; Fagin and Shylock are types as artistic as they are tremendous. Bad passions rage most violently in strong souls, as certain fevers are said to display their full force only in vigorous physical frames.

But not in the direction of earthly love or hate, of avarice or patriotism, has the force of the Hebrew nature exerted itself most strikingly. When it has been directed toward heavenly objects, it has constituted the most fervent piety which the world has ever seen. Those majestic prophets of old are counterparts of their countrymen to-day, only in them the national force shot strongly upward. They grasped heavenly things so vividly that even their bodily senses seemed to lay hold of God and angels. Spiritual presences faced the bodily sight in wilderness or burning bush, or above the ark of the covenant. The earthly ear caught tones from the other world in some still small voice, or pealing from a bare mountain peak. And here it is that the Jew has accomplished his most extraordinary achievement. His faith furnished the stock upon which Mahomet grafted the creed of Islam,—upon which one mightier than he fixed a scion, whose leaves, as the branch has extended itself, have been for the healing of the nations.

So stands the Jew to-day—his astonishing history behind him, his soul alight with such extraordinary fire, and set off with such intense, picturesque traits. What other human type has such vividness and color! It is not altogether surprising arrogance then when the Jew lays claim to a remarkable eminence. The Christian and the rationalist, on different grounds to be sure, are ready to say that there has been nothing in the world so wonderful as the career of the Israelitish nation. Certainly no intelligent man can fail to see with Freeman that the phenomenon of the Jewish race is one of the strangest in history. The more it is thought of, the more its utter strangeness appears—that its position is completely unique. To attempt some sketch of the progress of this people during its long history, to depict its ancient state, to sketch the depth of humiliation through which it has been forced to pass, and the signs that can now be discerned that it is about to issue into a time of extraordinary triumph,—this certainly is a theme of interest.

CHAPTER II.

THE MORNING-TIME IN PALESTINE.

THE southwestern corner of Syria, known as Palestine, the Holy Land, is a country small in extent. Its boundaries are somewhat indefinite; for in different ages the power of the Hebrews was extended now over a greater, now over a smaller tract. It was about one sixth as large as England, scarcely larger, in fact, than the State of Massachusetts. From a high mountain peak in the centre, it would be quite easy for an observer in a clear day to behold on every side the most distant limits—to the south the ranges bordering upon Arabia, to the north the summits of Lebanon; the Mediterranean to the west would seem not far distant; so, too, the unproductive steppes into which, on the eastern frontier, the pasture lands are gradually merged. Short as the journey would be between the farthest points, consuming scarcely half a day with our ways of travel, great contrasts of scenery would be encountered. The lofty mountains of Lebanon rise far toward the line of eternal snow, their flanks are covered with forests, the elevated valleys with the vegetation of high latitudes. Passing south from these, while the country remains hilly, fruitful plains frequently occur, extending to the margin of the western sea. In the south the land wears a look less hospitable; the desert lies close at hand, and already vast wastes of sand are seen, crossed by lines of hills upon which grows no tree or blade of grass. From the northern uplands a tumultuous river, the Jordan, makes it way in cataracts and rapids to the lower levels. Early in its course it rests in a tranquil expanse of water known anciently as the Lake of Merom. Midway, again, the floods pause in the Sea of Tiberias, also called Gennesereth and Galilee. At last, in the south, the turbulent stream cuts its way deep through the land to lose itself in a gloomy lake, sunk far beneath the level of the ocean, whose brackish waters and sulphurous shores have caused it to be called the Dead Sea.

Palestine is still, in parts, a beautiful land. A traveller arriving at certain seasons of the year from the dreary regions to the south and east, at the rich central fields and green northern valleys, even now might greet it as the land of promise. It is capable of being redeemed in great part to luxuriance. In ancient times before its resources had become wasted and when it was held by free and thrifty tribes, it is easy to understand how it could be said to flow with milk and honey. In the harvest time great tracts, no doubt, waved with corn. Up the sunny slopes, in terrace over terrace, smiled the vineyards. Olive forests everywhere bore rich burdens of fruit. Groves of palm rose where in the lowlands the breath of the south could be fully felt; while the high ledges of the northern hills were fringed

JACOB AND RACHEL.

with mighty cedars. There were abundant pastures white with flocks; there were balm-fields on the plain of Sharon; in Bashan was the lowing of innumerable herds; the grapes of Eshcol ripened into such clusters that even the shoulders of strong men found them a heavy burden. This land of promise the children of Israel at length, after a severe struggle, possessed, and for many centuries it continued to be their home.

The Israelites, Hebrews, or Jews, as the race is indifferently called, belong to the great Semitic branch of the human family, long believed to be descended from the eldest son of Noah, Shem. Since the lapse of time which we have to consider is so vast, much of the history of the Hebrews must be passed over in most rapid review. If we date the origin of the Jews at the time when Abram went southward from Haran, we are taken back to a most remote past. As the mists of the morning time arise, a group of allied tribes, Moabites, Edomites, Ammonites, and Israelites, may be descried in Southern Palestine, of which group the Israelites are found in the territory extending westward. About 1500 B.C. we can trace the Israelites in Goshen, fertile pasture lands in northern Egypt, where they acknowledge the dominion of the Pharaohs, but retain their own manners and institutions. The patriarchs Isaac and Jacob have played their part. Joseph, sold into bondage, has found favor in the eyes of the splendid monarch. Mindful of his brethren, he withdraws them from the outer desert and gives

JOSEPH INTERPRETING PHARAOH'S DREAM.

them pleasant seats in the plain watered by the beautiful river, where instead of the famine which has constantly threatened them, they enjoy a perpetual abundance among the Egyptian flesh-pots. At length come darker days. Rulers succeed who forget the hospitality of their predecessors. The Hebrew strangers are reduced to slavery, in which state they languish, until beneath the blow of Moses the Egyptian task-master is smitten to the earth. The bold rebel develops presently into a national champion and leader, to whom the oppressed people surrender their hearts. The Red Sea is passed and Pharaoh is overwhelmed in the pursuit. The Law is given at Sinai, followed by the long wandering in the desert. Moses, his aged eyes refreshed on Mount Pisgah by the sight of the promised land, goes to his rest in the sepulchre over against Beth-Peor, whose place no man knoweth unto this day; and the people pass into Canaan, finding homes in the south, not far from those of their ancestors, in the days before the sojourn on the Nile.

Up to this time we see in Israel no settled nation. In the day of Moses the old patriarchal system of families and clans prevailed ; the people was an unorganized collection of tribes of the same stock, but not at all closely combined. The authority of Moses came from his success in leading them out of Egypt. He established the holy administration of the Law or Torah, an institution which preceded a formal polity, but at length came to serve as the foundation pillar upon which the state rested. The basis of the unity which prevailed from the earliest

MOSES IN THE BULRUSHES.

times in Israel was an intense conviction in their breasts that they were the chosen people of that one God whom alone they recognized, Jehovah. As they entered Palestine, his sanctuary was established at Kadesh Barnea where usually stood the sacred ark of the covenant. The camp, however, it has been said, was the "smithy in which the tribes were destined to be welded into a nation,"* and the ark of the covenant, carried by the hands of the Levites, was the standard, which the Hebrews bore in their midst as they entered upon their conquests.

According to Josephus, the ark was a shrine of precious wood, five spans in length, three spans in breadth, and three in height. It was covered with gold, both within and without, so that the wooden part was not seen. A lid united to the side by golden hinges closed the casket; in each side were fastened two golden rings, through which gilded bars were passed, that it might be borne upon the shoulders of the priests. Upon the cover were two cherubim, flying creatures, their form not like to any of the creatures which men have seen, though Moses said he had seen such creatures near the throne of God. The ark contained the two tables of stone, brought down from Sinai by Moses, upon which were inscribed the ten commandments. On the march, the tribe of Levi was the especial guard of the ark, which was borne in the centre of the people. On the east proceeded Judah, on the south, Reuben, on the west, Ephraim, on the north, Dan, each tribe beneath the banner marked with its en-

* Wellhausen.

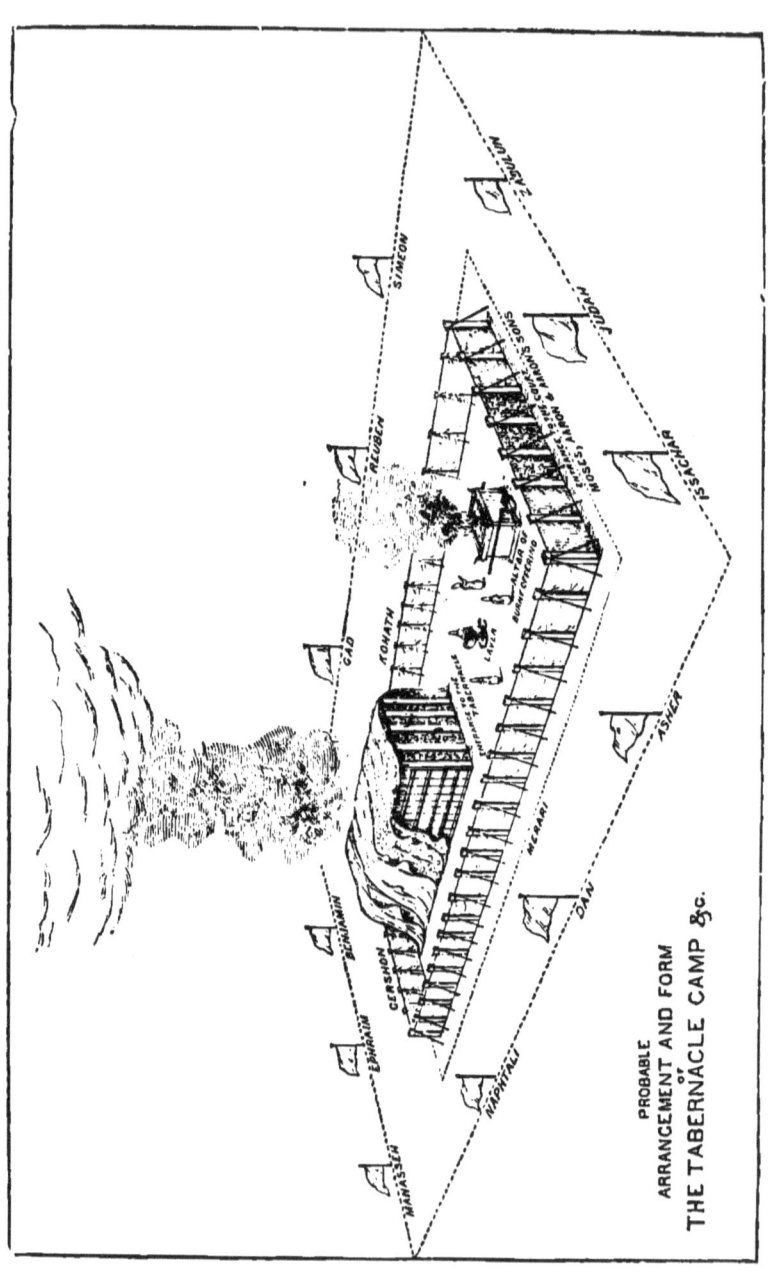

PROBABLE ARRANGEMENT AND FORM OF THE TABERNACLE CAMP &c.

sign. When in camp, the ark rested in the Holy of Holies of the Tabernacle, in the midst of the tribes, each in its fixed place. The Canaanites, against whom the Israelites went, were a people superior to them in numbers, perhaps also in civilization. These they did not extirpate, but subdued and absorbed, deriving their power to do so from the fierce conviction which inspired them, that they among all the races of the earth were the especial favorites of Heaven.

Joshua, Gideon, Jephthah, show their prowess. The tribes of Simeon and Levi undergo annihilation; Judah is hard pressed, but maintains itself at last through the might of Caleb. The south of Palestine is gained; at length, the central plateau, and the ark is brought from its sanctuary on the borders of the desert northward to Shiloh. The Canaanites, at discord among themselves, oppose but feebly. The north at length is laid open by the defeat of the king of Hazor at Lake Merom. Sisera for a time is formidable, but Deborah fires the hearts of her countrymen; a new leader is found in Barak, and the Canaanite dies with the nail of Jael driven into his temple. A more terrible enemy from the towns of the coast at last threatens. The Philistines overpower even Samson, and are victorious on the plains of Sharon, carrying devastation even to Shiloh, and bearing away the ark of the covenant. A great exaltation of religious feeling pervades the Hebrews at the desecration. It expresses itself in songs and dances; the tribes are full of frenzy to redeem themselves from such humiliation. Through the proph-

THE SETTING UP OF THE TABERNACLE

et Samuel, the champion Saul is discovered. A giant in form, and of a fiery disposition, he wins victory, and is anointed king in the ancient camp of Joshua at Gilgal. Jonathan, his son, assisted by his armor-bearer only, drives the Philistines into retreat. But a greater leader is at hand. A smooth stone from the sling of a Hebrew youth smites in the forehead the giant of Gath, and David stands revealed.

Through him the foes from the coast are beaten and humbled. The ark is brought back, to the joy of the people. The Lord stands on the side of Israel. David hears him in the rustling of the leaves of the balsam-trees, close at his hand. One of the Hebrew captains brandishes his spear over eight hundred slaughtered foes; another wields his sword until his hand grows rigid about the hilt and cannot be unclasped. "The king was in an hold and garrison of the Philistines, and longed and said: 'Oh, that one would give me a drink of the water of the well of Bethlehem, which is by the gate!'" Then three mighty men, Adino, Eleazar, and Shammah, brake through the host of the Philistines, and drew water out of the well of Bethlehem that was by the gate, and took it and brought it to David. Then the king would not drink thereof, but poured it out unto the Lord, saying: "Is not this as it were the blood of the men that went in jeopardy of their lives?" Thus, in undoubting confidence that Jehovah is with them, the Hebrews, with valiant deeds and great sacrifices, fight on. The country to the north is to a large extent subjected. The mountain fortress of the Jebusites is seized, destined to become

THE RETURN OF THE ARK.

Jerusalem, the most famous city of the world. Moab, Ammon, and Edom, to the south and east, are subdued; the recovered ark finds a new sanctuary upon Mt. Zion; the Hebrew power is at its height.

With the close of David's career, a period was reached when the character of the Hebrews underwent a certain change. Up to that time their hold upon Palestine had been precarious; each Israelite had been compelled to be a soldier, prepared by force of arms to resist opposition in every quarter. With Canaan subjugated, however, a time had come for attention to the arts of peace. The woodmen upon Lebanon felled timber for the architects, who built new cities as the people multiplied. The waters of Merom and Galilee yielded a harvest to the fishermen. The vineyards flourished, the broad cornfields upon the plains were tilled by hands that had turned the sword into the plough-share. An unwholesome contagion, moreover, from luxurious neighbors on the borders began to sap the ancient Hebrew vigor, and a dangerous tolerance came to be shown toward the strange gods of the Gentiles. In these times were heard in the land the voices of the prophets, men who were believed to receive into their souls special messages from Jehovah; their venerable forms, on the mountain-side, in the market-place, on the highroad, now stimulated the indifferent, now denounced apostates, now threatened coming woe to the degenerate.

The magnificent Solomon, loving peace better than war, organized the great districts which David had subdued, and maintained a gorgeous court. To extend and embellish Jerusalem lay near his heart, and, in accomplishing this, he indulged to the full a strong passion for architecture. He constructed a vast citadel, in the midst of which rose the walls of the Temple. The Temple of Solomon! Of all edifices reared by human hands, there is no other that has interested such multitudes. Solomon began to build it in the fourth year of his reign, about 1010 B.C., employing preparations which had already been made by David. In return for the corn, oil, and wine, which fertile Palestine produced abundantly, he obtained from Hiram, King of Tyre, skilled workmen and precious materials. The Temple's utmost height was two hundred feet, built up from deep foundations, with colossal masonry and great beams of cedar from Lebanon. The stones were so laid "that there appeared to the spectator no sign of the hammer, but as if all had naturally united themselves together."* Plates of gold were so nailed upon the surfaces that the whole Temple shone. Doors of cedar overlaid with gold afforded entrance, and before these hung veils of blue, purple, and scarlet of the brightest and softest linen, wrought with curious flowers. The deepest recesses of the Temple contained the Holy of Holies. This enclosed two cherubim of gold of fifteen feet in height, whose outstretched wings, reaching to the right and left, the northern and southern walls, touched one another, also, in the centre, and so formed a covering for the ark, which was placed between them; but nobody can tell, or even conjecture, what was the

* Josephus.

shape of these cherubim. In the chamber adjoining the Most Holy Place, stood the altar of incense, made of cedar, covered with gold, and also a great number of candlesticks, one of which was always lighted. Upon a multitude of tables were put many thousand vessels of gold and silver; but upon the largest was set forth the shew-bread, lawful to eat for the priests alone.

In the court before the Temple stood the brazen altar upon which sacrifices were offered, and the vast basin called the sea of brass, which rested on the backs of twelve brazen oxen, and held water for the ablutions of the priests before the sacrifice. To the right and left of the porch rose to the height of thirty feet two pillars of hollow brass. Their circumference was twenty feet, and the metal of four finger-breadths in thickness. The Tyrian workmen embossed upon them the forms of lilies and palms, and two hundred pomegranates in two rows; the pillar to the right bore the name Jachin, and that to the left the name Boaz.

The splendid details of the Temple are described by Josephus, and also in the books of Kings and Chronicles, and there is no reason to doubt the substantial correctness of the descriptions. Seven years were consumed in its erection, and when all was done the people far and near were gathered together for a solemn dedication. The king himself, with the Levites, went before, rendering the ground moist with oblations, and so filling the air with incense that it touched the senses even of those who were far off. Neither king nor people grew weary of singing hymns or dancing; but as the priests approached, who bore upon their shoulders the ark, the multitude gave way. The ark held, as of old, nought besides the two tables of stone, upon which the finger of Jehovah was believed to have inscribed the ten commandments. It was set reverently beneath the golden wings of the cherubim, and near at hand were put the seven-branched candlestick and the golden altar. As the priests went forth, after setting all in order, it is related that a thick cloud spread itself after a gentle manner within the Temple, so darkening the place that one priest could not see another. A fire, moreover, came running out of the air, and, rushing upon the altar in the sight of all, it consumed speedily the sacrifices that were placed thereon. It was believed that Jehovah thus gladly pitched his tabernacle within the Temple, and signified his pleasure in the victims that were offered.

Thus Jerusalem became beautiful, and the fame of the wisdom and magnificence of Solomon spread throughout the world. But the vigor of David's rule was sadly missed. A Syrian kingdom was allowed to establish itself undisturbed at Damascus to the northward, and turbulent Edom in the south became again independent. The wisdom of Solomon became the worst folly. When he died at length, the simplicity and discipline of the earlier Hebrews were becoming sadly relaxed, and a way was prepared for heavy calamities in the future.

Great discords came to prevail. The nation of the Hebrews was split into two divisions, Judah at the south with Jerusalem for the capital, and Israel at the north with the new city of Samaria as the seat of its kings. The two kingdoms were sometimes in harmony, but often at feud. The purity of the ancient worship, moreover, became commingled with Phœnician and Egyptian elements, against which protested the prophets Elijah and Elisha. In the softening of manners which existed, when agriculture had replaced the ruder life of the shepherd and herdsman, and the spirit of commerce was beginning to prevail, the national force was debilitated, and though huge fortifications surrounded the towns, there was a want of worthy defenders. So speedily did the ancient rugged virtue decay, that even in the time of Rehoboam, the successor of Solomon, Jerusalem was sacked by the Egyptians, who bore away, together with much wealth, the trophies of David. Damascus sent conquering armies to the very gates of Jerusalem. At length approached a most noteworthy crisis: the purple Assyrian invaded the land with chariot and spear.

We have followed already the story of the Jews for more than a thousand years. In the annals from the days of the patriarchs to the period we have now reached, it is often difficult to separate authentic history from legend. With the Assyrians we arrive at an age, however, when the mists of the morning-time are dissipated and the clearest sunlight prevails. We can well afford here to take a closer look. Within little more than a generation, discoveries have been made which give an extraordinary interest to this part of the ancient history of the Jews, and there is no period in which their characteristics are more plainly displayed. Of the many foreign nations which play a part in the older Hebrew annals, none is so prominent as Assyria. In the most ancient Hebrew documents we find them mentioned. An antediluvian existence indeed is attributed to the nation in the second chapter of Genesis; but without dwelling upon uncertainties, we find that in the eighth century before Christ, the power of Assyria becomes very conspicuous. The books of Kings and Chronicles are largely concerned with the relation of her conquests. In the expedition of Jonah we have the only instance of a prophet's going to a distance from Judæa to exercise his prophetic functions. Among the more ancient prophets whose writings remain to us, Amos, about 790 B.C., first hints at danger from Assyria. Hosea, soon afterward, is much occupied with the calamities impending from this quarter. Isaiah, later still, from first to last, indicates how great was the pressure upon the Hebrews of this mighty force from the Tigris. Micah, his contemporary, and Nahum, a little after, prophesy only to threaten vengeance upon these terrible foes. Zephaniah, 640 B.C., predicts the destruction of Nineveh, the Assyrian capital; and Ezekiel, in a subsequent generation, after the destruction had been accomplished, describes it at length. The whole population of Israel, the kingdom lying to the northward, is swept away into slavery. At length, 587 B.C., the capital of Judah, Jerusalem itself, is destroyed, and the poor remnant of the Hebrews carried captive to Babylon, which, until shortly before, had been a dependency of Nineveh.

The crisis which we have reached in the story of the Jewish nation is so momentous, our knowledge of the period is so clear, to a large extent gained so recently and in such interesting ways,—that it becomes proper to employ in our narrative greater detail than heretofore.

CHAPTER III.

ISRAEL AT NINEVEH.

AN old Greek historian, Diodorus, relates, that when Semiramis, the Assyrian queen, had subdued many nations, loaded with spoil she broke into Ethiopia. There she came upon a wonderful lake, whose waters were vermilion in color, and of a sweet flavor like that of old wine. Whoever tasted it became mad and confessed his misdeeds. The intellect of the modern world, after adding to her empire realm after realm of knowledge, has invaded, with arms strengthened by her conquests, the domain of ancient history. Suddenly before her stretches a shining lake. Hitherto of its waters she has known nothing, except as an old annalist or poet, here and there, has preserved in his vase a few glittering drops. But now the full expanse begins to spread itself before her, rich with gorgeous tints and flashing light. She grows dizzy over the spectacle, and is disposed to recall many of her boastful claims to superior power and knowledge.

In the great halls of the British Museum none are more impressive than those which contain the vast collections made by Layard among the ruins of Nineveh. Against the walls are ranged sculptured slabs, dingy with the discolorations of 2,500 years. Upon these tower the figures, bearded, colossal, just as they were cut by the Assyrian sculptors. One may touch the chiselling of the winged creatures, or the muscles that stand out so strangely from the gigantic limbs, or the flowing robes or locks, thinking, as the fingers pass along the groove in which worked the tool of the old artist, how many and how mighty the events have been since the stone was thus wrought. Greece has risen and gone to decay; so Rome, and so a score of empires. As strange and quiet as they stand now, rose those figures, when the prophets of Israel, in the very same palaces and temples in which the sculptures formerly stood, spoke their messages. Some of the carvings represent the very kings and soldiers of whose deeds we read in the Bible, under whose chariot-wheels the people of Judæa were again and again crushed. The slabs line the walls, and in the centre of the halls are colossal sculptured figures — lions with wings and human heads—figures sitting and standing — representations of kings heavily bearded, with faces of power, the very monarchs in whose presence the prophets spoke, and whose armies destroyed the towns of the Jews. In the presence of relics so very wonderful, it can hardly be otherwise than that the heart beats quick. As the modern visitor passes through the solemn halls, his shadow falls athwart the giant sculptures, as the shadow of Jonah once fell. Standing at one end and glancing backward, the sculptures so uncouth, yet so marvellously majestic, loom in that dim London atmosphere preternaturally large, so that to the figures is imparted an air of weird enchantment.

JONAH CALLING NINEVEH TO REPENTANCE.

Let us try to gain a clear idea of that indomitable force and pride—that extraordinary confidence in himself—which have marked the Jew everywhere, from the earliest history to the latest, and which are among the most important causes of the vitality and solidarity of the race. We shall appreciate it most vividly perhaps if we get at it by means of a side-light. We wish to understand their ancient force; let us understand the force and splendor of that which they confronted unabashed, which overwhelmed them utterly and yet did not smother them. Let us behold a picture of one enemy whom the Jew in his ancient day was compelled to meet, by whom, for a time, he was overborne, whom, however, he has survived for many ages.

"Assyrians," says Ezekiel, "captains and rulers clothed most gorgeously, horsemen riding upon horses, girded with girdles upon their loins, exceeding in dyed attire upon their heads, all of them princes to look to." Brilliant though the Assyrians were, mighty and gorgeous though the empire was which they established, men felt until a generation since that all authentic knowledge of them had been lost. But little correct information was to be obtained except from the books of the Old Testament, and there the mention of Assyria, though abundant, as has been seen, was scarcely coherent or trustworthy. This scriptural mention was enough to stimulate curiosity, but not to gratify it; the same can be said of the accounts of the Greek historians Ctesias, Diodorus Siculus, and Herodotus, from whom it has been possible to glean here and there only a shred or a patch with which scholars have tried to piece out the scanty story.

But did this mighty race live and die and leave no records of its own? By no means. It has left behind whole libraries of records. The oldest nations, with the chisel, or the brush dipped in indelible colors, wrote down upon tablets of rock, or upon the walls of their buildings, all that they knew. Upon such indestructible pages were inscribed their history, their knowledge of the arts and sciences, their philosophy and poetry. A house was something more to an Egyptian or a Ninevite than a mere place to dwell in; it was a book as well. The libraries were the towns and cities, crowded with volumes large and small, from the pyramid and temple down to the humble home of the laborer. Some were bare and plain, where poverty had time and means to cut only a few characters or paint a line or two. Others were crowded with inscriptions from base to cornice, the tracery most elaborately wrought, and often illuminated from end to end with the most brilliant hues. Everywhere, in the square, on the palace-front, on both sides of the way, the whole lore of the world was so displayed that he who ran might read.

To this day moth and mildew have continued to spare these old libraries. Thebes and Baalbec, Memphis and Babylon, half covered in sand or overgrown with brambles, still preserve on their solemn walls the memorials of their founders. The traveller hears the lonely desert wind sweep by him; the wild beast is scared from his desert lair at the unusual sound of a human foot-fall, but there in the desolation stands the record, sometimes as distinct as if each century, instead of obliterating, had been an Old Mortality, to deepen the chiselling, or had come with a brush to renew the splendor of the tints. One may read of the whole life of human beings, three thousand years ago; of long-lost arts, which modern civilization has not grasped; of empires whose memory is fast disappearing under the accumulating years, as their ruins have been buried under the drifting sands of the waste; of Nimrod and Sesostris, and many a forgotten hero.

Such was the record which the Assyrians left behind. They cut and stamped their history not only into their buildings, but also into the rocks and mountains. If we were Assyrians we should take perhaps Kenesaw Mountain, smooth a side of it into a precipice with an overhanging ledge, then, underneath, carve in colossal dimensions the figure of the soldier who won the battle there, and the whole story of the march to the sea. At Richmond would rise an immense pyramid, sculptured from base to summit with the achievements of Grant; while at Washington would stand a palace containing a few miles of halls lined with pictured slabs to tell the story of the administration of Lincoln.

If the record was so elaborate, the natural question is, why has it not endured? Sculptured cliff and obelisk have indeed remained in sight, but in solitudes where the eye of civilized man has rarely beheld them. Temple and palace have been buried from sight by the dust of the accumulating centuries. The site of the grave of all the buried splendor had almost been forgotten, when the 19th century at length resolved upon a resuscitation and wrought out a wonderful result. The discoveries have been made in Western Asia, in a half-desert region remote from the way of commerce. A few miserable Turkish cities in the last stages of decay are situated within the territory, but it is resigned for the most part to the wild Arabs. Everywhere over the surface of the ground there are scattered relics—now a mound or wall—now a heap of sculptured stone—here a space paved with inscribed bricks or pieces of pottery—there a crumbling tower. Desert, though it is at present, there is hardly a portion of the earth that has such historical interest. It was the seat of the Saracens, whose Caliphs, celebrated in the "Arabian Nights," shone at Bagdad until their fragile state was shattered by the Tartars. The apostate Julian came here to die, the old Pagan splendor of Rome shooting forth its last ray from his glazing eye as he falls. Earlier still, this earth felt the heavy soldiery tramp of Xenophon and the ten thousand, of whom the school-boy reads in the Anabasis, and the chariot-wheels of the Persians who swept after them. In yet older times than these, here came the Pharaohs as conquerors, and here prophets from Israel thundered forth the messages of the Lord.

From an early period the antiquities of Babylonia and the region lying farther to the eastward have been recognized as the remains of Nineveh and Babylon. In Strabo and Pliny mention is made of the ruins, as also in the books of travellers belonging to the middle ages of our own era. Of the modern explorers, Niebuhr may be regarded as the pioneer, who visited the localities a century ago. In the decade from 1840 to 1850, the famous archæologists, Botta and Layard, at length, startled the world with a marvellous uncovering. But the possession of these long-buried treasures would be of comparatively little value, were it not for a contemporaneous discovery. The palaces and temples into which Botta and Layard penetrated, contain upon their vast walls innumerable sculptured slabs, in which the figures and scenes are accompanied by inscriptions. The characters of which these are composed are combinations of a certain mark resembling a wedge or arrow head, broad at one end and tapering to a point at the other, from which circumstance it has received the name of the arrow-headed, or, more commonly, the cuneiform, wedge-shaped character. Some idea of Assyrian grandeur might have, no doubt, been obtained from the pictorial representations alone, but for any satisfactory knowledge an acquaintance with the cuneiform was necessary. The inscriptions are numerous, being cut not only upon the slabs with the sculptures, but stamped more or less thickly upon almost every brick or article of pottery. Ability to decipher the cuneiform was gained at the very time it was so much needed, and the history of the achievement is a marvellous record of ingenuity and patience. The task cannot yet be regarded as fully accomplished. Modern scholarship is, however, mastering her wedge-shaped tools, and now the last bars are yielding that have so long kept a beautiful captive from the gaze of the world. We know each year more and more of her robes and gems, her hanging gardens and castles of alabaster, her crimson pomp and mighty sway.

Two thousand years before Christ a powerful empire existed upon this territory, whose inhabitants had acquired the art of working metals, and were so far refined as to make some progress in astronomical knowledge. Shadowy is the history of those old Chaldæans. They flourished in the world's morning time before the mists had cleared, and a cloud must always hang over them. Through it we discern dimly the moving to and fro of a great people, the tramp of armies, the glare of forges, the majestic figures of sages versed in unknown lore. To this ancient power Assyria succeeded, becoming the most important country of the East perhaps as early as the thirteenth century before Christ. Her kings became constantly more vigorous and aggressive, and at length opened the era of magnificence. Before speaking of their power and state, a word or two must be said as to the nature of the dominion of the Assyrian kings, which will be needed to understand the description which follows. Their occupation was conquest, but the vanquished states, although under a most absolute despotism, were allowed in the earlier periods to retain their nationality, no difference being made in their internal administration. The subjugated potentates retained court and title, but were forced to pay tribute and render certain personal services. Western Asia was at this time densely peopled, and divided into a multitude of petty kingdoms, most of which became tributaries of Assyria. But the dominion of the Great King, though splendid, was precarious. Any untoward circumstance was sure to bring about revolts, involving often the repeated subjugation of the same state. At a later period, expedients were adopted to repress the tendency to rebellion. Satraps were appointed over conquered nations in place of the kings who were dethroned; and sometimes, where the vanquished were especially dreaded, the whole nation was torn from its home, and driven to remote districts of the empire.

We have no concern with the activity of these warrior-kings, except as it affects Palestine. The record of this comes down to us written on the rock, and has just been restored to the world after an entombment of twenty centuries. In the book of Kings there figure two monarchs of Syria, which lay to the north of Palestine, between the power of Nineveh and the seats of the Jews. We may read on the rock how one, the fierce Ben Hadad, was smitten with a loss of twenty thousand men; and of the fall of Hazael, the other, with his eleven hundred chariots dashed to pieces. The kingdoms of Judah and Israel see coming nearer and nearer the terrible tempest that has been impending for years. Damascus and Syria have fallen, and there is no other intervening height upon which the threatening storm can discharge itself. The prophets Amos and Hosea threaten imminent woes, and at length they come. The tribes of Gad, Manasseh, and Reuben are swept away, and at length, beneath the Assyrian battering-rams, the city of Samaria falls. Three years the city struggles, mindful of her glory under Jeroboam, when the state of Solomon himself was paralleled. According to the inscriptions on the slabs, the number of families that were driven from Samaria was twenty-seven thousand two hundred and eighty. These are the ten lost tribes of the house of Israel, and one may see them sculptured on slabs like those in London, some going to augment the splendor of Nineveh with unrewarded toil, some to people distant and barren regions far to the east. There is no mistaking the Jewish faces; the same lines mark them which mark the faces of the Abrahams and Mordecais of to-day.

The power and glory of Assyria have now reached the culminating point, Sennacherib succeeds to the throne. He it is of whom it has been written :

"The Assyrian came down like the wolf on the fold,
And his cohorts were gleaming with purple and gold."

Upon this brilliant period the light of history falls abundantly. Sennacherib, of all the Assyrian kings, most engages the writers of the Old Testament. We find mention of him in profane history, and whole acres, covered with ruins of palaces and temples, attest his grandeur. This grandeur, for a moment let me try to paint, for the Jews have their part in it.

It is eight hundred years before Christ. The good King Hezekiah rules in Judah, whose counsellor is the venerable prophet Isaiah. It is so far back in time that Rome is just being founded by Romulus. Greece is but in the infancy of her glory, and over her unstoried soil, to the music of Dorian flutes, the hardy bands of Sparta go marching to their earliest battle-fields. Long centuries must pass before there will be any mention at all of Teuton, Sclave, or Celt, but the Jew, even then, is old upon the earth. The dominion of Assyria stretches to the ocean on the south, and farther west to the middle provinces of Egypt, the lower banks of the Nile being dependencies of the Great King. Northward, the mountain princes to the base of Ararat, and even to the Euxine, bring him tribute. In the East the yoke has at length been fastened upon the neck of the intractable Mede. The Mediterranean washes the western border; Cyprus, lately won by the prowess of an Assyrian king, being the outpost. Nineveh at last has become the metropolis and the most beautiful city of the empire. The territory in its neighborhood, to-day almost a desert, is, at the time of which we write, very fertile. It is intersected by canals, supplied by the Tigris and Euphrates, which grow smaller and smaller as they proceed, and interlace with one another in every direction. Through this arterial system, a double life-giving stream pours into Mesopotamia, refreshing the soil and wafting its vast commerce. On the banks stand machines for irrigation, so that every rood of ground teems with fruitfulness. In the useful arts the Assyrians have made considerable progress. Copper and lead are mined and wrought with skill. Iron is worked in various forms and manufactured into excellent steel. Glass is made of various degrees of fineness, from that fitted for coarse utensils, to the crystal lens through which the lapidary is to trace microscopic engraving. The potters furnish a variety of ware, from the rude vessel for the use of the captive, to the elegant vase, enamelled and gilded with tasteful designs, intended for the palace of the satrap or the Great King. The textile fabrics of Assyria have been famous from an early day. In part the materials of their manufacture are produced at home, in part imported from distant lands. Rich stuffs of cotton, wool, and silk come from the looms. Dyes of a brilliancy, perhaps, surpassing any now used by Europeans are employed, and the splendor of the more costly fabrics is still further increased by weaving in threads of gold. The Assyrians are acquainted with many mechanical contrivances,—the roller, the lever, the pulley, the wheel, and, it may be certain, engines now lost. An art resembling printing was in general use. In most of the structures built of brick, each brick is stamped with the same inscription, consisting often of several words, and sometimes of a series of sentences. The stamping is believed to have been performed by means of a single engraved plate. The process was, therefore, quite similar to modern stereotyping, except that the impression was received upon clay instead of paper.

Does the reader think, that the Jews are forsaken, as we occupy ourselves in this way with the details of Assyrian industry? It must be remembered that in this time there was no industry but that of slaves, and that a vast multitude of captive Hebrews were already in servitude on the Tigris. The instruments just described were in the hands of enslaved Jews,— the accomplishments narrated were the achievements of their toil. Our story only follows them into thraldom, as we dwell thus upon the details of Assyrian civilization.

The commerce of Assyria was immense. Mesopotamia was a great mart between the East and the West from immemorial antiquity down to the discovery of the passage around the Cape of Good Hope. Up the Tigris from the Southern Ocean came silk and cotton from India and China, and precious metals from regions unknown. From Southern Arabia, by caravans, came spices and perfumes. The Phœnician cities to the west sent the produce of trading voyages extended even to Britain and the shores of the Baltic. From the mountains on the north great rafts of lumber were floated down upon the Tigris by the winter floods. Fine wool and droves of cattle and horses were sent from the pastures of Armenia and the Syrian uplands.

Concerning the state of the Great King one hardly dares to speak. The reader will think that the "Arabian Nights," or the vagaries of some mad hashish-eater have crept in among the authorities; but only the statements of matter-of-fact modern scholars and artists are followed. We are far removed in all our tastes and institutions from that ancient life. In the blood of the cold Northern races there is no especial passion for splendor; in the strong and civilized nations of the world to-day, any considerable accumulation of power by single individuals, to be exercised without let or hindrance, is impossible. Even in Russia, despotism is hemmed in by many restraints. In Assyria, however, a race of princes of marvellous energy, possessed to an inordinate degree of that passion for magnificence which has always characterized the Orientals, sat upon the throne. Their immediate subjects, a warlike people, knew no law but the sovereign's will. A long course of victory had put a hundred powerful nations under their absolute control. If the Great King saw fit, and he often did, he could draw from a tributary the last ounce of treasure, or utterly depopulate a vast district to furnish workmen for any given undertaking. It was unmitigated despotism, exercised by a wonderfully vigorous, unscrupulous, and splendor-loving dynasty. Assassination was the only restraint. No wonder the results of such conditions are almost incredible. The Great King sat on his ivory throne, a true Aladdin ; and the genii, controlled by his signet-ring, were all the opulent and industrious states of the East. What phantom world could furnish a mightier company?

Viollet le Duc and Fergusson, the historians of architecture, have paralleled in their department the feat of the naturalist, who from a bone or a scale, constructed with exactness, as it was afterwards proved, the form of an extinct animal. From the broken fragments of the palaces, they have constructed their former grandeur. In the midst of the level landscape rose, in the first place, an immense artificial hill. The excavations from which the soil came may still be distinctly traced in depressions and vast swamps. On all sides this elevation was faced with solid masonry, while upon the lofty platform on the summit was built the palace. Fortifications like cliffs rose near it an hundred feet high, and wide enough for three chariots abreast. At frequent intervals towers shot up to a still loftier elevation. The platform was ascended by a stately stair. The foot of the visitor trod upon slabs carved or inlaid with handsome designs. Sculptured portals, by which stood silent guardians, colossal figures in white alabaster, the forms of men and beasts, winged and of majestic mien, admitted him to the magnificence within. The façade of the palace at its base was covered with graven images. Upward, tier above tier into the blue heavens, ran lines of colonnades, pillars of costly cedar, cornices glittering with gold, capitals blazing with vermilion, and between them voluminous curtains of silk, purple and scarlet, interwoven with threads of gold. The wind from over Media came breathing through these aërial pavilions, and far down to the alabaster lions and the plumed divinities in the court beneath, they whispered of the glory of the Great King. In the interior, stretching for miles, literally for miles, the builder of the palace ranged the illustrated record of his exploits. The inscriptions were deeply cut in the cuneiform character, and parallel with them in scarlet and green, gold and silver, ran the representations of the scenes themselves. There were commemorated the exploits of the chase, the building of palaces, and scenes of feasting. More numerous, however, were the pictures of war, the battle, the siege, the torture, the long procession of captives. In places of honor, the portrait of the monarch himself was set, with his foot upon the neck of some tributary prince or worshipping before his gods. Through lion-guarded portals admission was gained to still other halls, lined everywhere by the endless record. The mind grows dizzy with the thought of the splendor,—the processions of satraps and eunuchs and tributary kings winding up the stair and pouring in a radiant stream through the halls,—the gold and embroidery,—the ivory and the sumptuous furniture,—the pearls and the hangings. Nor let it be supposed it was merely barbaric splendor. In modern times, in Italy, memorials have been discovered of a refined people who were precursors of the Roman power,—delicate vases, and gold and silver chased in forms of grace, for which the beholder finds no word but perfect. The old Etruscan art is believed to-day to have been transplanted from Assyria. Architecture found in the balconies of Nineveh the beautiful Ionic column. Highest distinction of all, it is believed that sculpture, the art of arts,—the white Phidian blossom, so pure and peerless in the chaplet of ancient Greece, budded in the chambers of the Assyrian kings.

CHAPTER IV.

THE DESTRUCTION OF SENNACHERIB.

LET us imagine ourselves, for the moment, viceroys or princes, personages of sufficient dignity to be guests of the mighty Sennacherib, and that we have ascended with him, the possessor of all this pomp, to the carven roof of the towering palace, where stand altars for sacrifice. Hundreds of feet below, the Tigris washes the foundations, and shoots its waters into the artificial channels winding everywhere through the land. From an unfinished temple close at hand comes the hum of uncounted captives, the keen eye and hawk nose of the Jew appearing among them, slaves since the subjugation, in the previous reigns, of Northern Palestine. In the distance, along the river, in gay barges, approaches the train of some subjugated prince bearing offerings. Mesopotamia, as it were in bondage too, bound under the silvery watercourses beneath the eye, as if by an interlacing net, prepares for the master her punctual tribute of corn and wine. The Great King turns his haughty, bearded face to the southward, where the messengers of Hezekiah, King of Judah, approach, bearing thrones and couches. There are camel-trains from Solomon's seaport of Ezion-Gebir with the wealth of Ophir; trains, too, from Southern Arabia, laden with spice, frankincence, and myrrh, caravan upon caravan, until all the robber winds of the desert, from rifling their bales, fling perfumes everywhere through the wilderness. Sennacherib turns his face to the east, and in his dark Assyrian eye there is a light as he thinks of the Mede scourged into servitude. Northward rise peaks covered with snow. He calls to mind, perhaps, how as his chariot bands swept past the base of one of them, down upon them, shroud and sepulchre at once, an avalanche swept over their purple pennons. But what mattered it in so great a multitude! It was a trifle, and the cymbals of the spearmen clashed on loud as ever through the narrow defiles. The Great King looks westward long and thoughtfully. His breast heaves under its covering of gems, and new pride sits in his haughty face. Was it not there, with the dash of the Mediterranean in his ear, that he pressed his foot upon the necks of the great Phœnician princes, lords of the continuous city stretching northward from Acre two hundred miles to Aradus? Was it not there that the laboring galleys put to sea out from Sidon, to bear even to distant Tarshish, and the still more distant amber-coasts, the fame of his might? Was it not there, too, that the ships of the rich Tyrian captains swept past him as he sat on his throne; their mighty oars, in the words of Ezekiel, made of tough oak from Bashan, their planks of fir-trees from Senir, their tall masts cedars of Lebanon, their sails of embroidered linen, the rowers, as they swept the deep, seated upon benches of ivory carved in his own Nineveh? How, as the pageant rushed through the waters, even the sea threw off its blue that it might assume the purple light of their sides and the glitter of the shields on their prows! By the side of the Great King, upon an altar set about with beryl and chrysolite, burns eternal fire, kindled in Chaldea once by sages who had looked upon the face of Noah. Well may he bow and worship the gods of Asshur, who have set their favored son on such a pinnacle.

It is scarcely possible to make too brilliant the picture. It was a nation not much behind the modern world in many of the useful arts; and in those which contribute to luxury and splendor, the arts among them especially cultivated, they were perhaps far before. The people, whose prowess and magnificence have just been hinted at, the Jew was called to confront, when at its mightiest. It is for us to see how he bore himself. The good King Hezekiah labored to restore the ancient usages and glory of the Jewish nation, whose power had languished since the reign of Solomon. The old polity was restored, and the sceptre of Judah stretched over several of the neighboring countries. At length growing bolder, and relying upon the support of Egypt, Hezekiah dared to throw off the yoke of Assyria, of which he had been a tributary. Presently from his high throne came rushing the insulted sovereign. The passes in the mountains to the north are choked with his host. The waters of the Jordan in its lower course trickle feebly in a diminished stream, so great is the multitude of men and animals who drink at its source.

Samaria is crossed already desolate; the frontiers of the tribe of Benjamin are invaded, and like trees, one by one isolated and consumed by a flood of lava, city after city is enveloped and crushed by the red and glittering array. Hezekiah strips the very temple of its treasures, giving up the sacred utensils, and tearing from the pillars their heavy golden plates in order to appease Sennacherib; but the imperious monarch is determined to establish the altars of Asshur in the soil of Mt. Zion.

"Like the leaves of the forest when summer is green,
That host with their banners at sunset were seen,"—

for the resources of Sennacherib have been stretched to the utmost. When this insignificant handful of Jews has been crushed, there is to be an invasion of Africa. From the sculptures which in our day have come to be an object of study, we may behold in detail the battle order.

The host is in array, for scouts in the van bring tidings of the approach of a hostile army from the southward. The light-armed troops are slingers and archers. They are dressed in short embroidered tunics, with their hair surrounded by bands. Like the Saxon bowmen, the archers draw their arrows to the ear. Their weapons are handsomely decorated. The heavy infantry carry spears and shields; on their heads they wear helmets of burnished brass; cross-belts support small-arms at the side, and shining discs of metal cover their breasts. They stand in regular ranks, file behind file. To-morrow, when the host of Judah makes its onset, the first rank kneeling, the second stooping, will form with their spears a bristling hedge, and from behind, the bowmen will discharge their arrows. In a similar way, twenty-five centuries hence, the brigades of Napoleon, at the battle of Mt. Tabor, not far distant, will receive the charge of the Mamelukes. But the strength of the host is in the swarming cavalry and chariots. The horses are spirited steeds from Arabia and Armenia. The riders sit upon decorated saddles, clad in armor, with helmets and lances. The chariot bands are the chivalry and flower of Asshur. The coursers are caparisoned with purple silk and embroidered cloth; from their heads hang plumes and heavy tassels. As they hurry to and fro, flashing behind them with gold and jasper, with ivory and enamel, roll the formidable vehicles. The warriors within, the veterans of many wars, are clad from head to foot in steel; embossed upon their shields are the heads of lions; lofty standards of precious stuffs, embroidered, hang over their plumed helmets, and all along the line hover pennons of scarlet. In the rear are the rams and other warlike engines, the ladders for escalading, the steel tools for the mines, already battered and blunt with hard service before the fenced cities of Judah. In tents of costly and gaudy stuffs, the concubines and eunuchs of the Great King and the Ninevite nobles outnumber even the soldiers. Everywhere, from fertile Jericho to the sea-coast of old Philistia, range the foragers, and innumerable as a locust swarm, the beasts collected for burden and provision consume the pastures. Here and there some great officer—the chief cup-bearer, or the inso-

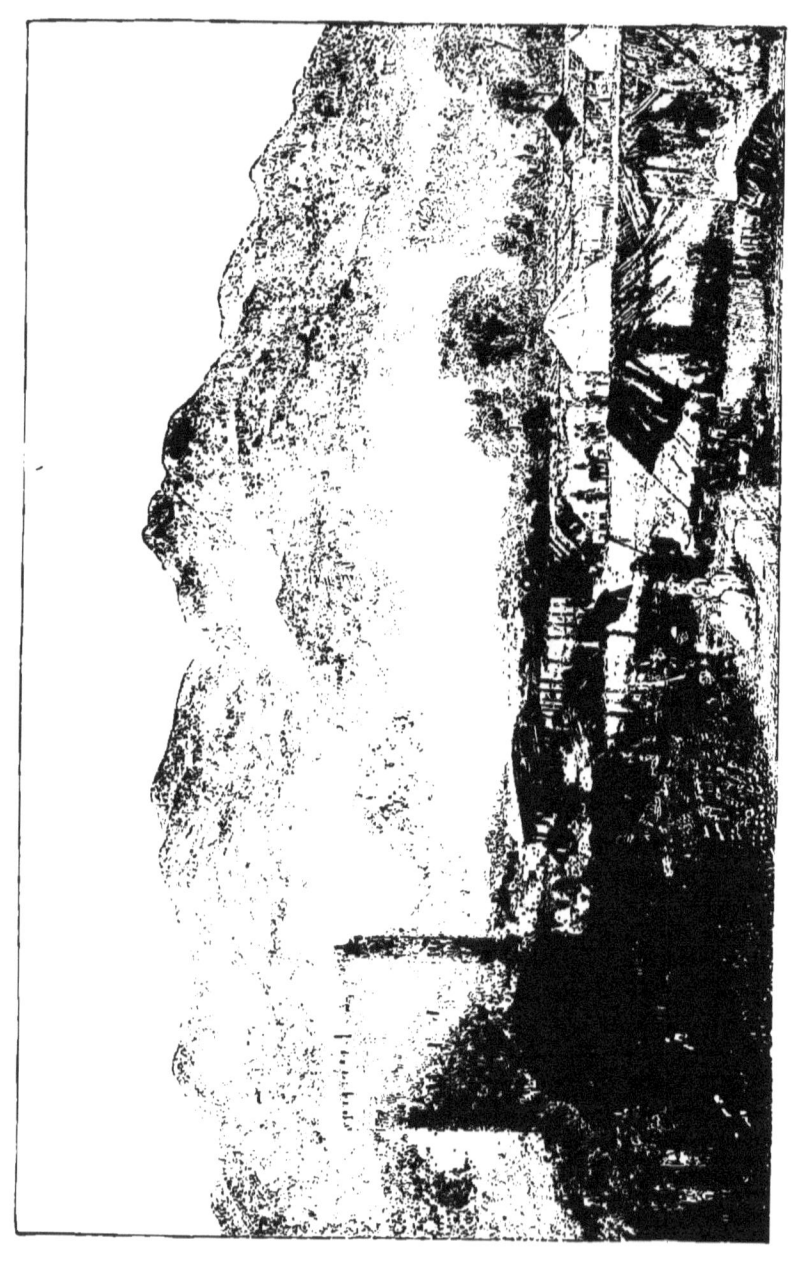

JERICHO.

lent Rabshakeh, or perhaps even Sennacherib himself—goes by in his canopied chariot attended by stately body-guards.

Doubtless that eve there was panic in Jerusalem; but all true Israelites, confident in having the Lord upon their side, surveyed from the battlements with contempt even this array, so magnificent and appalling. The youth of true Hebrew fire, from his high watch-tower as the sun descended, looked down upon the scene. Into his mind came crowding the grand traditions of Judæa—how Jephthah smote the Ammonites hip and thigh from Aroer even unto Minnith; how Caleb slew the Anakim in the fastnesses of Hebron; and how the mighty Joshua had said in the sight of Israel: "Sun, stand thou still on Gibeon, and thou, Moon, in the valley of Ajalon," and the sun stood still and the moon stayed until the people had avenged themselves on their enemies. When from the glittering Assyrian lines the drums and dulcimers throbbed out upon the still air of twilight, clear and far out of the height from a Jewish trumpet rang a blast of defiance. The Lord's chosen people would abide the battle!

By the side of Hezekiah as counsellor stands a venerable figure. In the year that King Uzziah died, half a century before (this is his own account of himself), he had seen the Lord sitting upon a throne high and lifted up, with a train that filled the temple; and while he looked an attendant seraph, seizing a coal from off the altar, had laid it upon his lips, and the voice of the Lord had bidden him go forth and speak his will until the land was utterly desolate. Now this interpreter of the Lord's messages, the great prophet Isaiah, determines the counsels of the king. Thus he speaks:

"This is the word that the Lord hath spoken concerning Sennacherib: 'The virgin, the daughter of Zion hath despised thee and laughed thee to scorn. The daughter of Jerusalem hath shaken her head at thee. By thy messengers thou hast reproached the Lord, and hast said, with the multitude of my chariots I have come up to the height of the mountains, to the side of Lebanon, and will cut down the tall trees thereof, and the choice fir-trees thereof, and the forest of his Carmel. With the sole of my foot I have dried up all the rivers of besieged places. But the house of David shall take root downward and bear fruit upward.' Therefore, thus saith the Lord concerning the King of Assyria: 'He shall not come into this city, nor shoot an arrow there, nor come before it with a shield, nor cast a bank against it. By the way that he came by the same shall he return, and shall not come into this city,' saith the Lord."

That was the prophecy which Isaiah poured forth with hot utterance, and according to the old Hebrew story this was its fulfilment: "And it came to pass that night that the angel of the Lord went out and smote in the camp of the Assyrians an hundred and four score and five thousand, and in the morning, behold, they were all dead corpses.

" And there lay the rider, distorted and pale,
   With the dew on his brow and the rust on his mail;

And the tents were all silent, the banners alone,
The lances unlifted, the trumpets unblown,
For the might of the Gentile, unsmote by the sword,
Had melted like snow in the glance of the Lord."

And Sennacherib returned and dwelt in Nineveh, and it came to pass as he was worshipping in the house of Nisroch, his god, that Adrammelech and Sharezar, his sons, smote him with the sword, and Esarhaddon, his son, reigned in his stead.

Such was Assyria at its height, but a rapid decadence ensued, and at length, seven hundred years before Christ, Cyrus the Mede smote her with the sword and lighted her funeral pyre. Until the late discoveries, the tale of the splendor of ancient Oriental nations was believed to be enormously exaggerated, if not fabulous. But after all it was not so far short of the truth. Grant that the records of the kings are boastful, yet the vast artificial mounds, crumbling so long, but so mountain-like, the palaces covering acres, the leagues of sculptured masonry, are testimony to the power and state of the kings not to be invalidated. They are remains of a nation, not much behind the modern, in the useful arts; and in those which contribute to luxury and splendor, the arts among them especially cherished, they were perhaps far before.

It is not strange that the modern world becomes somewhat dizzy with the spectacle, and feels inclined to recall some of its claims to increase of power and knowledge. Think,—it may be that this venerable empire will be remembered when the fame of modern nations has quite passed away. The slabs in the

British Museum have already held their sculptured record twenty-five hundred years. Which has the best chance to-day of enduring to a remote future, that imperishable rock, or the paper and paste-board books in the library close at hand, to which we have entrusted our annals? Do you know the story of the great library of Alexandria into which had been gathered the parchments and books of antiquity? Its treasures of learning were disposed on countless shelves, and quite untold. Not the Caliph Omar, as has been believed, but a mob of Christian monks, infuriated with fanaticism, set the library on fire. While the frail receptacles perished, one can imagine the temple-fronts of the Pharaohs, the pyramids, and the obelisks, looming up in the glare, crowded thick with the inscriptions of an older time. In the bright light appeared the deep-cutting, low relief, the indelible tints,—monuments like those to which the monarchs of Nineveh entrusted the story of their grandeur. Literature had lost her frailer page, but high on her ancient strongholds, she defied, from those imperishable tablets, as they flushed red from line to line in the midnight blaze, the impotent torches of man.

If we follow one school of geologists, we know that a time may come when this present geological era, amidst the rush of oceans or the bursting forth of volcanic fires, may come to an end. In that case how quickly will these perishable memorials of ours which we know as books, shrivel and disappear. But that old literature, entrenched securely within its rocky tablets, will mock the very forces of nature, as it defied in Egypt the torches of the Arabs; and new orders of beings, searching among the fossils and deposits of a by-gone age, may read there the story of the Assyrian kings.

But what use in being long remembered unless we can be remembered with blessing! The red and shining characters in which is written the story of Nineveh, repeat a terrible tale of violence and wrong. The glory of the old empire beams like the pearl indeed, but, like the pearl, too, it is no normal or healthy growth. The glitter upon her ivory and jasper is from the tears of captives. Her scarlet and vermilion dyes are from the life-stream of crushed nations. "The stone cries out of the wall and the beam out of the timber shall answer it: Woe to him that buildeth a tower with blood and establisheth a city by inquity!"

CHAPTER V.

JUDAS MACCABÆUS, THE HEBREW WILLIAM TELL.

THE kingdom of Judah escaped destruction at the hands of Sennacherib, but its respite was short. Soon afterwards Babylon, closely related to Assyria, and the heir of its dominion, swept into captivity in distant Mesopotamia nearly all that were left of Hebrew stock. For a time the nation seemed to have been wiped from the face of the earth. The ten tribes of Israel that had been first dragged forth never returned to Judea, and their ultimate fate, after the destruction of Nineveh, whose splendor they had in their servitude done so much to enhance, was that of homeless wanderers. The harp of Judah, silent upon the devastated banks of the Jordan, was hung upon the Babylonian willows, for how could the exiles sing the Lord's song in a strange land! But the cry went forth at length that Babylon had fallen in her turn, just as destruction had before overtaken Nineveh. In the middle of the sixth century B.C., Cyrus, the Mede, made a beginning of restoring the exiles, who straightway built anew the Temple walls.

In David's time the population of Palestine must have numbered several millions, and it largely increased during the succeeding reigns. Multitudes, however, had perished by the sword, and other multitudes were retained in strange lands. Scarcely fifty thousand found their way back in the time of Cyrus to the desolate site of Jerusalem, but one hundred years later, the number was increased by a reinforcement under Ezra. From this nucleus, with astonishing vitality, a new Israel was presently developed. With weapons always at hand to repel the freebooters of the desert, they constructed once more the walls of Jerusalem. Through all their harsh experience their feelings of nationality had not been at all abated; their blood was untouched by foreign admixture, though some Gentile ideas had entered into the substance of their faith. The conviction that they were the chosen people of God was as unshaken as in the ancient time. With pride as indomitable as ever, entrenched within their little corner of Syria, they confronted the hostile world.

But a new contact was at hand,—for the Jews, and for the world at large, far more memorable even than that with the nations of Mesopotamia,—a contact whose consequences affect at the present hour the condition of the greater part of the human race. In the year 332 B.C., the high-priest, Jaddua, at Jerusalem, was in an agony,* not knowing how he should meet certain new invaders of the land, before whom Tyre and Gaza, the old Philistine stronghold, had fallen, and who were now marching upon the city of David. But God warned him in a dream that he should take courage, adorn the city, and open the

* Josephus.

THE REBUILDING OF THE TEMPLE.

gates; that the people should appear in white garments of peace, but that he and the priests should meet the strangers in the robes of their office. At length, at the head of a sumptuous train of generals and tributary princes, a young man of twenty-four, upon a beautiful steed, rode forward from the way going down to the sea to the spot which may still be seen, called, anciently, Scopus, the prospect, because from that point one approaching could behold, for the first time, Jerusalem crowned by the Temple rising fair upon the heights of Zion and Moriah. The youth possessed a beauty of a type in those regions hitherto little known. As compared with the swarthy Syrians in his suite, his skin was white, —his features were stamped with the impress of command,—his eyes filled with an intellectual light. With perfect horsemanship he guided the motions of his charger. A fine grace marked his figure, set off with cloak, helmet, and gleaming arms, as he expressed with animated gestures his exultation over the spectacle before him. But now, down from the heights came the procession of the priests and the people. The multitude proceeded in their robes of white; the priests stood clothed in fine linen; while the high-priest, in attire of purple and scarlet,—upon his breast the great breast-plate of judgment with its jewels, upon his head the mitre marked with the plate of gold whereon was engraved the name of God,—led the train with venerable dignity.

Now, says the historian, when the Phœnicians and Chaldeans that followed Alexander thought that they should have liberty to plunder the city, and torment the high-priest to death, the very reverse happened, for the young leader, when he saw the multitude in the distance, and the figure of the high-priest before, approached him by himself, saluted him, and adored the name, which was graven upon the plate of the mitre. Then a captain named Parmenio asked him how it came to pass that, when all others adored him, he should adore the high-priest of the Jews. To whom the leader replied : " I do not adore him, but that God who hath honored him with his high priesthood ; for I saw this very person in a dream, in this very habit, when I was at Dios in Macedonia, who, when I was considering how I might obtain the dominion of Asia, exhorted me to make no delay, but boldly to pass over the sea thither, for that he would conduct my army, and would give me the dominion over the Persians." Then when Alexander had given the high-priest his right hand, the priests ran along by him, and he came into the city, and he offered sacrifice to God in the Temple, according to the high-priest's direction, and magnificently treated both the high-priest and the priests. He granted all the multitude desired ; and when he said to them that if any of them would enlist themselves in his army on this condition, that they should continue under the laws of their forefathers, he was willing to take them with him, many were ready to accompany him in his wars.

When the high-priest Jaddua and Alexander the Great went hand in hand up into the mount of the Temple, then for the first time came together the Jew and the Aryan. In the days of the early world, in some mysterious region of Central Asia, a choice strain of men began to grow numerous and powerful. As the home became contracted, a band departed southward, whom we find, when history begins, advancing from the north into India. In hymns which have come down to us in the Vedas, they sang in honor of fire: "Neighing like a horse that is greedy for food, thy path, O fire, is dark at once"; and in honor of the dawn: "She shines upon us like a young wife; she is the leader of the clouds, golden-colored, lovely to behold." Their descendants, pressing forward, have possessed at length the whole of India.

But this Aryan troop that went southward is less interesting to us than companies that departed westward, for in these westward marching bands went the primeval forefathers, from whose venerable loins we ourselves have proceeded. They passed into Western Asia, and from Asia into Europe—each migrating multitude impelled by a new swarm sent forth from the parent hive behind. At the head of the Adriatic Sea an Aryan troop had divided, sending down into the eastern peninsula the ancestors of the Greeks, and into the western peninsula the train destined to establish upon the seven hills the power of Rome. Already the Aryan pioneers, the Celts, on the outmost rocks of the western coast of Europe, were fretting against the barrier of storm and sea, across which they were not to find their way for many ages. Already Phœnician merchants, trading for amber in the far-off Baltic, had become aware of wild Aryan tribes pressing to the northwest—the

Teutons and Goths. Already, perhaps, upon the outlying spurs of the Ural range, still other Aryans had fixed their hold, the progenitors of the Sclave. The aboriginal savage of Europe was already nearly extinct. His lance of flint had fallen harmless from the Aryan buckler; his rude altars had become displaced by the shrines of the new Gods. In the Mediterranean Sea each sunny isle and pleasant promontory had long been in Aryan hands, and now in the wintry forests to the northward the resistless multitudes had more recently fixed their seats. In the Macedonians, the Aryans, having established their dominion in Europe, march back upon the track which their forefathers long before had followed westward, and now it is that the Jew for the first time touches the race that from that day to this has been the master-race of the world. It was a contact taking place under circumstances; it would seem, the most auspicious—the venerable old man and the beautiful Greek youth clasping hands, the ruthless followers of the conqueror baffled in their hopes of booty, the multitudes of Jerusalem, in their robes of peace, filling the air with acclamations, as Alexander rode from the place of prospect up the heights of Zion, into the solemn precincts of the Temple. It was the prologue, however, to a tragedy of the darkest, to a persecution of two thousand years, the flames of which even at the present hour can scarcely be said to have died down.

The successors of Alexander the Great made the Jews a link between the Hellenic populations that had become widely scattered throughout the East by the Macedonian conquests, and the great barbarian races among whom the Greeks had placed themselves. The dispersion of the Jews, which had already taken place to such an extent through the Assyrian and Babylonian conquests, went forward now more vigorously. Throughout Western Asia they were found everywhere, but it was in Egypt that they attained the highest prosperity and honor. The one city, Alexandria, alone, is said to have contained at length a million Jews, whom the Greek kings of Egypt, the Ptolemies, preferred in every way to the native population. Elsewhere, too, they were favored, and hence they were everywhere hated; and the hatred assumed a deeper bitterness from the fact, that the Jew always remained a Jew, marked in garb, in feature, in religious faith, always scornfully asserting the claim that he was the chosen of the Lord. Palestine became incorporated with the empire of the Seleucidæ, the Macedonian princes to whom had fallen Western Asia. Oppression at last succeeded the earlier favor, the defences of Jerusalem were demolished, and the Temple defiled with Pagan ceremonies; and now it is that we reach some of the finest figures in Hebrew history, the great high-priests, the Maccabees.

There dwelt at the town of Modin,* a priest, Mattathias, the descendant of Asmonæus, to whom had been born five sons, John, Simon, Judas Maccabæus, or the hammer, Eleazar, and Jonathan. Mattathias lamented the ravaging of the land and the plunder of the Temple by Antiochus Epiphanes, and when,

* Josephus and the Books of the Maccabees.

in the year 167 B.C., the Macedonian king sent to Modin to have sacrifices offered, the Asmonæan returned a spirited reply. "Thou art a ruler," said the king's officers, "and an honorable and great man in this city, and strengthened with sons and brethren. Now, therefore, come thou first : so shalt thou and thy house be in number of the king's friends, and thou and thy children shall be honored with silver and gold and many rewards." But Mattathias replied with a loud voice : "Though all the nations that are under the king's dominion obey him, and fall away every one from the religion of their fathers, yet will I and my sons and my brethren walk in the covenant of our fathers. God forbid that we should forsake the law and the ordinances! We will not hearken to the king's words to go from our religion, either on the right hand or the left."

An heroic struggle for freedom at once began which opened for the Jews full of sadness. An apostate Jew, approaching to offer sacrifice in compliance with the command of Antiochus, was at once slain by Mattathias, who struck down also Apelles, the king's general, with some of his soldiers. As he fled with his sons into the desert, leaving his substance behind him, many of the faithful Israelites followed, pursued by the Macedonians seeking revenge. The oppressors knew well how to choose their time. Attacking on the Sabbath-day, when, according to old tradition, it was a transgression even to defend one's life, a thousand with their wives and children were burnt and smothered in the caves in which they had taken refuge. But Mattathias, rallying those that remained, taught them to fight on the Sabbath, and at all times. The heathen altars were overthrown, the breakers of the law were slain, the uncircumcised boys were everywhere circumcised. But the fulness of time approached for Mattathias; after a year his day of death had come, and these were his parting words to his sons: "I know that your brother Simon is a man of counsel; give ear unto him always; he shall be a father unto you. As for Judas Maccabæus, he hath been mighty and strong even from his youth up. Let him be your captain and fight the battles of the people. Admit among you the righteous."

No sooner had the father departed, than it appeared that the captain whom he had designated was a man as mighty as the great champions of old, Joshua and Gideon and Samson. He forthwith smote with defeat Apollonius, the general in the Samaritan country, and when he had slain the Greek, he took his sword for his own. Seron, general of the army in Coele-Syria, came against him with a host of Macedonians strengthened by apostate Jews. The men of Judas Maccabæus were few in number, without food, and faint-hearted, but he inspired them with his own zeal, and overthrew the new foes at Bethoron. King Antiochus, being now called eastward to Persia, committed military matters in Palestine to the viceroy, Lysias, with orders to take an army with elephants and conquer Judæa, enslave its people, destroy Jerusalem, and abolish the nation. At once the new invaders were upon the land; of foot-soldiers there were 40,000, of horsemen 7,000, and as they advanced many Syrians and renegade Jews joined them. Merchants marched with the army with money to buy the captives as slaves, and chains with which to bind those whom they purchased. But Judas Maccabæus was no whit dismayed. Causing his soldiers to array themselves in sack-cloth, he made them pray to Jehovah. He dismissed, those lately married and those who had newly come into great possessions, as likely to be faint-hearted. After addressing those that remained, he set them in the ancient order of battle, and waited the opportunity to strike. The hostile general, fancying he saw an opportunity to surprise the little band of Hebrews, sent a portion of his host against them, by secret ways at night. But the spies of Judas were out. Leaving the fires burning brightly in his camp, to lure forward those who were commissioned to attack him, he rushed forth under the shadows against the main body, weakened by the absence of the detachment. He forced their position, though strongly defended, overcame the army; then turned back to scatter utterly the other party who were seeking him in the abandoned camp. He took great booty of gold and silver, and of raiment purple and blue. He marched home in great joy to the villages of Judæa, singing hymns to God as was done in the days of Miriam long before, because they had triumphed gloriously.

The next year Lysias advanced from Antioch, the Syrian capital, with a force of 65,000. Judas Maccabæus, with 10,000, overthrew his vanguard, upon which the viceroy, terrified at the desperate fighting, retired to assemble a still greater army. For a time there was a respite from war, during which Judas counselled the people to purify the Temple. The Israelites, overjoyed at the revival of their ancient customs, the restoration of the old worship in all its purity, and the relief from foreign oppressors, celebrated for eight days a magnificent festival. The lamps in the Temple porches were rekindled to the sound of instruments and the chants of the Levites. But one vial of oil could be found, when, lo, a miracle! The one vial sufficed for the supply of the seven-branched golden candlestick for a week. This ancient Maccabæan festival faithful Jews still celebrate under the name of the Hanoukhah, the Feast of Lights.

Judas subdues also the Idumeans to the southward, and the Ammonites. His brethren, too, have become mighty men of valor. Jonathan crosses the Jordan with him and campaigns against the tribes to the eastward. Eleazar is a valiant soldier, and Simon carries succor to the Jews in Galilee. But at length the Macedonian is again at hand, more terrible than before. The foot are 100,000, the horse 20,000; and as rallying-points, thirty-two elephants tower among the ranks. About each one of the huge beasts is collected a troop of 1,000 foot and 500 horse; high turrets upon their backs are occupied by archers; their great flanks and limbs are cased in plates of steel. The host show their golden and brazen shields, making in the sun a glorious splendor, and shout in their exultation so that the mountains echo. In the battle that follows fortune does not altogether favor the Jews. In particular, the champion Eleazar lays down his life. He had attacked the largest elephant, a creature covered with plated armor, and carrying upon his back a whole troop of combatants, among whom it was believed that the king himself fought. Eleazar had slain those in the neighborhood; then creeping beneath the belly of the elephant, had pierced him. As the brute fell Eleazar was crushed in the fall. Judas was forced to retire within the defences of Jerusalem, where still further disaster seemed likely to overcome him. Dissensions among themselves, however, weakened the Macedonians. Peace was offered to the Jews, and permission to live according to the laws of their fathers—proposals which were gladly accepted, although the invaders razed the defences of the Temple.

The peace was not enduring. New Macedonian invasions followed; new Hebrew successes, the Maccabees and their partisans making up, by their fierce zeal, their military skill, and dauntless valor, for their want of numbers. But a sad day came at last. Judas, twenty times outnumbered, confronts the leader Bacchides in Galilee. The Greek sets horsemen on both wings, his light troops and archers before the heavier phalanx, and takes his own station on the right. The Jewish hero is valiant as ever; the right wing of the enemy turns to flee. The left and centre, however, encompass him, and he falls fighting gloriously, having earned a name as one of the most skilful and valorous of the world's great vindicators of freedom. For three years he had been high-priest, and as such had resolved to form an alliance with a new power, far to the west—of whose conquests the Oriental world in those days was just beginning to hear—the power of Rome. When the messengers of Judas Maccabæus stood before the Senate, the City of the Seven Hills saw then, for the first time, the Jew,—the race she was in time destined to conquer, at whose hands she herself, in a spiritual sense, was destined to undergo conquest. It was the beginning of a very memorable connection, but as yet all was unknown. Simon and Jonathan, the brethren, received the body of the hero by treaty, and buried him solemnly at Modin by the sepulchre of their father.

Like Eleazar and Judas, John, the eldest son of Mattathias, undergoes a soldier's death. At one time the land is given to apostates, and the faithful undergo such sufferings as have not been seen since the Babylonish captivity. Simon and Jonathan survive, however, and possess the Asmonæan heart and arm. If there are times of humiliation, times of triumph succeed. The splendor of Jerusalem is renewed; messengers bring to the Maccabees vessels of silver, purple garments, buttons of gold, as signs of favor. Jonathan is confirmed in supremacy over Judæa and four prefectures, and Simon is made general over the country stretching from Tyre to Egypt. They in their turn die, not on the field, but by the hand of treachery. One following the other, each has been high-priest, and now with lamentations the people entomb them in magnificent sepulchres at Modin with the other mighty priests, Judas and Mattathias. Each has tried to confirm the alliance with Rome, for the masterful quality of the Italian power in those years unfolds itself more and more.

Though the old father has gone, and all his sons, the Asmonæan vigor still lives, in grandsons and great-grandsons. As one traces the details, a multitude of traits, pathetic, picturesque, terrible, heroic, appear upon the page. An Asmonæan prince, John Hyrcanus, like his ancestors, high-priest, besieges Jericho during civil dissensions, a city defended by a kinsman, who holds in his keeping the mother and brethren of the prince. These are brought upon the wall and tortured before the prince's eyes. Threats are made that they will be cast down headlong if the siege is persisted in. The mother spreads out her hands and begs John Hyrcanus to persist in spite of the fate that may overtake her and her children; but when he sees her beaten and torn to pieces, his courage fails.

The same John, besieged at another time in Jerusalem, by still another Antiochus, begs for a truce of seven days at the time of the Feast of the Tabernacles, that the festival may be worthily honored. The truce is granted, and more; for as the feast begins, lo, from the enemy's camp proceeds a magnificent sacrifice, messengers bearing sweet spices and cups of gold and silver, and leading bulls with gilded horns, sent by Antiochus to be offered upon the altar of the Lord.

Miraculous portents abound in the Asmonæan days. Heliodorus, sent by his Macedonian master, undertakes to rob the Temple. "Throughout the whole city no small agony was felt. Priests, prostrating themselves before the altar, besought that things given them to be kept might be safely preserved. The people rushed in terror from their houses. Women shrouded in sackcloth abounded in the streets; and the virgins, that were ordinarily kept in, ran, some to the gates, some to the walls, and some looked out of windows. All made supplication, and it would have aroused any one's pity to see the falling down of the multitude of all sorts, and the anguish of the high-priest. Heliodorus, however, unmoved, set about the fulfilment of his commission; but there appeared unto him a horse with a terrible rider, and adorned with a very fair covering; and he ran fiercely and smote at Heliodorus with his forefeet. His rider wore a complete harness of gold; moreover, two other young men appeared before Heliodorus, notable in strength, excellent in beauty, and comely in apparel, who stood on either side and scourged him continually. The desecrator fell to the earth and was compassed about with great darkness. When he had been carried away in a litter, he came at length to himself, and with softened heart offered sacrifices." Still more memorable than the wonders seen by Heliodorus, was the appearance in the heavens, at a time of confusion, of a vast and magnificent army. From buckler and spear-point flashed, as it were, lightnings. Above the clouds there gleamed innumerable golden helmets. Rank on rank they moved in shining arms.

So passed the time of the Asmonæans, with its sufferings, its heroism, its solemn portents. In each generation the league was knit with Rome, and after a hundred years, in 63 B.C., the Roman came. Pompey, with his centurions, overpowered Jerusalem and lifted the veil before the Holy of Holies; and Crassus, on the way to his Parthian grave, stripped the Temple of its treasures. Palestine became tributary to the new conquerors, and Herod ruled, a vassal king.

CHAPTER VI.

THE BEAUTY OF HOLINESS.

THE short-lived independence of the Jews, brought to pass two thousand years ago by the prowess of the Maccabees, and closed by the encroachments of Rome, is a very memorable period in Hebrew story, because then, for the last time, they were, as a nation, their own masters, in their ancient seats. The boundaries of Judah were extended, and a certain degree of internal prosperity was attained. Although as bondmen they had beheld and in part created the splendor of Nineveh and Babylon—at length, indeed, stood sometimes in places of honor in the midst of the brilliant life in Mesopotamia,—it is not probable that the Israelites, after their return to Palestine, established a splendid civilization. Unlike so many of the ancient countries, there are no ruins in the Holy Land to show that there once stood there magnificent cities. The Hebrews were not great builders; if the Temple of Solomon was of beautiful architecture, it was made so by the skill of the Tyrian workmen, whom the king obtained from Hiram, his Phœnician ally. It is not probable that other arts flourished. The prohibition of Moses against the making of graven images, or likenesses of any thing in the heavens above, or on the earth beneath, or in the waters under the earth, crippled completely painting and sculpture; and even music, an art in which in modern times the Jews have shown themselves so accomplished, was probably in a rude condition. The people were generally farmers and shepherds, men of simple ideas. Commerce, with its influences so stimulating in the way of giving breadth and intelligence, had made but feeble progress.

The Jews were sharply divided into a higher and lower class: the former claiming to be the "holy seed," descendants of the unmixed Hebrew race who had returned from Babylon for the rebuilding of the Temple; the latter of blood more or less commingled, the hybrid progeny of Israel and stocks of Canaanitish or other foreign derivation. Of the holy seed were the twenty-four orders of priests and the townsmen of higher rank; of the lower class, the villagers and peasants, who, in the times to which we have descended, had lost the ancient Hebrew tongue, employing a dialect known to scholars as the Aramaic.

Since the independence of the Hebrews might have been preserved far longer and their career as a nation been far grander, but for the violent internal dissensions into which they fell, some account of the sects and factions into which they became broken is proper. Popular belief assigned to Ezra, the great leader who in the middle of the fifth century before Christ restored the Jews to their former home in Palestine, the establishment of the Canon of the Old Testament;

but it was, probably, gradually formed during two or three centuries.* From the time of the Maccabees, the Old Testament appears as a whole, though it is probable that even yet the separate parts were not placed on an equal footing, or regarded universally with equal reverence. A little later Josephus designates as the Canon, or books of authority, the five books of Moses, or the Law, the Torah; thirteen books of the prophets; and four containing hymns or directions for life. So, substantially the Canon has stood until the present day. A number of Jewish writings, of comparatively late origin, are sometimes bound up with the Bible under the name of the Apocrypha, but these are held to be without authority. To the Canon of the Old Testament, the Jews, wherever dispersed and of whatever station, have always shown the greatest reverence. In 277 B.C., at the request of the king of Egypt, seventy learned men were sent by the high-priest from Jerusalem, who made in Alexandria the Greek translation known as the Septuagint. Paraphrases of Scripture, made in the Aramaic dialect, were communicated orally to the people, to the mass of whom Hebrew had become an unknown tongue; some of these, finally committed to writing and handed down to later times, are called the Targums.

It was a Hebrew belief that Moses, upon Sinai, received not only certain laws which he wrote down, but likewise a second revelation interpreting the first and containing also additional precepts. When he descended from the mount, it was said that he sum-

* Smith: "Dict. of the Bible."

moned Aaron, to whom he gave first the tablets, and then recited the later, more complete communication, in the same order in which it had been imparted. Moses recited the oral Law to the sons of Aaron, also; then, to the Sanhedrim, or grand council of the nation; and, lastly, to all the Israelites who were disposed to hear. Moses then withdrawing, Aaron repeated the oral Law as he had received it; his sons did likewise, and after them the Sanhedrim. Through these frequent rehearsals the oral Law became firmly fixed in the minds of its first recipients, by whom it was handed down from father to son, age after age. With the original communication, much became, in process of time, incorporated which did not properly belong to it. Ezra, therefore, besides arranging the written Law, in the case, also, of the oral Law, carefully separated the original nucleus from the subsequent accretions, and the revised code, handed down as before, was held in undiminished respect by the nation in general.

A minority of the nation, in the days following the time of Ezra, neglected the oral code, declaring that duty was fulfilled by observing the regulations of the written Law. Such observance made men worthy of the title "Zadikim," or the righteous. The majority, who superadded to the observance of the written Law, that of the traditional Law also, of which the requirements were in many respects more strict, took the name "Chasidim," or the pious, accounting themselves to be more holy. The former sect became known in time as the Sadducees, taking their name from Sadoc, one of their teachers. From the

"Chasidim," who united with the observance of the traditional Law a disposition to hold themselves aloof from all Gentile contact, arose in time the Pharisees.

The Sadducees denied not only the authority of the traditional law, but also the immortality of the soul, the existence of angels and spiritual beings, and among the canonical books of Scriptures attached importance only to the five books of Moses. They believed in the freedom of the human will, and, hence, were noted, when they sat in judgment, for the severity of their sentences. Though fewer in number than the Pharisees, they surpassed them in wealth and quality. They looked with kinder eyes, moreover, upon the Gentiles, and out from their number at last was developed the party of Herodians, a body which, taking a name from the tributary princes whom at length the Romans had set up, favored strongly the Roman influence.

The Pharisees derived their name from a Hebrew word meaning to separate; and received the title either from the fact that their superior strictness set them apart from their fellows, or because they wished to avoid all contact with the world about them. The observance of the minute injunctions of the oral Law brought it to pass that their conduct became very ceremonious and scrupulous. They practised washings and fastings without number, were distinguished by the breadth of their phylacteries (bands of parchment inscribed with scriptural passages, and attached to their garments, or even their faces), and were intolerant toward dissent from their own ideas. They thought themselves defiled by contact with publicans and sinners, observed the Sabbath exactly, paid their tithes with care, and made long prayers in public places. Though not the richest and highest placed of the Jews, they formed a very large and influential class, comprehending most of the scribes and the lawyers, among whom was preserved the lore of the nation. While they believed in the freedom of the human will, they are also said to have held that all events are predestined, in some way reconciling doctrines which appear conflicting. They believed in the resurrection of the dead and immortality, holding in the earlier period the idea of the transmigration of souls. Angels and spirits played a large part in their scheme; they were zealous in making proselytes, to which practice the Sadducees were indifferent. Converts were, however, never admitted to an equal footing with themselves, since none of Gentile birth could stand with those of Hebrew blood. The Pharisees came to constitute the vital portion and core of the Jewish race, absorbing, as time went on, more and more of its vigor. As from the Sadducees sprang the lax Herodians, so from the Pharisees proceeded the Zealots, in whom Pharisaic strictness of every kind was carried to extreme.

There was still another remarkable division. In the days which we have reached, there might have been often seen, moving austerely among the tribes that came up to Jerusalem to the Temple service, or going from house to house in the villages on kindly missions of healing or comfort, certain figures robed in white and belted about by a peculiar distinctive girdle. These were Essenes, a body everywhere held in honor, but about whose real origin and character a certain mystery has always prevailed. Some regard them as an offshoot of the Pharisees, originating in the deserts in a time of persecution; some hold them to have been, at a later time, neither more nor less than a company of Christians.* A portion, though not all, were austere—indeed, monastic in their habits; they lived in seclusion, taking upon themselves vows of charity and chastity, and holding their goods in common. In their places of retirement, in the intervals of religious exercises they cultivated the soil; they condemned wedlock, keeping up their number, like the modern Shakers, by the adoption of children. Unlike the extreme Pharisees, they respected the foreign rulers; they were much venerated by the people, who believed them to possess prophetic power. The Essenes rendered a substantial service as physicians, for they made it a point to understand the healing properties of herbs. Philo, a famous Alexandrian Jew, writing just after the beginning of the Christian era, describes one class of the Essenes, the Practici, in such terms that one would say they must have formed an almost ideal community. The whole duty of man was comprised within the three definitions—love of God, love of virtue, love of man. All men were held to be equal before God, and slavery was condemned. Large cities and wicked places were avoided through fear of temptation; in this, perhaps, we may see a

* See De Quincey's essay, "The Essenes."

touch of over-scrupulousness, as also in their abstinence from trade as promoting covetousness. Strife of words was unknown among them, as well as strife with the sword, for peace was held to be the proper state. They had recourse to arms, however, in self-defence. Among themselves their charity was perfect; they held their goods in common, and the sick and weak never suffered. Much time was spent in the study of moral and religious duties, the relation of man and wife was held in honor, children received careful nurture, and age was reverenced. After death an immortality for the soul was anticipated. The ascetic Essenes correspond remarkably in habit and discipline with the monastic orders of later ages, which undoubtedly borrowed many usages from these ancient recluses.

We must also glance at the followers of Hillel,[*] an enlightened teacher, who, coming from Babylon, appeared in Judea not far from the time when the Herodian rule displaced that of the Asmonæans. Anticipating work which was, as we shall see, to be performed at a later time, he had already made a beginning of writing down the Mischna, as the oral Law was called, of whose transmission an account has just been given. His doctrine was in some respects near that of the Pharisees, but he gave a far nobler, more generous interpretation to the words of Moses. His disciples are said "to have made the Law light, not because they lightly esteemed its authority, but because they revived the beneficent spirit of the original."

[*] C. R. Conder: "Judas Maccabeus."

Among those whom the unmixed Israelites, the holy seed, regarded as of corrupt derivation, the Samaritans received the greatest scorn. They were not distinct enough to be regarded as a separate nation, and yet they were too distinct to be properly a sect. The Jews declared that they were originally a separate people, Cutheans, and idolaters. Their territory became an asylum for renegade Jews who had rendered themselves obnoxious to punishment by breach of the law. In process of time the Jewish element came to prevail in the Cuthean nation; idolatry was abolished, the authority of the law established, and Jehovah recognized. This drawing near of the Samaritans to the Hebrews did not win from the latter favor, and as years passed events brought about the highest pitch of hatred. The builders of the new Temple after the return from Babylon, were actively annoyed by Samaritan forays; for the mongrel race had built a shrine of their own upon Mt. Gerizim, which they maintained to be the only place where Jehovah could be properly worshipped. The Samaritans accepted of the scriptures, only the five books of Moses, and rejected also the traditions, in this resembling the Sadducees. Sadoc, founder of the Sadducees, was reported, indeed, to have learned his doctrine while an exile among the Samaritans. The Pharisees, however, the bulk and the most earnest part of the Jewish race, prevented the upspringing of any sympathetic feeling. As years passed, hatred increased, until finally a bitter Hebrew curse was pronounced upon Samaria, involving land and people. The fruits of the earth were declared to be as swine's flesh, unclean; to taste even water of Samaria was pollution. A Samaritan remnant still haunts the ancient seats of the people, in the vale of Shechem, about the well of Sychar. Their faces yet give evidence of their kinship with the Hebrews, and they have preserved to the present time, upon mouldering scrolls of parchment, a copy of their holy law, which is one of the most ancient manuscripts in existence.

Thus disunited, Palestine, though free from the Macedonian yoke, invited subjection at the hands of Rome. Religious observances absorbed a large amount of the time and energy of all. Twice in each year every male Jew was under obligation to visit Jerusalem and remain one week. Of the twenty-four orders of priests, one each week conducted the Temple service. The new order arrived on Friday, the old left on the first day of the week; so that on the Sabbath there was always a double company, and every order visited the Holy City twice in each year. In a similar way the whole nation was divided, a certain proportion of the laity going to the Temple with each company of priests. Thus the tribes went up, the tribes of the Lord, to give thanks unto the name of the Lord. The position of the "standing men," the representatives of the congregation, was one held in great respect. After a special purification these were admitted to the Inner Temple, where they stood in an elevated place before the court in which rose the altar. Below them in a great square enclosure gathered the main congregation, the women occupying galleries above. On steps leading to the gate Nicanor, the Levites were ranged for chanting the Songs of Degrees, and the priests, in a position above all, blessed the congregation. These constant gatherings to Jerusalem and the Temple service gave opportunity to people of remote districts to become acquainted with one another, and so the nation was bound together.*

The feasts and the fasts were occasions of great importance, observed, in great part, even to the present day, by every faithful Jew with scrupulous care. Each new moon was celebrated by a festival of trumpets. The heavens were carefully watched for its appearance everywhere in Judæa, and whoso saw it first hastened to inform the Sanhedrim at Jerusalem, to whom was committed the principal authority. Such witnesses sometimes hurried to Jerusalem by scores. A beacon was forthwith lighted upon the Mount of Olives, answered by fires on the more distant hills, till the whole land was alight. Early in April was celebrated the Passover; at the end of May, the Pentecost; at the beginning of October, the Feast of Tabernacles. The Feast of Purim, commemorating the national deliverance through Esther, and the Hanoukhah, Feast of Lights, in remembrance of the renewal of the Temple worship by Judas Maccabæus, were later additions to the list of holy times. Besides the feasts there were six solemn fasts, in commemoration of national calamities. Of these, the great Day of Atonement,

* Conder.

at the end of October, was most important, when the scapegoat, dedicated to the spirit of evil, was led forth, burdened with the sins of the people, to be dashed in pieces from a cliff in the dreary desert near Jericho.

No period, no race, is satisfied with its present condition. There is always a looking back to some golden age in the past, from which there has been a degeneration, and an anticipation of a happy time in the future, when all shortcomings shall be made good. Among the Hebrew race such anticipations were coupled with the vivid expectation of a Messiah, a heaven-sent leader, under whose guidance the chosen people were to attain the splendor and supremacy which were appropriately theirs. Many passages in Scripture were believed to foretell the coming of the great national Saviour. Even in the ancient Law it stood written: "The Lord thy God will raise up unto thee a prophet from the midst of thee, of thy brethren, like unto me; unto him ye shall hearken." The desolated holy places were restored, in the expectation that "there should come a prophet to show them what should be done." According to Isaiah, "he was to be a rod from the stem of Jesse,"—"a branch of the house of David," according to Jeremiah; and so again and again, until at least seventy scriptural passages were believed to have a Messianic character. In the time of Judas Maccabæus, it was a great prophet rather than a mighty prince upon whose coming the hopes of the nation were fixed. As the glory of the Asmonæans faded, and the Romans were called in as arbitrators in their quarrels, the Jews consoled themselves by the hope of a future king, whose right to the throne of the Hebrews should be undisputed, and who should magnificently vindicate his race. The expectation became more and more intense, some holding that the empire of the Messiah to come was to be purely spiritual, while the people generally looked for a glorious temporal prince, to be born at Bethlehem of Judæa of the house of David.

The Hebrew strength had long been wasting itself in oppressive ceremonials, and the dissensions of factions. Independence, won at such cost by the children of Mattathias, had been for many years lost, when at length there went out a decree from Cæsar Augustus, the Roman arbiter of the Israelitish destinies, that all the world should be taxed, and all went to be taxed every one into his own city. From the town of Nazareth in Galilee a man named Joseph, with Mary his espoused wife, people poor and simple, but of illustrious lineage, went up to Bethlehem of Judæa, to pay the tribute. Mary, being great with child, brought forth a son, and because there was no room for them in the inn, she wrapped this, her first-born, in swaddling clothes, and laid him in a manger. In the same country shepherds watching their flocks by night had seen great portents. While the glory of the Lord shone about them, an angel had announced tidings of great joy, the birth at last of the Saviour; and while the angels sang "Glory to God in the highest," the shepherds, departing, came with haste, and found Mary

BETHLEHEM.

and Joseph, and the babe lying in the manger. Wise men from the East, moreover, came, saying: "Where is he that is born king of the Jews, for we have seen his star in the East, and have come to worship him?" and lo, the star which they saw in the East went before them till it came and stood over where the young child was. When Herod, the tributary prince, who under Rome now ruled the country, heard of these things, he was sore troubled, feeling that his power was threatened, and he slew all the children of Bethlehem, and in all the coasts thereof, from two years and under, hoping thus to destroy the newborn king; but Joseph, warned in a dream, had departed with the young child and his mother into Egypt, where they remained until the death of Herod made it safe to return.

It is the most familiar of tales. The child whose life had been preserved by the flight into Egypt, become a boy of twelve, is lost by his parents at Jerusalem, whither they had gone, after the custom of the nation, to observe the Passover. Sitting in the midst of the doctors in the Temple, he astonishes all that hear him by his understanding and answers, for he is already about his Father's business. John the Baptist, while the people muse whether he be the Christ or not, proclaims the mightier one who shall come, the latchet of whose shoes he is not worthy to unloose; the young man Jesus is baptized, the Holy Ghost descending in bodily shape upon him like a dove, while the heavenly voice declares him, "My beloved Son, in whom I am well pleased." He is led into the wilderness to be tempted of the

Devil, and at last enters upon his wonderful mission. The predictions of ancient seers are fulfilled; the blind are made to see, the deaf to hear, the lepers are cleansed, the dead are raised up, and the poor have the gospel preached to them.

The preaching of the gospel--this last and greatest—and what is this gospel? To love God and our neighbor, to do justly, to love mercy, to walk humbly with God, to be meek, to be peace-makers, pure in heart, to be persecuted for righteousness' sake, not to remember the old prescription, "an eye for an eye, and a tooth for a tooth," but to love them that curse us, to bless our enemies, to pray for those who despitefully use and persecute us,—these are the things which make us children of our Father who is in Heaven; even as he is perfect, so we are to be perfect.

The agony in Gethsemane is undergone, Judas betrays, the high-priest rends his clothes, saying, Jesus has spoken blasphemy; Pilate, after scourging him, delivers him to be crucified between the two thieves. As he yields up the ghost, the veil of the Temple is rent in twain, the graves are opened and the bodies of saints which slept arise and appear unto many. The angel of the Lord, descending from heaven, rolls back the stone from the door of the sepulchre. His countenance is like lightning, and his raiment white as snow, as he tells Mary Magdalen and the other Mary that Christ is risen from the dead and goes before them into Galilee. And when the disciples see the risen one, they worship him, but some doubt. And he bids them go and teach all nations, baptizing them in the name of the Father, and of the Son, and of the Holy Ghost, teaching them to observe all things, whatsoever he had commanded them, and promising to be with them always, even unto the end of the world.

The disciples go forth and teach, and those whom they teach in turn bear the message to others ; and so it came about that the zealous Stephen, arousing wrath, was cast out of a city and stoned, the murderers laying down their clothes at a young man's feet whose name was Saul. Saul consented to his death, and breathing out threatenings and slaughter, went upon another mission of persecution. But suddenly there shined about him a light from heaven, and he fell to the earth and heard a voice, saying : " Saul, Saul, why persecutest thou me ? " and when he had been instructed, there fell from his eyes as it had been scales, and straightway he preached Christ, that he is the Son of God. Thus the band gained the great apostle to the Gentiles, who at length could give this summing up of work and danger: " In labors abundant, in stripes above measure, in prisons frequent, in death oft : of the Jews five times I received forty stripes save one, thrice was I beaten with rods, once was I stoned, thrice I suffered shipwreck, a day and a night I have been in the deep: in journeyings often, in perils of waters, in perils of robbers, in perils by mine own countrymen, in perils by the heathen, in perils in the city, in perils in the wilderness, in perils in the sea, in perils among false brethren, in weariness and painfulness, in watchings often, in hunger and thirst, in cold and nakedness."

THE SITE OF THE ANCIENT TEMPLE.

What preachers of a great cause have ever suffered more! What preachers of a great cause have ever won success so triumphant!

Not all, even of those who claim the Christian name, have believed that in this first-born of a Jewish mother, God became flesh and dwelt with men. Not all have been able to believe that about the plain facts there has been no accretion of myth; that the stories of the multitudinous heavenly host appearing among the clouds, of the water blushing into wine, of the new pulses of life in the corrupting bodies of Lazarus and the son of the widow of Nain, or of the multiplying of the loaves and fishes, are to be received with faith as undoubting as that a great teacher once walked by Galilee, and spoke to his countrymen from the Mount. Whether ordinary occurrence or unparalleled marvel, the ancient record narrates the circumstances with equal simplicity and directness. Fortunately it does not belong to him who writes this story of the Jews to say whether or not the narrative shall be accepted without reservation; or, if it be granted that some things are to be questioned, to try to ascertain the line beyond which a just faith becomes credulity. To some this child of the Jew is the incarnate Deity; to others, while not divine, he is nevertheless superhuman; to others still he is a man with no other inspiration than "the light which lighteth every man that cometh into the world." But whatever differences of view may exist as to the nature of Jesus of Nazareth and the real facts of his career, Jew, Christian, Heathen, all have, at any rate, this standing-ground in common—that there is no higher wisdom or excellence than is contained in his precepts and was lived out in his life. It is the very beauty of holiness; and the remembrance of this life, the hope of the realization of its promises, and the faith in the truth of its teachings, have been the support and the inspiration of thousands upon thoussands of weary pilgrims, patient sufferers, and noble martyrs in the long ages that have passed.

CHAPTER VII.

VESPASIAN AND JOSEPHUS.

MORE than a century had passed since the Jews had paid tribute to Rome, when Gessius Florus, a man of tyrannical nature, became procurator. The Jews resisted his exactions, in spite of the exhortations of the more prudent spirits among them, who foresaw that Rome would make a pretext of the refusal to raise a charge of rebellion, and after that destroy the nation. The counsel prevailed among the Jews to refuse the offerings sent by the Romans for the Temple service, but this was a practical casting-off of the Roman yoke. The party known as the Zealots, fanatical maintainers of independence, gained power, and at length Roman blood was shed, upon which Florus marched against Jerusalem with the 12th legion. At a battle in the suburbs of the city, the masters of the world were roughly handled; nevertheless, made bold by dissensions which broke out among their adversaries, they entered the city and besieged the rebels, who took refuge in the Temple. Making a tortoise with their shields, so that with backs and heads perfectly protected they could work directly beneath the walls, the Romans brought the besieged to great straits. Florus, however, who as a leader was inferior, drew his soldiers off when success was just at hand. As he retreated through difficult passes, his rear was attacked, and he and his army came near meeting the fate which a generation or two before had overtaken Varus in Germany. Leaving four hundred of his bravest legionaries to make head against the furious pursuers, four hundred who, like Romans, died almost to a man, he gained time to escape with the main body, losing, however, together with the detachment, his baggage and the great war engines, which were an immense gain to the victors.

Open war henceforth existed, and Josephus, a Jew of the lineage of Aaron, trained according to the best discipline of his race, and who had also been well received at Rome, was put by his countrymen in command of the province of Galilee. Afterwards as an historian he described the events. Soon a very different leader took the place of the weak Florus. The veteran, Vespasian, the best soldier of Rome, appeared with an army of 60,000. Galilee was at once attacked, whose people, following the orders of Josephus, fled to their fenced cities. He himself, with the bravest, finding it impossible to make head against the invaders, shut himself up in Jotapata, on a high precipitous hill. It could be approached only from the north, and here a mighty wall formed the defence. Vespasian spent four days in building a road by which his army could approach nearer, encamping at last at the distance of a mile. For five days the works were stormed with desperate fighting on both sides. Then the Romans drew off, and determining to use slower means, reared opposite the defences a high bank, upon which were set one hundred and fifty engines, discharging javelins, lighted brands, and stones. The besieged, no less energetic, dragged away in sorties the mantlets which sheltered the workmen, and set fire to the timbers, As the bank continued to rise, Josephus on his side built the wall of the city higher, protecting the workmen with raw hides of oxen stretched upon stakes, against which Vespasian's missiles fell powerless. Thus the height of the wall was increased by thirty feet, and the Romans, for the moment disheartened, ceased in their efforts to overtop it.

A strict blockade was now resorted to that the stronghold might be starved out. While there was food sufficient, water was scanty, the sole supply being cisterns, which in summer were nearly dry. Of this the enemy had a suspicion, but Josephus deceived them by making the people dip garments in water and hang them, dripping, over the wall. Meantime he sent messengers, disguised in skins so that they might pass for dogs at night, who made their way by steep overgrown paths, which the Roman sentries overlooked, out into the country, to arouse all Galilee. Vespasian renewed his assaults. The Jews were lighter and quicker than the heavy-armed Romans; but the catapults were never quiet, and at length the dreaded rams, of the length of the mast of a ship, headed with iron, and hung from a high frame by the middle, began to shake the wall. A great company of men, protected by hurdles and hides, dashed the mighty beam against the works,

THE SEA OF GALILEE.

made top-heavy by the added height, while the Arabian auxiliaries, with bows and slings, tried to prevent the interference of the besieged. Josephus managed to let down sacks filled with straw, which received the thrust of the rams: the Romans, by blades of iron fixed to long poles, cut the ropes by which the sacks were suspended. In sorties the Jews burned the hostile engines with bitumen, pitch, and sulphur. Vespasian was wounded by a spent javelin; but the siege was pressed with loud noise from the machines and the whizzing of the stones. One suspects from some of the descriptions of Josephus, as he speaks of the effects of the machines, that he himself knew how to draw a long bow. He declares that the head of a man at his side, struck off by a stone from a catapult, was driven nearly half a mile. There is no reason, however, to doubt his substantial accuracy.

The Romans at length made a breach, and against the impending storm Josephus ranged his bravest soldiers. "Shut your ears against the shouting of these men," he said, "and as for their missiles, kneel and hold your shields over your heads till the archers have spent their arrows. Fight when the stormers come." Cries and the sound of the trumpets announced the Roman charge; the day was darkened by their arrows; the column climbed slowly upward pressed together, with a roof of shields closely overhead, like an armored serpent. The Jews, however, poured upon the testudo boiling oil, which, creeping under the armor of the assailants, covered them from head to foot. A slippery paste, made from boiling the herb fenugreek, cast liberally upon the gangways which the Romans had prepared, made the footing uncertain. Again Vespasian was foiled. He built a bank, however, placing upon it three towers fifty feet high, cased with iron.

On the forty-seventh day of the siege, Vespasian learned from a deserter that the defenders slept in the last watch of the night. Assembling the army at that hour, Titus, son of Vespasian, and the centurion, Domitius Sabinus, succeeded in reaching the wall unperceived. In a heavy mist, they slew the guards, opened the gates, and the destruction of the city was accomplished. Together with forty of the chief men of the town, Josephus found a hiding-place in a cavern opening out from a well, but through treachery the place of concealment was made known. Vespasian, anxious to take the Jewish leader alive, sent the tribune, Nicanor, who had been his friend, to induce him with fair promises to surrender. Josephus was about to give himself up, but was prevented by his companions. "We will care," said they, "for the honor of our country." At the same time they offered a sword and "a hand that shall use it against thee." Josephus called every one by name: "at some he looked sternly, as a captain might do, and another he would take by the hand, and another he would beseech by many prayers, turning as a wild beast when it is surrounded by the pursuers, to each one as he came near." He proposed that they should perish together, but by the hands of one another, instead of suicide. Lots were cast. He who drew the first offered his neck to him who stood next, and so forward. Finally, through marvellous fortune, Josephus and one other alone were left, and here the slaughter ended. The two survivors surrendered to the Romans. A great concourse of soldiers collected to see Josephus brought before the general, and many demanded that he should be put to death. The magnanimous Titus, however, stood his friend, and by his great influence with his father, thwarted the ferocity of the troops. Josephus now played upon the superstitions of the victor. "Have I not been sent to thee of God?" he exclaimed. "Thou shalt be emperor—thou and thy son after thee. Bind me, therefore, and keep me, to see whether my words are true or no." The flattering prophecy brought for Josephus a respite, for he was held in honor, though not yet relieved of chains.

The subjugation of Galilee followed, after the fall of Jotapata, with all the terrible circumstances of ancient warfare. Jerusalem for a time was spared, its strength making it formidable. At Rome, moreover, the emperor died, and the purple, passing to short-lived successors, fell at last, according to the prophecy of Josephus, upon Vespasian, who cut the chains from the limbs of the captive, in sign that all dishonor was removed, and assigned to his son Titus the task, so long deferred, of humbling the mighty towers of Mount Zion.

The capture of Jerusalem by Titus is one of the most memorable events in the history of mankind. It caused the expulsion of an entire race from its home. The Roman valor, skill, and persistence were

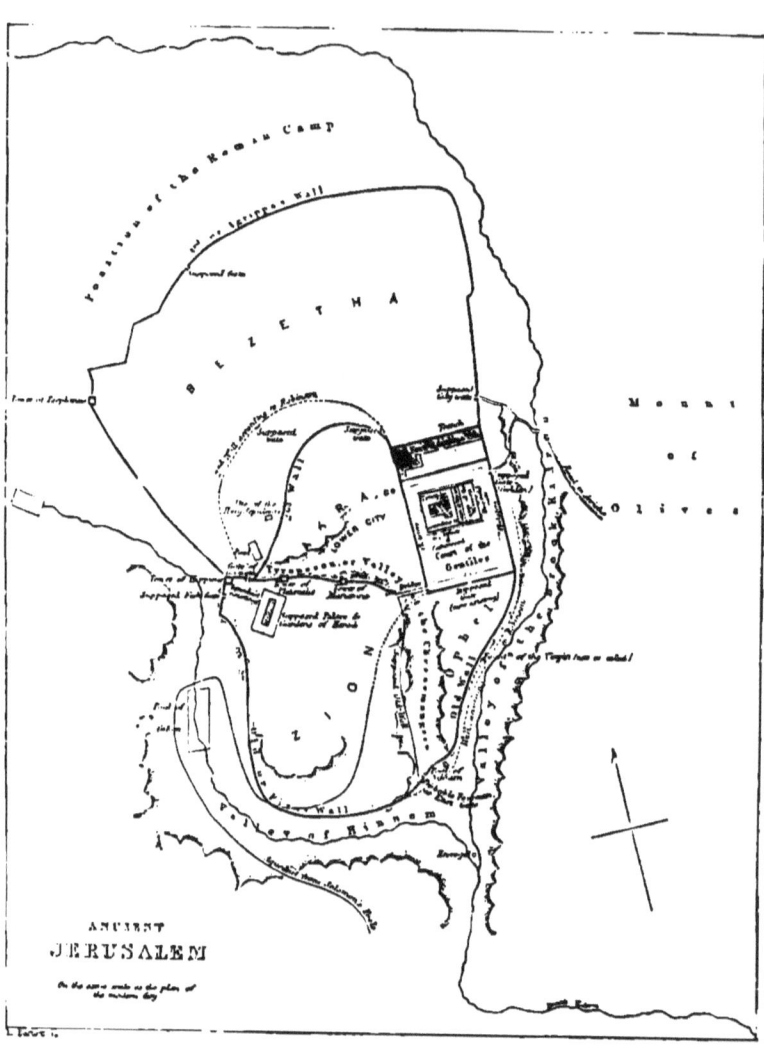

never more conspicuously displayed. No more desperate resistance was ever opposed to the eagle-emblemed mistress of the ancient world. There is no event of ancient history whose details are more minutely known. The circumstances in all their appalling features are given to us by the eye-witness Josephus, so that we know them as vividly as we do the events of the career of Grant. To understand fully the story of the siege, we must first look with some care at the city.

The site on which Jerusalem stands is bounded on three sides by deep gorges. Of these, one on the east, called anciently Kidron, or the "Valley of Jehosaphat," runs north and south; another to the west, called Hinnom, running at first parallel to Kidron, turns at last eastward—the bottoms of the two gorges meeting at a point full five hundred feet below the hills which they cut. The ravines form thus a rough parallelogram, with the northwest side left open. They are everywhere deep, with here and there precipices of red rock. The area, more than five miles about, thus bounded contains a basin-shaped depression called the Tyropœon, to the east of which, immediately over Kidron, rises Mount Moriah, upon which stood the Temple. On the west of the Tyropœon, a narrow neck of high ground swells out southward, into a high, broad hill, almost cut off from approach by the surrounding gullies. This was Mt. Zion, the original city of David, afterward known as the "Upper City," by nature the strongest point in Jerusalem. The Tyropœon formed before the Temple a kind of amphitheatre, within which was built much of the city. Streets ran along the upper edge, others lower down and parallel, all connected by cross-ways which descended from the higher ground toward the bottom of the basin.

On Moriah rose first the great walls of Solomon. Spacious courts, paved throughout with marble, covered immense reservoirs, containing large supplies of water, which gushed out by mechanical contrivances. The enclosure within which the Temple stood was square, an eighth of a mile on each side. On one side was precipice, where the gorge came close up to the foundations; on the others Solomon's wall, some of the stones of which were sixty feet in length. The cloisters by which it was surrounded were roofed with cedar; upon the pillars of the outer court, the Court of the Gentiles, was written in Greek: "Let no stranger enter the Holy Place." Ascending a flight of fourteen steps, the inner court was reached, where the Holy Place became visible through its lofty porch. No doors were within the gate, that it might be signified that the heavens are always open. Over it was trained a golden vine with clusters as large as a man's body, and it was draped with Babylonian curtains, whose colors symbolized the elements,—blue for air, yellow for earth, scarlet for fire, and purple for the sea. Within stood the golden candlestick of seven branches, typifying the planets; the table, whose twelve loaves of shew-bread typified the signs of the zodiac; and the altar, whose incense signified that God was the possessor of all things. From this spot the Holy of Holies was approached, within whose solemn vacancy it was lawful for no man to look. Of the Temple gates, that called "Beautiful" was the finest, full seventy-five feet in height, fifty feet wide, and built of Corinthian brass. Its doors were so ponderous that twenty men could shut them only with difficulty. "The outward face of the Temple in its front wanted nothing that was likely to surprise either men's minds or their eyes, for at the first rising of the sun it reflected back a very fiery splendor, and made those who forced themselves to look upon it, to turn their eyes away, just as they would have done at the sun's own rays. It appeared to strangers when they were at a distance, like a mountain covered with snow, for those parts of it that were not covered with gold were exceeding white."

Vast and splendid the Temple certainly was. The Romans were then at the height of power, and familiar with all the magnificence of the earth, yet it seemed to them one of the wonders of the world. No doubt it far surpassed in greatness and beauty the structure of Solomon, upon whose foundations it was reared. The Herods had lavished upon it vast treasures.

The Temple possessed, besides its splendor, all the strength of a fortress; but just north of it rose a stronghold more formidable, the Antonia, named for Mark Antony, who had been, a century before, a redoubtable figure in all this region. The Antonia stood upon an elevated crag, of which the sides were faced with smooth stones, and the top surmounted by a wall enclosing a great tower or keep of the height of sixty feet. Turrets stood upon the corners of this,

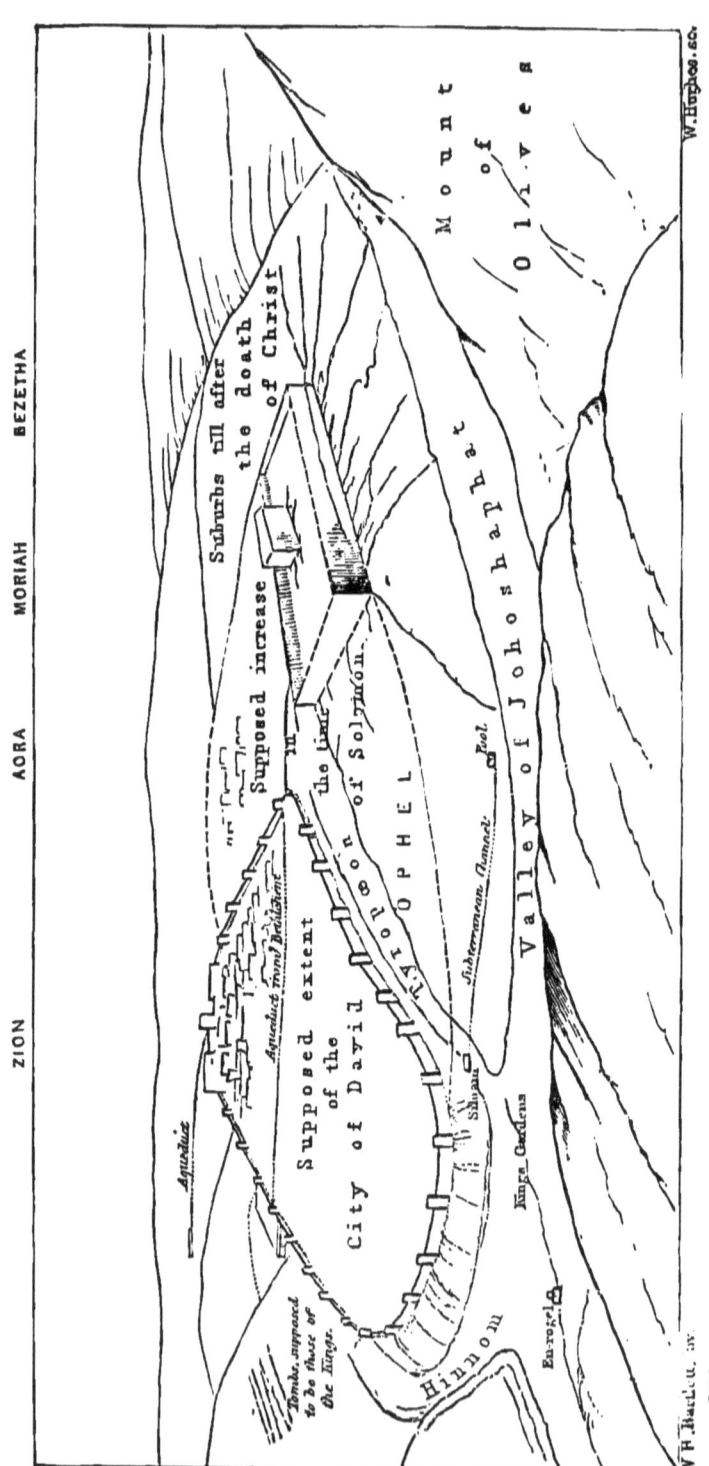

GRADUAL FORMATION OF JERUSALEM.

one rising to a height of more than a hundred feet, which commanded a view of the whole interior of the Temple. The fortress comprehended spacious apartments, courts, and camping grounds. During the Roman occupation, it was always garrisoned by a legion, who, by convenient passages, could march forth into the Temple or the city, if it were the governor's will.

For external defences, the city had before it three walls, except where protected by deep ravines, in which places there was but one. The construction was most massive, the walls rising to the height of thirty feet, with frequent towers, provided with chambers and cisterns for the rain, on which the city was largely dependent for its water. The number of these towers was one hundred and sixty-four. Akra and Ophel were quarters of the city closely adjoining the Temple; while Bezetha, a populous suburb, had shortly before been included within the defences by Herod Agrippa, the builder of the third wall. With such citadels and defences, manned by men fanatical in their patriotism, the city may well have seemed impregnable.

Forebodings of calamity, however, filled the minds of the people. The most direful portents were believed to have been seen. At the feast of the Passover, a light like noonday had been beheld within the Temple in the ninth hour of the night. The great bronze door of the gate Beautiful, with its bolts of iron and posts of stone, the door which twenty men could scarcely move, opened of itself in the sixth hour of the night. Before sunset, seven chariots had been seen driven across the sky; hosts of men in battle order surrounded cities in the clouds, and prophets, going about the streets, foretold woe to Jerusalem.

CHAPTER VIII.

TITUS ON THE RUINS OF ZION.

THE respite which the city had was long, but Vespasian at length was firmly seated on the imperial throne, and the news spread that Titus was approaching. It was the month of April of the year 70 of our era. The Roman army numbered fully 100,000 men, as it advanced from Cæsarea. There were the three legions which Vespasian had formerly commanded, hardened in the fierce campaign in Galilee. With these the 12th was joined; the 5th, too, marched to meet Titus by Emmaus, and the redoubtable 10th by Jericho. The ranks of all were filled to the full complement, and there were multitudes of Syrian auxiliaries. In the order of their march the auxiliaries formed the vanguard. Titus, with the spearmen came later, followed by the great engines,—the rams, the balistæ, the catapults. Then proceeded the legions, marching six men abreast,— the terrible short swords for the time in the scabbard, the eagles glancing in the sun, and the trumpets waking every echo. Rome itself had perhaps never before made a more formidable display of power.

Besides the buckler, lance, and sword, each footman carried a saw, basket, pick-axe, and axe, a thong of leather, a hook, and provisions for three days. The horsemen were as thoroughly accoutred, as well for siege as battle, and the entire host, by the marvellous Roman discipline, was linked and welded together into a fearful machine. "Not the bodies of the soldiers only but their souls were trained by their preparatory exercises. Death followed not only desertion, but any slothfulness; at the same time great rewards were ready for the valiant. The whole army was, as it were, but one body, so well coupled together were the ranks, so sudden their turnings about, so sharp their hearing as to what orders were given them, so quick the sight of their ensigns, so nimble their hands when set to work. What they did was done quickly,—what they suffered was borne with the greatest patience. What wonder is it that the Euphrates on the east, the ocean on the west, the most fertile regions of Libya on the south, and the Danube and Rhine on the north, are the limits of this empire! One might well say that the Roman possessions are not inferior to the Romans themselves."

Imposing, however, as was the Roman array, it might, perhaps, have dashed itself in vain against the rock-fenced city, had it not been for the factions among its defenders, which hated one another scarcely less than they hated the invaders. Of these, there was a moderate party, at the head of which stood the high-priest Ananus, which at first secretly favored making conditions with Rome, in the idea that her victory was inevitable and it was only inviting destruction to oppose her. Against these stood the Zealots, who would hear of no compromise. Troops of robbers, who, from the ravaged country, were now driven into the city, were ready for any violence. Crowds, less ill-disposed, also sought refuge within the walls. From Galilee in particular came a noteworthy figure, a fierce and fanatical chief, John of Giscala. The foe had destroyed his town and driven its population forth, but he nevertheless declared that the Romans had suffered much and could be easily defeated. The warfare between the factions was no mere strife of words. The Zealots, reinforced by John of Giscala, and entrenched within the Inner Temple, summoned to their help the Idumæans from the south, a population brave and intensely patriotic. The Idumæans, arriving outside the walls, found the entrances barred by the party of Ananus, and while a tempest beat upon them, against which they sheltered themselves by locking their shields over their heads, they encamped for the night outside the walls. But the guards of Ananus slept, and the Zealots, taking the sacred saws of the Temple, found means, while the wind and thunder drowned all sound, to cut through the bolts of the gates and admit their allies; upon which ensued such a strife that the Temple swam in blood.

As the Romans drew near, the dissensions only grew more complicated. Among the Zealots, the most violent separated themselves from John of Giscala, and seized upon the Inner Temple. John made himself master of the Outer Temple, while the city beyond still remained in the hands of the friends of Ananus. The high-priest, however, had fallen in the battle with the Idumæans, and the head of his party, the new champion, was now a certain Simon Gioras. The doughty John of Giscala, between two foes, built on the one hand towers to defend himself against the violent Zealots, while, with war-engines made from consecrated timber, cedars of Lebanon of great size and beauty, he defied, on the other hand, the party of Simon Gioras.

The Romans had hoped with good reason that Jerusalem, thus distracted, would make but a feeble defence, and becoming unwary, narrowly escaped, at the beginning of the siege, no less a disaster than the capture of their leader. Titus, leaving his host in camp in the Valley of Thorns, more than a league from the city, set out upon a reconnoissance with a party of six hundred horse. We may suppose that he rode forth from the northward upon the spot called "Scopus," the place of prospect, where, four hundred years before, Alexander had paused to receive the greeting of the people and the priests. As Titus approached the walls no soul was in sight, the gates were shut, and he rode too intrepidly forward. At the last moment, when the blast of the Roman trumpets could actually be heard, the factions had united, and all confronted the common danger. The combined host of the defenders acted at once with the greatest promptness and courage. A sudden sally from the town, and Titus was cut off from his escort. Without helmet or breastplate he faced almost alone a crowd of foes, making his way at last to safety only with the greatest difficulty.

The Roman leader now stationed his host warily, placing the tenth legion in the post of special danger, on the Mount of Olives, to the east, whence, across the narrow ravine, they fronted the city close at hand. But before the legionaries had entrenched themselves in their advanced position, so fierce a sortie was made from the gates that these, the very flower of the army of Titus, were with difficulty saved by a strong rescue party, which the commander himself brought to their aid as they were on the point of being overthrown. Retreating for a moment, the Jews, upon the signal of a cloak waved from the lofty battlements, attacked again, and it was only by desperate fighting that they were beaten off. The Romans at last prevailed, and presently the practised soldiers had reared for themselves an entrenched camp—a fortress too strong to be stormed, upon whose banks stood engines that threatened the walls at close range.

The host of Titus now levelled the plain on the northern side to the walls, and the camps of the other legions were drawn to within quarter of a mile of the towers. One day a Hebrew troop came out from a gate, apparently driven forth by those within. While Titus prepared to receive them kindly, they cunningly attacked his escort, which had too incautiously approached. It had been only a ruse, and Titus again suffered disaster. The hardened Romans, however, were above panic or discouragement. Slingers and archers swarmed behind the great banks which were built; pent-houses of skins and wicker-work defended them against the Jewish

JERUSALEM BESIEGED BY TITUS.

missiles; the great engines were vigorously plied. The catapults of the tenth legion cast stones of a talent in weight a distance of two furlongs. Watchmen stationed upon the walls, seeing the great white stones coming, exclaimed, "It cometh," giving the defenders opportunity to seek shelter. The Romans at last blackened the stones, and they could no longer be seen as they approached.

The Jews opposed the Roman artillery with the engines captured from Cestius, which had been kept in the great arsenal of Antonia. When the battering-rams were brought to bear by Titus, they sallied forth again with fire and sword, but Titus forced them back, slaying twelve with his own hand. Stripping the whole country of its timber, he built five towers, seventy-five feet in height. One, defended with iron, fell, through its enormous weight, upon its builders, to their great consternation and loss. But at length the immense ram called the "Conqueror," made a breach, and on this day, the fifteenth of the siege, the Romans became masters of the third wall. Four days later the second wall was also taken, and Titus, to make an impression of moderation, commanded that no prisoners should be slain, nor houses burned. He caused his army to display its strength before the besieged. Resting for a few days from toil, and strengthened by the distribution of an abundance of provisions, the Romans marched before the first wall in magnificent review. First went the infantry, clad in breastplates, and with arms uncovered; the cavalry appeared with horses splendidly caparisoned; the whole space near glittered with warlike pomp. Josephus, now the friend of Titus, approached to advise his countrymen to yield, declaring that the invaders would now show mercy, but upon further resistance would become implacable. Many of the Jews began to regard their position as desperate, and were moved by the words of Josephus. But the leaders never wavered; they rejected all overtures, and relentlessly slew all who could be suspected of entertaining the design to submit.

Very appalling was now the situation of the defenders. The hot summer sun beat upon the crowds in the city, still immense in number, though war had swept them off in troops. From the Mount of Olives, across the narrow Kidron, hurtled day and night the projectiles which crushed houses and their inmates. Exactly what the power may have been of those engines of the tenth legion we do not know, nor how it was obtained and applied. But by the twisting of great cables, and the skilful employment of elastic timber, the Roman engineers, it is plain, had secured a force which, though of course inferior to gunpowder, was still very formidable. Through the ravines surrounding the city prowled the hostile parties, on the watch to secure any unguarded footpath, or to scale the precipices, if there was any negligence in the watch. To the north, in their new positions within the captured lines of wall, the ruthless legions, refreshed by their rest and abundant food, crouched ready for the spring that was to carry the last defences. But worse even than these outer dangers, a dreadful famine began to prevail. The fighting men, ravenous, sought for food within the houses, and put to the torture the wretched inmates, to make them disclose their hidden stores. Wives snatched food from their husbands, children from their parents, mothers from their babes—for the closest bonds had become loosened. Certain poor wretches made their way by night beyond the walls, in search of herbs that might support life. Part were caught by the Romans, and, for an example, crucified before the defences. Those who managed to return were, as they climbed back, robbed by the Jewish soldiers. The battlements of the Antonia frowned, the Temple front flashed white from Moriah far over the hills. Beneath them what scenes of pain and death in the city like an amphitheatre that had once been so proud! It was now an arena for the rioting of terror.

Notwithstanding his successes, Titus had not yet gained his end. Four legions worked seventeen days to build new banks, but John of Giscala ran a mine deep into the earth beneath them, which he stored with pitch and sulphur. At the right time it was fired, and the legionaries and their constructions perished in the sudden volcano. Even while the devouring crater thus opened beneath the feet of Titus, and his army was for the moment astounded, Simon, son of Gioras, at the head of a furious column, with the wildest war shouts and weapons naked, rushed forth in a sortie, burning the ruins with fire, and smiting hundreds with the sword. The confusion among the Romans was but for a moment. In three days Titus surrounded the city with a wall nearly five miles in circuit, producing by the blockade distress so great that the bodies of those who had perished by famine were cast out into the ravines, and lay in the streets of the city in heaps. Many desperate Jews leaped from the walls. Horrors so multiplied that even the stern Titus called God to witness that he was not responsible. But still he pressed the siege. Timber was brought from twelve miles distant for new towers and engines. Attacking once more with the rams, holding their shields linked into a tortoise over their heads, the Romans broke four great stones out of the last wall, and made a breach. Lo, John of Giscala had built another wall behind, and stood on its summit defiant!

But now the end was really near. It was announced one day that twenty soldiers with the standard-bearer of the fifth legion had scaled the wall of Antonia, and sounded their trumpets from the top. Titus was at hand with supports and the fortress was presently in his possession, John and Simon fleeing to the Temple to stand at bay. Choosing thirty from each company, with a tribune over every thousand, and Cerealis, a valiant leader, captain over all, Titus sent a chosen band to attack by night, while he oversaw all from a watch-tower. The last days of Jerusalem had come, but the death-throes were Titanic. From the ninth hour of the night to the fifth hour of the day neither side had advantage. The Antonia was destroyed to facilitate access to the Temple walls, and the Romans swarmed upon the roof of a cloister by which the Jews might be approached. But the besieged preparing a conflagration with wood, sulphur, and bitumen, consumed them in a terrible holocaust. From hour to hour it was constant sortie and repulse, until at length for the Hebrews a direful day arrived, the anniversary of the destruction of the Temple by the power of Babylon. A soldier, then, upon the shoulders of a comrade, succeeded in casting a torch through a door in the wall which led to the chambers on the north side of the Temple. Titus would have avoided this, for he was reluctant to destroy what was the glory of the whole world. The conflagration spread, however, fanned by a tempest; in the flames, besiegers and besieged, locked into the final struggle, perished until the bodies were piled against the very altar, and the blood ran down the steps. The ground could not be seen for the dead. The furious priests brandished for weapons the leaden seats and spits of the Temple-service, and rather than yield, threw themselves into the flames. Titus and his captains, entering the Holy Place, found it beautiful and rich beyond all report. The fire fastened upon all but the imperishable rock; the Roman standards were set by the eastern gate, and Titus received the salutes of the legions as emperor.

Joshua, the priest, surrendered the candle-sticks, the tables, and the cups, all of gold—the curtains and garments of the priests—the precious stones, the dyes, purple and scarlet,—the cinnamon, cassia, and spice for the making of incense. The last place of refuge in the upper city yielded and the Romans shouted from the walls. All was at length over. John of

Giscala died in prison of starvation. Simon, having put on a white tunic beneath a purple robe and surrendered, appeared afterward at Rome in the great triumph of Titus. The city was razed, excepting three towers and part of the wall, which were preserved that all might know how great a city Rome had taken. The soldiers were rewarded with crowns of gold, with spears having golden shafts, with chains and ensigns of silver. Of the Jews, says Josephus, 1,100,000 had been slain, 97,000 survived as captives, of whom the handsomest young men were sent to Rome to grace the triumph of the conqueror; the rest were sold into slavery.

What a picture is suggested to the imagination by the fearful tale! From the northern mountains, the forests were fairly swept to furnish timber for the military engines. The herds and harvests disappeared upon the plains, that the invaders might have food. In the ruined cities, the people had been slain, or had fled from the sword to take refuge in Jerusalem. How the mind of the world in those days was fastened upon those heights, so fearfully contested! The grim veteran wearing the purple at Rome thought of his son there in armor, and exulted or trembled as the messenger galleys brought the varying news,—now that Titus had stormed a line of wall,—now that John or Simon had destroyed a cohort by a mine or brought down a tower. Far and wide, from Asia, from Africa, from Europe, had been gathered the soldiery which the genius of Rome had been able to turn into such an instrument of iron.

In all the corners of the earth men and women hung expectant upon word from the great Hebrew stronghold, for sons and neighbors were there among the strivers. It was indeed brought low, but at the cost of what devastation to the victors!

The narrative of Josephus is made vivid by many personal incidents. Antiochus of Commagene, a young Syrian prince of Macedonian descent, comes with a band trained after the manner that had given victory to Alexander, and haughtily depreciates the conduct of the Romans, who allow theselves to be so foiled. Titus gives the prince an opportunity to show his own prowess. His band attack bravely, but the Jews soon teach them to estimate more correctly the difficulty of the task which the Romans have undertaken. The horseman Pedanius, the Jews having made a sortie, catches by the ankle a young soldier, as they retreat. The youth is robust of body and in his armor; but so low does Pedanius bend himself downward from his horse, even as he is galloping away, so great is the strength of his right hand, and so firm his horsemanship, that he prevails. He seizes upon his prey as upon a precious treasure, and carries him captive to Cæsar. Artorius in the holocaust being surrounded with fire upon the roof calls to him Lucius, a fellow-soldier, a tent-fellow who is in safety. "I do leave thee heir of all I have, if thou wilt come and receive me." When Lucius comes, Artorius throws himself down upon him, saving his own life, but dashing his friend to death against the stone pavement.

In such terrible colors Josephus portrays the destruction of Jerusalem. It is not probable that the horrors are exaggerated, nor the desperate valor of the besieged, nor the unshaken persistence of the besiegers. Vast as are the multitudes put to the sword and swept into captivity, the well-established character of ancient warfare makes the account of all the ruthless slaughter and devastation entirely credible. The whole land was nearly depopulated, and the Jews have henceforth been wanderers without a country. In some respects the story of Josephus must be received with abatement. He himself can scarcely be regarded as other than a renegade, living at ease among the Romans with quite too much equanimity while his countrymen undergo such terrible ruin. Probably his portraiture of Titus is too favorable, as on the other hand his picture of Simon, John of Giscala, and other defenders of the city, is quite too dark. He has, however, narrated a great chapter in the world's story, with a patient fulness of detail almost unexampled among the writers of antiquity, and we stand in his debt. He follows Titus to Rome, and appropriately continues his account of the wars of the Jews, with a description of the splendid and cruel triumph of Titus.

Vespasian welcomed with joy his victorious son, and on the appointed day the emperor and the conqueror, coming from the temple of Isis, appear before the multitudes of Rome, crowned with laurel, and wearing the ancient purple habits belonging to their family. Seated in ivory chairs upon a tribunal before the cloisters, without arms, and clad in silk instead of steel, the stern soldiers viewed the streaming pageant, and received the acclamations of the legions, marching past with all possible military pomp. Josephus finds it impossible to describe the multitude of shows, the silver, gold, and ivory, contrived into innumerable shapes, and so borne along, that it did not appear as if carried, but ran on like a river of splendor. The richest purple hangings, Babylonian embroidery, precious stones in crowns of gold and ouches, spoils of the conquered,—of these there was such a number that none could think them to be rarities. A crowd of captives, whose costly adornment concealed the cruel wounds received in battle, and the emaciation produced by hunger in dungeons, bore along the objects, once the possession of their countrymen, but now the booty of the victors. Great structures rolled forward three or four stories in height, draped and spread with rich carpets and set off with precious metals. Upon these were presented with all possible vividness portraitures of war. There was to be seen a happy country laid waste, entire squadrons slain, the flight of fugitives, the seizure of captives. High walls were represented overthrown by machines, upon which an army poured itself through the breach. Then followed the supplications of enemies no longer able to defend themselves, the conflagration of temples, the casting down of houses upon their owners. Rivers, also, after they came out of a large and melancholy desert, ran down not into a land cultivated, nor as drink for men or cattle, but through a land still on fire on every side,—for the Jews related that such a thing they had undergone during the war. The workmanship of all this was so lively and magnificent that it seemed to the spectators as if they were really present at actual scenes.

Then, after a great number of ships and other spoils had passed, was borne along the booty from the temple. These were the golden table of many talents weight, the golden, seven-branched candlestick, the sacred tablets inscribed with the laws of the Jews. The broken-hearted Hebrews were forced to behold these objects, heretofore preserved in their innermost shrines, and possessed of the utmost sanctity, now exposed to the gaze and touch of the Gentile rabble. Rome, however, exulted in the humiliation. Images of victory were carried aloft, following the trophies. When the long train had slowly moved past, Vespasian, Titus, and his brother Domitian, descending from their lofty seats, proceeded after, while all the people shouted for joy. Vespasian built a shrine to Peace, in which were laid the golden vessels and instruments from the Jewish Temple: the tables of the Law and the purple veils of the Holy Place were deposited in the royal palace itself. Conspicuous in the great procession had moved the captive Simon, son of Gioras, the brave defender of Jerusalem. No trace of magnanimity appeared in the treatment accorded to him. A halter was set upon his head,—by way of mockery a train of seven hundred of the handsomest captives attended him,—as he proceeded he was tormented by his conductors. He was slain at last at the temple of Jupiter Capitolinus.

The arch of Titus still spans the ancient Sacra Via at Rome, at the top of the Velian ridge. Its beautiful proportions make it one of the most interesting monuments of the eternal city. Its noble sculptures, unfortunately, have not been well preserved, but still within the vault can be traced the seven-branched candlestick, the golden table, and the sorrowful train of Jews, as the captives bear the desecrated relics of the destroyed Temple beneath the cruel eyes of their conquerors. So, after eighteen hundred years, the solemn marble commemorates a tragedy than which calamity was never more complete!

Is the volume closed? Is the career of the Jew finished? Not so. In a century or two, he has accomplished as an outcast the most momentous of human conquests. We have already followed in brief the career of the Aryan races, in their majestic descent from their mysterious mountain cradle until they possess Europe,—then at last in the power of Greece, and a little later, in the power of Rome, come into contact with the Jew. The Aryan races go forward, as the centuries lapse, to make Europe, among the divisions of the world, the especial seat of power and civilization. As upon the night of barbarism, there flashed first the splendor of the Hellenic beacon, followed soon by the blaze of Rome, so, in his turn, came the Goth, kindling slow like anthracite, then through long centuries making bright the central plains and the islands of the sea. A torch, late, but vivid with promise, shone at last upon the

ARCH OF TITUS.

Northeastern steppes. Meanwhile the Atlantic barrier of tempest and surge was at last broken, and the Western world, even to the Ocean of Peace, has become all alight. So the Aryan, with face ever toward the setting sun, has run his flashing series, till the West is East again, and the round world is becoming belted with his light. It is a tale of conquest never ending,—of the spreading of a radiance that never grows dim.

There was one, however, to master even the master,—to bring light even to the light-bringer. In the midst of his path the exultant Aryan encountered this swarthy, burning-eyed Semite of the Syrian hills and plains. His limbs were marked by the weight of the fetters he had worn as a bondman in Egypt. Scarcely had he been able to cope with the puny tribes of Syria, with Philistine, and Amorite, and the men of Moab. Driven by the lash of taskmasters, he had constructed the palaces of Nineveh. In Babylon he had been broken and sundered. Suffered at last to return from exile, as he built anew his temple-walls, his feeble hands could scarcely quell the attacks of the petty freebooters of the wilderness. What respect could a creature, so crushed and dismembered, receive from the superb brethren of the great Aryan household, robust of limb, imperial in brain, trampling the world into servitude! He was but a despicable opponent. So thought the sons of the captains of Alexander, and they tore him anew beneath the harrow of invasion. So thought the power of Rome, and the ambitious Titus made the neck of the Jew a stepping-stone to the imperial throne. Where in the history of conquests has there been annihilation so utter? But it was only a superficial victory that the Aryan won. From the foot of a cross upon which had died an obscure disturber of the peace, of peasant birth, went forth twelve poor men who had loved him. How trifling the circumstance! One day at Athens, upon Mars Hill, the travel-worn tent-maker, Paul, addressed, not far from the altar to the unknown God, a supercilious crowd. What mattered that small event! At Rome the passionate agitator, Peter, crucified at last head downward, died, confessing to the last the teacher in whose name he had spoken. But such things were done every day. What could a Jew effect? In the grapple between Aryan and Semite, the Semite was apparently crushed out of life; but even while the knee of the ruthless victor was upon his breast, the victim spoke a calm, strong mandate which abashed and overcame. "Yield to me," said the prostrate Jew, "in that point where the soul of man feels most deeply,—his thought of the great invisible world. Your deities, Zeus, Mars, Odin, are not gods but phantoms. Elysium, Tartarus, Walhalla, it is all unreal. Straightway dash in pieces your altars, though the smoke of sacrifice has ascended thence for ages. Straightway dismiss every hymn and precept, every rite and rule. Ended forever be libation and augury, obeisance of flamen, chant of vestal, the oracular whisper of the sacred oaks, the frenzy of the Pythoness aglow with the God. Dismiss it all as false. Take from me a faith which shall last you for ages, burn in your deepest soul, inspire you to the grandest which you shall ever undertake. Accept Jehovah, my God, as the only God. Accept my race as the chosen race ; accept its literature as sacred and infallible. Reverence my land as a holy land. Accept a man of my race, not only as the Redeemer of the world, but the incarnate God himself. That your subjection may be the more marked and utter, this crucified Galilean whom I force you to receive as Lord and Saviour, I myself will utterly reject and contemn, requiring you to reverence what I despise as folly and superstition!"

Thus spoke the eagle-faced, burning-eyed captive, homeless, broken, humiliated, to his Aryan subduer at his very proudest. Did the Aryan obey? Straightway the Aryan obeyed. Greek, Roman, Celt, and Teuton pass under the yoke of the Jew. In his turn comes the Sclave, equally submissive, all the stronger brethren of the Aryan household enthralled really by the Semite, though superficially they seem to have vanquished him—their subjugation maintained through all these nineteen slow-lapsing centuries!

Is it a supernatural conversion, as the Christian world has always maintained, or can it all be explained according to the natural sequence of cause and effect, as the rationalist will assert? Whether natural or supernatural, the little race that has thus brought the world to its feet has possessed a pre-eminent force which has made its history unique. What the Jew has wrought is a marvel among marvels. It has been no strange thing upon the earth for beings in human guise to be made gods. Hercules, Odin, Alexander, Cæsar, and many another have been raised to the heavens and worshipped. Only, however, in the case of this first-born child of a Jewish mother has the apotheosis endured.* He stands in this exaltation, not in the wild fancy of barbarians, but in the trained and cool judgment of the races whose brain and vigor have made them foremost among men. These have felt that he spoke as never man spoke, and was the embodiment of his own gospel of love in his life and in his death. Who will say that his name is not above every name? If we refuse, as some men do, to ascribe to him a superhuman character, then how astonishing the miracle, that a Hebrew peasant has been able to so influence the destinies of mankind!

* Disraeli: "Tancred."

PART II.

THE MEDIÆVAL HUMILIATION.

CHAPTER IX.

HOW THE RABBIS WROUGHT THE TALMUD.

THE year 70 of our era brought the dreadful tragedy of the destruction of Jerusalem. In the next generation the champion Bar Cocheba, whom many Jews believed to be the Messiah, headed a revolt which was soon put down by the Emperor Hadrian. The taking of his stronghold, Bethar, was the *coup de grace;* Palestine was utterly devastated; even the olive-trees had disappeared; the land was full of graves, the markets with slaves; the towns were given over to wolves and hyenas. Even the name of Jerusalem was lost; a pagan city, Aelia Capitolina, rose upon its site; a temple of Jupiter stood upon Mt. Zion, about which was gathered a population of Roman veterans, of Greeks, Phœnicians, and Syrians. So long as the Roman empire endured, no Jew could enter the city under pain of death.

Long before these events, the Jews, as we have seen, had begun to wander. The ten tribes that had disappeared in the Assyrian days were still to a large extent present in their descendants in Mesopotamia, or were scattered abroad in unknown regions. The prosperity of the great colony at Alexandria had given evidence of the constant favor of the Ptolemies. At Rome the Jewish face had become well known, and they had penetrated with the legions into Spain and Gaul. " How unjust," said often the suffering Jew of the Middle Ages, "to persecute us because Christ was crucified, when our fathers had left Jerusalem long before his time!"—a plea often well founded.

The religious faith they gave to others they rejected themselves. Christianity became from its very origin the possession of the Gentiles, the Jewish following being always insignificant. These unbelievers, where have they not gone upon the face of the earth? It is said they are to be found in China and the depths of India, upon the steppes of Tartary, in inner Africa, in every market and capital of Europe and America. Alike among Christians, Moslems, and Heathen they have been outcasts and subjects of persecution, exposed to suffering not due entirely to the bigotry of the races among which they have been cast, but largely owing to their own exclusiveness and proud assertion of superiority. In entering upon an account of events in which the Christian world appears in a light so discreditable, it is only fair to state distinctly, that in the position which the Hebrews have constantly occupied toward the races among which they have sojourned, there has been much to exasperate men just rising out of barbarism—much indeed which those well-civilized have hardly been able to bear with equanimity. The Christian has bitterly persecuted; but when has the Jew been conciliatory? or, except in the

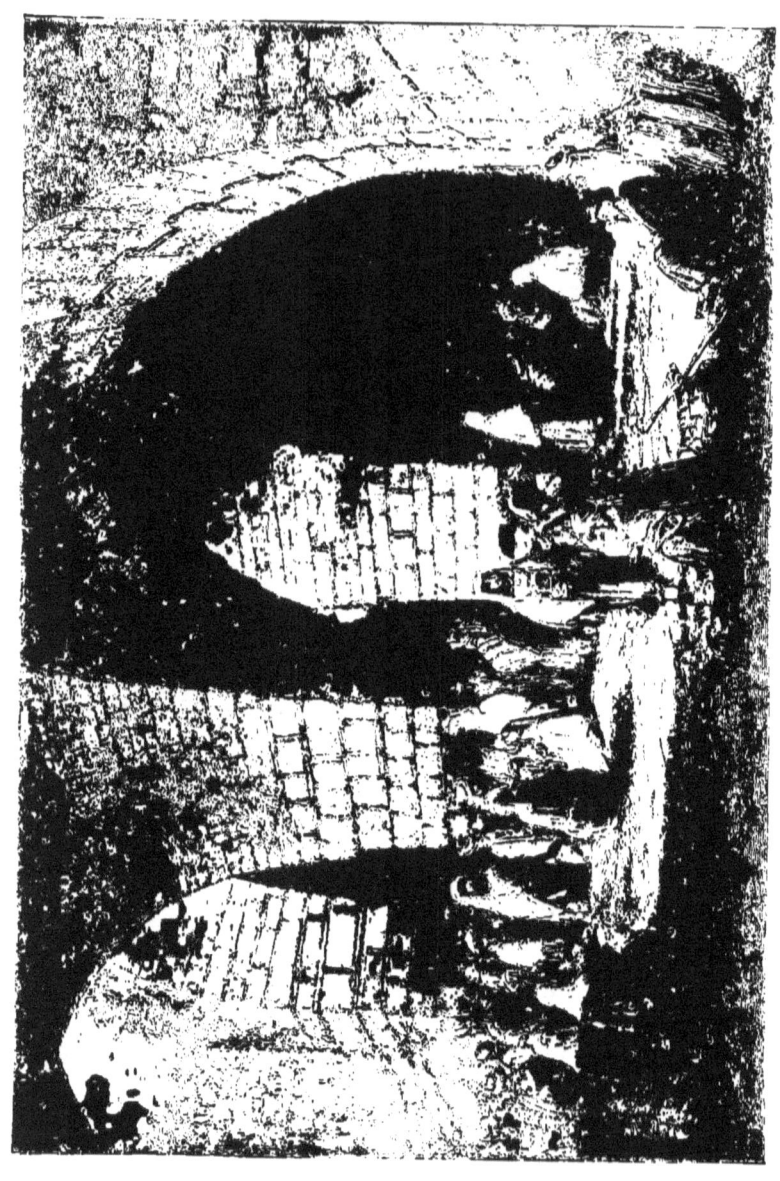

ROMAN MASONRY, JERUSALEM.

case of the nobler spirits of his race, whom he has usually made haste to cast forth, when has he shown the wide-extending sympathy which recognizes cordially the brotherhood of the human race, and looks toward the tearing down of walls of separation between man and man? In this story of humiliation, therefore, the victim is not to be held quite blameless. Let no Christian, however, presume to claim that the guilt is not mainly with his houshold of faith.

The Jews, originally, had no special turn for trading.* In the earlier day their life we have seen to be that of herdsmen, tillers of the soil, and handicraftsmen of the simplest sort. Their traffic was insignificant even after their return from the exile, until the Macedonian days, when mercantile intercourse with other nations became among them a more frequent pursuit. Even then commerce was far from absorbing them. But in the countless lands into which they were at length carried by the dispersion, they were often forced to follow quite other paths than the old. The prejudice of the races among which they came frequently forbade to them the ownership of land and the following of the handicrafts. Commerce became to them the easiest, most natural resource; as they practised it, their dexterity increased. The success they reached aroused a disposition which their ancestors did not possess. The awakened trading-spirit favored the dispersion; the dispersion, on the other hand, stimulated the trading-

* Herzfeld: "Handelsgeschichte der Juden des Alterthums," 271, etc.

spirit, until, through the interaction, the Jews were everywhere scattered and everywhere merchants.

That the Jews have been in the latter ages prevailingly traders, has been made a reproach to them, but for the reasonable of our day it needs no excuse. Honest trading is recognized as by no means worse than any other legitimate and necessary occupation. It may be claimed perhaps, that it has contributed more than any other to the elevation and comfort of man. During the breaking down of the Roman empire, the Jewish merchants were the connecting links between Asia and Europe. At the beginning of the Middle Ages they were an economical necessity. Forced into this channel by the fate which had overtaken them, confined to it more and more closely as fanaticism, growing more and more suspicious, shut before them the doors of other callings, they deserved not contempt but gratitude, as they helped the comfort, the prosperity, the civilization of so many peoples. As to the honesty with which they have trafficked, Israelite historians successfully show that they were honorably distinguished in antiquity. Not Phœnician or Babylonian, not Greek or Roman, equalled them. They were not Jews who made the same divinity stand at once as the god of thieves and of merchants. In later days also, in spite of the slanders of the learned and the unlearned, the impartial investigator will find the Jews in their business relations rather above than below the level of common morality, their faith in this as in every other department requiring of them an ideal purity.*

* Herzfeld.

After its wonderful seizure of the Aryan soul, Judaism encountered presently a form of faith more nearly related to itself than Greek, Roman, and Teuton ideas. It might be expected that from Mahometans, the Jew would receive somewhat better treatment than from races unallied. The Arabs, a stock which like the Israelites looked to Abraham as a progenitor, gave to Islam its prophet. In reality it is only at times, that the outcast people has received kindness at their hands, fiery Mussulman intolerance bringing more often to pass a persecution scarcely less bitter than that from Christian hands. Throughout Arabia, Mesopotamia, and Babylonia, however, the Hebrews spread, in the cities establishing thriving colonies, and maintaining at various points schools where a learning profound, though fantastic, was taught by the Rabbis to crowds of pupils. They followed with their congeners in the path of the advancing crescent through Northern Africa, and helped essentially in the conquest by means of which the old Visigothic power of Spain was displaced. The bloom of Moorish civilization followed; Averroes and Avicenna, with torches kindled upon Greek altars, lighting in the west the fire of philosophy. An art came to flourish which could create the Alhambra; a poetry was developed that softened and ennobled manners; many a truth of physical science was anticipated—a night, meantime, almost unbroken enveloping every part of Christendom. It was, on the whole, a happy time for the Jews. Given free course under the tolerant sway of the Caliphs, their striving was an important factor in producing the beautiful result. When at length to the rest of Europe came the Renaissance, the Jews, going and coming in their intercourse with their brethren everywhere, now in the land where the arts were thriving, and now in regions where all was waiting, were among the chief mediators who bore the fructifying pollen from the sunny, blossoming spots to the more shadowed regions which awaited impregnation.

Among the Saracens in their time of power the lines of Israel did not fall ill, nor was its position one of difficulty when the modern world first began to emerge. Under Charlemagne, Jews were tolerated— indeed, befriended and honored. In the famous embassy to Haroun al Raschid, the honored figure is that of the Jew Isaac; and, in other positions than diplomatic, Hebrews were friends and helpers of the great path-breaker. Under the immediate successors of Charlemagne, still greater good fortune was enjoyed; but we cannot pass even the threshold of the Middle Ages without encountering a Hebrew persecution which is perhaps the most dreadful page of history.

Not a single Christian people has kept itself clear from the reproach of inhumanity to the Jews. To afflict them has been held to be a merit. The times when religion has been most rife and the conscience most sensitive have witnessed the sharpest scourgings and the most lurid holocausts. When the nations were aroused to redeem the Holy Sepulchre from dishonor, when the cathedrals were rising, gushes of devotion from the popular heart, fixed in stone to stand for centuries, it was precisely then that the faggots were heaped highest and the sword was most merciless. The Jews and the Saracens were allied stocks, between whom a secret understanding may sometimes have existed. "If we are to fight infidels," said fanaticism, "why not fight them at home as well as in Syria?" Men and women chivalrous and saintly have denounced and wrung the Jew almost in proportion to their chivalry and sanctity, and this has endured almost to the present hour,— Richard Cœur-de-Lion, St. Louis of France, Ferdinand and Isabella, Luther, Savonarola, Maria Theresa,—yet how great is the debt of civilization to these men so cruelly hounded! They had become a trading race, indeed, but not entirely so. They had a large share in the restoration of learning and the cultivation of science in the time of the Renaissance. Through them many Greek writers were translated into Arabic, thence to be rendered into the tongues of Europe and made accessible to the young universities of the West. Through them medicine was revived, to become the parent of physical science in general. They were universal translators, publishers, and literary correspondents. Their schools at Montpellier in France, Salerno in Italy, and Seville in Spain, abounded in erudite men and scientific experimenters. While superstition reigned elsewhere, they were often comparatively free from it. The deserts of the Hebrews in these respects must never be forgotten, though perhaps here they accomplished less than as merchants, almost the only representatives of commerce as they were, "the fair, white-winged peacemaker" flying across field and flood among the distant cities of men, binding them into a noble brotherhood.

We are to follow the footsteps of the broken nation into the lands of their exile, so utterly cold for them—footsteps of blood in a wintry landscape. But before taking up the story, something must be said about the standards which the Hebrews held in honor, now that their independence as a nation was destroyed,—standards venerated without abatement down to the present hour; a veneration almost universal, and a principal cause why the Jews, though so sundered and smitten, have maintained a solidarity.

First, the Jew held in honor the Scriptures, containing the Law of Moses, the sacred Torah, the Prophets, and the Hagiographa, or sacred writings. The Canon, as we have seen, had been formed in the age of Ezra: the centuries which had followed had deepened respect for it; and as the Gentile world gradually became Christian, that, too, received the canon of Ezra, under the name of the Old Testament, with faith as undoubting as that of the Hebrews themselves.

But the reader will remember that when the written Law was brought from Sinai, a body of precepts was, it was believed, at the same time imparted, which was for many ages handed down orally. This was called the Mischna, and not until the time of the teacher Hillel, a generation or two before Christ, was any beginning made of reducing these traditions to writing. In the sad days which resulted in the destruction of Jerusalem, no one was found to carry out the work of Hillel, but a time came when it was brought to fulfilment, and the result was the Talmud.

The latest Jewish authority* declares the composition of the Talmud to be the most important fact of Hebrew history during the four centuries that follow the fall of Jerusalem. In order to strengthen the written Law and supplement it where it was silent, recourse was had to those oral traditions which all Israel believed had come down from Moses himself. During the period mentioned the Jewish doctors made these the subject of ardent and minute study,— a labor believed to be necessary, since the destruction of the Temple and ever-increasing dispersion of the nation no longer allowed tradition to perpetuate itself as formerly. As this second code became developed, it was much more detailed than the Torah, embracing in its prescriptions the whole civil and religious life of the Jews, and ensuring unity of faith by the uniformity which it brought about in ceremonial practices.

The Rabbis, however, were not satisfied with the drawing up of the "Mischna." An attempt was further made to develop and reconcile, to render an account of whatever was mysterious; in fine, to apply to real or fictitious cases which the ancient doctors had not foreseen, the principles which they had stated only generally. This labor, pursued with diligence in the schools both of Palestine and Babylonia,

* Reinach : "Histoire des Israélites depuis leur Dispersion jusqu' à nos Jours," Paris, 1885.

resulted in the "Gemara," which was given to the world at last in two immense compends, the Talmuds of Jerusalem and Babylon, the latter and most important of which, even in the partial form which has survived to us, comprises twelve large volumes. To all but the most patient students, the work would seem to be a hopeless chaos. The subtle Rabbis took a lively pleasure in puzzling over insoluble difficulties, discussing to an infinite extent the opinions of their predecessors, discovering difficulties, sometimes imaginary, and trying to harmonize things quite irreconcilable. The contents are most varied,—satirical allegories, popular proverbs, fantastic imaginary stories, historical recitals strangely distorted, scientific discussions, medical prescriptions in which Chaldaic superstitions play a large part,—an irregular familiar talk, often, without rule or plan.

The authority whom I follow maintains that whereas to the Talmud in some ages has been assigned an importance quite exaggerated, it is at present by many critics quite improperly decried and depreciated.* The character of the men to whom the Talmud addressed itself is forgotten. At the time when the dispersion of Israel was beginning, it was necessary to raise about Judaism, at every price, a double and triple moral barrier, an exterior wall, to protect it against dissolving influences from outside. The Talmud was such a wall. It was long the principal, if not the sole, intellectual food of the scattered Hebrews. Its destinies have been those of the

* For an example of such criticism see Depping: "Die Juden im Mittelalter," 14, 15.

Jewish race, and whenever it has been burned, the burning of the Jews themselves has been not far off. If some minds have become stultified in its debates, minute and often inane, others have gained by their study a subtle and penetrative power. Many a rabbi, trained by the study of the Talmud, has developed and made fruitful other sciences. The philosophy of many a beneficent Jewish thinker had here its root. The first translators of Aristotle and Averroes passed their youth in the rabbinical schools. If the Jews escaped in a measure the eclipse of the Dark Ages, so total over the Christian world, they owe it to the Talmud.

A Gentile has great difficulty in obtaining any coherent idea of this strange old work. The Rabbis seem to prescribe and condemn tolerance, to approve and forbid usury, to recommend and despise agriculture, to honor and depreciate women. It seems strange it should have been held in such honor. One Rabbi said the written Law was water, the Mischna wine, and the Gemara an aromatic liquor very precious. I give a passage from still another Jewish scholar of our own time, who is believed to have been a most accomplished Talmudist[*]: "Well can we understand the distress of mind in a mediæval divine, or even in a modern savant, who, bent upon following some scientific debate in the Talmudical pages, feels, as it were, the ground suddenly give way. The loud voices grow thin, the doors and walls of the school-room vanish before his eyes, and in their place uprises Rome the great, and her

[*] Emanuel Deutsch: "Literary Remains," 45, etc., 151.

million-voiced life. Or the blooming vineyards around that other city of hills, Jerusalem the Golden herself, are seen, and white-clad virgins move dreamily among them. Snatches of their songs are heard, the rhythm of their choric dances rises and falls. Often, far too often for the interests of study and the glory of the human race, does the steady tramp of the Roman cohort, the shriek and clangor of the bloody field, interrupt these debates, and the arguing masters and their disciples don their arms, and with the cry, 'Jerusalem and liberty,' rush to the fray.

"It shows us the teeming streets of Jerusalem, tradesmen at work, women at home, children at play, priest and Levite, preacher on hillside, story-teller in the bazaar,—nor Jerusalem alone, but the whole antique world is embalmed there, Athens, Alexandria, Persia, Rome. * * * A strange, wild, wierd ocean, with its leviathans and its wrecks of golden argosies, and with its forlorn bells that send up their dreamy sounds ever and anon, while the fisherman bends upon his oar, and starts and listens, and perchance the tears may come into his eyes."

While it is so difficult to derive from the Talmud any system or history, the poetical scholar goes on to compare these fanciful pictures to photographic slides, half-broken and faded, but startlingly faithful. As the most childish of trifles found in an Assyrian mound may lead the scholar to great results, so may the trifles in the Talmud. That the old volumes contain shrewd worldly wit as well as profound spiritual wisdom, the following sentences will show:
" Be thou the cursed, not he who curses. Be of them

that are persecuted, not of them that persecute. There is not a single bird more persecuted than the dove, yet God has chosen her to be offered upon his altar. He who offers humility unto God and man shall be rewarded as if he had offered all the sacrifices in the world. When the righteous dies it is the earth that loses. Thy friend has a friend, and thy friend's friend has a friend,—be discreet. Commit a sin twice and you will think it perfectly allowable."

Of the strange and beautiful romance of the Talmud, no better example can be taken than the story, to which Longfellow has given a form so charming, of Sandalphon.

> Have you read in the Talmud old,
> In the legends the Rabbins have told
>   Of the limitless realms of the air,—
> Have you read it,—the marvellous story
> Of Sandalphon, the Angel of Glory,
>   Sandalphon, the Angel of Prayer?
>
> How, erect, at the outermost gates
> Of the city celestial he waits,
>   With his feet on the ladder of light,
> That, crowded with angels unnumbered,
> By Jacob was seen, as he slumbered,
>   Alone in the desert of night?
>
> The angels of wind and of fire
> Chant only one hymn, and expire
>   With the song's irresistible stress ;
> Expire in their rapture and wonder,
> As harp-strings are broken asunder
>   By music they throb to express.
>
> But, serene in the rapturous throng,
> Unmoved by the rush of the song,

With eyes unimpassioned and slow,
Among the dead angels, the deathless
Sandalphon stands listening breathless
　　To sounds that ascend from below;—

From the spirits on earth that adore,
From the souls that entreat and implore
　　In the ferver and passion of prayer;
From hearts that are broken with losses,
And weary with dragging the crosses
　　Too heavy for mortals to bear.

And he gathers the prayers as he stands,
And they change into flowers in his hands,
　　Into garlands of purple and red;
And beneath the great arch of the portal,
Through the streets of the City Immortal,
　　Is wafted the fragrance they shed.

It is but a legend, I know,—
A fable, a phantom, a show
　　Of the ancient Rabbinical lore;
Yet the old mediæval tradition,
The beautiful, strange superstition,
　　But haunts me and holds me the more.

When I look from my window at night,
And the welkin above is all white,
　　All throbbing and panting with stars,
Among them majestic is standing
Sandalphon, the angel, expanding
　　His pinions in nebulous bars.

And the legend, I feel, is a part
Of the hunger and thirst of the heart,
　　The frenzy and fire of the brain,
That grasps at the fruitage forbidden,
The golden pomegranates of Eden,
　　To quiet its fever and pain.

As in antiquity the traditioual Law was rejected by the Sadducees, who indeed found nothing worthy of respect but the five books of Moses, so in the modern era a sect known as the Karaites rejected the work of the Talmudists, and a bitter strife came to pass between these protestants of Judaism, and the Rabbanites, who accepted the work of the doctors. They mutually excommunicated one another, wrestled in the sharpest controversy, and refused to one another all friendship and alliance. Though Orthodoxy prevailed, Karaism is still not extinct, lingering on in a few communities in Lithuania and the Crimea.

Before dismissing the consideration of Torah and Talmud, a word must be said as to a very valuable and practical part of their precepts. The hygienic rules which they contain are said to possess great wisdom.* The idea of parasitical and infectious maladies, of which we now hear so much, occupied also the mind of Moses. He indicates with great wisdom the animals to be used as food, excluding those liable to parasites, as swine, rabbits, and hares. He prescribes the thorough bleeding of animals to be eaten, and the burning of the fat; it has been established that it is precisely the blood and the fat which are most liable to retain parasitic germs and carry infection. The Talmud, moreover, directs that the liver, lungs, and spleen shall be carefully scrutinized. Precisely those organs are especially liable to disease. With reference to dwellings and clothing, and the satisfying of natural wants, the rules of

* Dr. Noël Gueneau de Mussy : Hygienic Laws of Moses. *New York Medical Abstract*, March, 1885.

Torah and Talmud are excellent ; in point of health, the advantage of a careful observance of the Sabbath is very great ; even circumcision can be defended as an excellent sanitary expedient. In several respects the Mosaic Law is declared to have anticipated modern science by several thousand years. Throughout the entire history of Israel the wisdom of the ancient lawgivers in these respects has been remarkably shown: in times of pestilence, the Hebrews have suffered far less than others ; as regards longevity and general health, they have in every age been noteworthy; at the present time in the life-insurance offices the life of a Jew is said to be worth much more than that of men of other stock ; Sir Moses Montefiore dies at one hundred, and in his great age as well as in so many other ways, he is only a type of his nation.

Clasping thus in his arms as his chief treasures the scrolls of the Torah and the Talmud, the incongruous mixture of divine wisdom with curious follies, of exalted poetry with grotesque and repulsive superstition, the Jew comes forward in his long pilgrimage through the centuries. From the time of those fierce figures whom we saw struggling to the last against Titus among the wild spear-brandishings and conflagrations in the midst of which Jerusalem went down, to the era of the revival of learning, there is no Hebrew character before whom we need to pause; but here we come upon a memorable personage.

An illustrious type of the noble students and thinkers of the Renaissance was Maimonides, a native of Cordova in Spain, who died in Cairo at the beginning of the thirteenth century. Even in youth he had mastered all the knowledge of his time, receiving inspiration especially from the great Averroes, the Moorish teacher to whom the revival of learning owed so much. Persecution from his brethren drove him from his birthplace, pursuing him elsewhere also, until at last he found himself at Cairo, where, winning the favor of the broad-minded Sultan Saladin, he became court physician, and stood in a place of high honor. At the same time he taught as Rabbi among his own people, spreading abroad through speeches in the synagogue, but more especially through abundant writings in Hebrew and Arabic, a multiform knowledge. He communicated instruction in medicine, mathematics, and astronomy; better than this, he sent far and wide a noble philosophy which anticipated in its freedom and reasonable spirit the thought of a far later day. Though he suffered harsh treatment at the hands of his fellow-Jews and the blind world in which his lot was cast, he found defenders and followers; his words communicated the hints from which the master-spirits of later ages have caught the inspiration which filled them; to-day men look back upon him, standing there, just where the dark ages are beginning to grow brighter, as a form lofty and venerable. Not that he was a man before his age. In some of his writings he dwells unduly upon Talmudic trifles and stupidities, and cherishes a true Hebrew scorn towards the notions of the Gentiles. But at other times he denounces astrology, draws up certain rules to be held as fundamental principles, which proclaim monotheism and the immortality of the soul ; and in a book called the " Teacher of the Perplexed," tries to make easy for the common man the understanding of Scripture. In this work he so over-rides the confusion of the Talmud, that he was long held by orthodox Jews as a heretic, or possibly a secret Christian. He won, however, respect in life, and a pure and widely extended fame. His house in Cairo was besieged by the sick, who found in him a healer kind and skilful. Some declared him to be the first man truly great who had appeared among the Jews since the time of Moses, and it was written upon his grave that he was " the elect of the human race."

CHAPTER X.

THE HOLOCAUSTS IN SPAIN.

WE are now to examine the Hebrew story as it is told in the annals of one Christian race. The Jews have claimed that their progenitors were in the Iberian peninsula even in the days of Carthaginian rule. The Romans and Visigoths in turn succeed, and at length, through the Visigothic King Sisebut, the Hebrews undergo their first sharp persecution. They gladly exchange the Christian for the Moslem yoke, and, as we have seen, flourish with the Moors in brotherly accord. With the ebb of the Saracen power Navarre, Castile, Arragon, take shape on the strand that is laid bare, until in the fifteenth century the Cross supplants the green banner of the prophet even in Granada, and the forces of the whole peninsula, blended so that they can be wielded by a single arm, become the mighty power of Spain. The Jew changed masters, not to his advantage, but his misfortunes did not begin at once. The Spanish Israelites, the "Sephardim," as they call themselves, have always claimed that they were of nobler rank than elsewhere; at first they were prosperous and wealthy, with no mark of the degradation induced by being forced to debasing means of extorting riches. They owned and tilled the soil, were the agents of commerce, cultivators of the arts. In particular, they were the physicians of the country. "Every one," says Milman, "sat under his shady fig-tree or cluster-laden vine singing hymns to the mighty God of Israel who again had mercy on his people." In the Crusades Spain took little part, embarrassment from infidels close at hand pressing much too sharply. The Jews, too, were spared for a time the outbursts of fanatical rage which overtook them elsewhere in Christendom, but the respite was brief. In 1212, a great battle having been lost against the Moors, as was said on account of the love of the king for a Jewess, twelve thousand Hebrews were massacred.

Christian cruelty, however, was at first fitful. The outburst of rage was speedily followed by favor, and for two centuries we trace alternations of cruelty and sufferance until the union of the crowns of Arragon and Castile. To avoid persecution many Jews became nominally Christian. The converts were almost universally still Jews at heart, though many ascended to positions of the highest eminence. Even in the Church the frock of the friar covered thousands whose confession was only a pretence. There were heads indeed surmounted with the mitre whose sincere homage was rendered not to the Host, but in secret, before the parchment tables of the Law. To discover how widely covert Jewish practices prevailed, it is said, it was only necessary to ascend a hill on their Sabbath, and look down on towns and villages below. Scarce half the chimneys would be seen to smoke, for the multitudes of secret Jews

celebrated their holy time. Among men of the
bluest Castilian blood were those of Hebrew strain.
The lordliest hidalgos bowing before the altar of
the Virgin in public, often, when in private, lifted a
tapestry, and by a secret door entered a shrine set
forth with Israelitish symbols. Such a shrine is thus
described by a descendant of the Spanish Hebrews,
following, probably, traditions handed down from
an ancient time.*

"The edifice was square, and formed of solid blocks
of cedar; neither carving nor imagery of any kind
adorned it, yet it had evidently been built with skill
and care. There was neither tower nor bell. A
door, so skilfully constructed as when closed to be
invisible in the solid wall, opened noiselessly. The
interior was as peculiar as its outward appearance.
Its walls of polished cedar were unadorned. In the
centre, facing the east, was a sort of raised table or
desk, surrounded by a railing, and covered with a
cloth of the richest and most elaborately worked
brocade. Exactly opposite and occupying the centre of the eastern wall, was a sort of lofty chest or
ark, the upper part of which, arched, and richly
painted, with a blue ground, bore in two columns
strange hieroglyphics in gold; beneath this were portals of polished cedar, panelled and marked out with
gold, but bearing no device; their hinges set in
gilded pillars, which supported the arch above. Before these portals were generally drawn curtains of
material rich and glittering as that upon the reading-desk. But this day not only were the curtains drawn

* Grace Aguilar, in the "Vale of Cedars."

aside, but the portals themselves flung open, as the bridal party neared the steps which led to it, and disclosed six or seven rolls of parchment, folded on silver pins, and filled with the same strange letters, each clothed in drapery of variously colored brocade or velvet, and surmounted by two sets of silver ornaments, in which the bell and pomegranate were, though small, distinctly discernible. A superb lamp of solid silver was suspended from the roof, and one of smaller dimensions, but of equally valuable material, and always kept lighted, hung just before the ark."

It was very seldom that the zeal of the monkish preachers won a new convert.*

One is struck with wonder at the energy of the fanaticism that should undertake to crush out a form of unbelief so widely spread and so strongly placed. The attempt was made, and the instrument employed was the most dreadful engine which superstition ever devised—the Inquisition. In the city of Nuremberg one may go into the ancient torture-chamber—a room preserved unchanged, still retaining all

* From ancient times to the present day, indeed, the Hebrews have yielded few proselytes to Christianity—a fact amusingly hit off not long since by *Punch*, who describes the work of the English Society for the Conversion of the Jews in language substantially as follows: "It appears from the report of the Society for the Conversion of the Hebrews, that during the past year there has been an outlay of £5,000, as the result of which four large Israelites and one little one have been converted to Christianity. To effect the change, therefore, costs £1,000 per Jew. Mr. Punch would respectfully intimate to his Hebrew friends that he is acquainted with large numbers of Christians who would be very happy to become Jews at a much smaller figure."

its dismal apparatus for causing suffering. No member of the body appears to be forgotten; for each is the appointed contrivance to wring and tear. Then by winding subterranean passages you are led to the vault in the bowels of the earth, where stands the "iron maiden," the apparatus for secret execution. At the touch of a spring the rude woman's figure flies apart, the blood-rusted spikes of its interior dreadfully visible in the light of the smoking torch, as in ancient days before the eyes of condemned men; and below, the yawning pit, from whose abyss sounds far down the splash of the sullen waters into which the mangled body fell. To speak of such things almost requires an apology. The man of modern times groans and shudders at these sights. "Whence came," he cries, "the people who made and used these engines? How can I believe that these beings are of the same nature with my own?" At Regensburg, at Salzburg, in Baden Baden, in those deep caverns hollowed out in the heart of the rock, where doors of stone close behind you with a heavy groan, and the loudest cry is muffled at once into a whisper, one may see the grisly apparatus of Nuremberg duplicated, and these cities are not alone. There are grim volumes on the history of torture, from which may be learned that through antiquity and mediæval times there was no lawful court which did not have, not far off, some such dismal appurtenance, the legitimate and recognized appliance, not only for the punishment of crime, but for the examination of witnesses. To my mind, there is no thing which so measures the length of the forward step the world has taken, as the sickening dread with which the modern man contemplates these things which were once every-day and matter-of-course.

In the Inquisition there was a wholesale employment of all this nightmare machinery. The Inquisition was established in the first instance to terrify into faithfulness apostate Jews, the sincerity of whose conversion to Christianity was suspected, and in almost all cases, with good reason. Seated in some vast and frowning castle, or in some sunless cavern of the earth, its ministers chosen from the most influential men of the nation, its familiars in every disguise, in every corner of the land, its proceedings utterly secret, its decrees overriding every law, it would be impossible to draw a picture which would exaggerate its accumulated horrors. Men and women disappeared by hundreds, suddenly and completely as a breath annihilates the flame of a lamp, some gone forever without whisper as to their fate; some to reappear in after years, halt through long tortures, pale and insane through frightful incarceration. When in the cities the frequent processions wound through the streets, with their long files of victims on the way to the place of burning, children bereaved of father and mother flocked to see whether among the doomed they might not catch a last look of the face of the long-lost parent. The forms that were observed were such a mockery of justice! In the midst of the torture came the cold interrogation of the inquisitor. Fainting with terror and anguish, the sufferer uttered he knew not what, to be written down by waiting clerks and made the basis of procedure. Grace Aguilar, in one of her stories, makes her heroine to disappear through the floor of a chamber of Queen Isabella herself, who had sought to protect her, borne then by secret passages to a vast hall, where a grandee of Spain superintends cruelties of which my words give but an adumbration. She recites the traditions that have came down in Jewish families, and history confirms all that they report. No earthly power could save; no human fancy can paint the scene too dark.

For a time the situation of the Jews who dared to profess their faith openly, was preferable to that of those who made Christian pretences while really unchanged. It was not that the latter were regarded with greater favor, but because the powers hesitated before the magnitude of the task of dealing with a class numbering hundreds of thousands and comprehending a vast proportion of the intelligence and ability of the nation. But fanaticism rose to cope with the undertaking, showing a force and persistence that have something admirable even while so devilish. In 1492 a decree was passed, that the Jews, a multitude though they were, and often in high places, must depart from the land. Isabella, though well-meaning, was completely under priestly influence, and soon assented to the plan. Ferdinand, through motives of policy rather than humanity, hesitated long. When the decision was at length made, a dramatic scene is said to have taken place in the palace. Abarbanel, a Jew of the highest position and worth, a man compared to the prophet

Daniel for his authority among his own race, and the respect he had forced from the oppressors of his people, penetrated to the presence of the sovereigns, and threw himself at their feet. He implored that his people might not be driven forth, and offered a bribe of 300,000 ducats that the decree might be recalled. Suddenly into the presence stalked, in his monkish robe, the gloomy form of the chief inquisitor, Torquemada, bearing a crucifix. "Judas Iscariot" cried he, unshrinkingly, to the abashed rulers, "sold his master for thirty pieces of silver; you wish to sell him for 300,000. Here he is; take him and sell him!" I do not know what sadder tale can be told than the relation of the scenes of their departure. The Hebrews had come to love Spain like their own Canaan. They visited the graves of their ancestors, bidding them a long farewell. Sometimes they removed the tombstones to carry them in their wanderings. Along the high-roads proceeded the long files of outcasts, sometimes to the beat of the drum which the rabbis and elders caused to be struck that the hearts of the people might not utterly sink, bearing with them the scrolls of their holy Law, and the remnant of their possessions. Valuable lands, in the forced sales, were exchanged for a little cloth; fine houses for a pair of mules. Vast sums that were owed them were confiscated; in every way they became the prey of the rapacious. Stuffing their saddles and furniture with such gold pieces as they could secure, they made their way to the harbors. Alone of the nations of the world, the Turks of the Levant were ready to receive them with some kindness. Those who made their way to Morocco and Algiers were sold into slavery, starved, ripped open by oppressors, who hoped to find jewels or gold which the persecuted ones had swallowed. Christendom was barred against them almost as with walls of brass. Italy alone showed some trace of mercy. The great trading cities tolerated them, though for purely selfish reasons. The general policy of the popes, too, be it said to their credit, contrasts favorably with that of other sovereigns, though it was harsh enough, and such features of leniency as it possessed, came usually from no good motive. But even in Italy there was tragedy of the saddest.

In Portugal there was at first a prospect of mild treatment, and the greater part of the outcasts went thither. But a marriage of the king with a princess of Spain, which soon took place, brought to pass woes deeper, if possible, than elsewhere. Not only must the Jews depart, but their children were taken from them to be brought up as Christians, till at last mothers in despair threw their babes into the rivers and wells, and killed themselves. The stories of massacres are wellnigh incredible. But Spain pursued the policy without relenting. Those whom she cast out were of the best middle class, which both created the wealth of the land and kept it in constant movement, like blood within the body. They were not only capitalists, merchants, physicians, and scholars, but farmers, artisans, and laborers. The spirit of enterprise and culture left Spain with the Jews. Her population became spiritless and diminished, and the land sank into a debasement which has never passed away.*

Following the details as given by the Israelite historian Graetz in his great work of eleven volumes, there are scores of vivid touches making all too plain this dreadful harrying and expatriation. "Spain," he says, "was full of the corruption of dungeons and the crackling pyres of innocent Jews. A lamentation went through the beautiful land which might pierce bone and marrow; but the sovereigns held back the arms of the pitiful." "The beautiful land!" so do the Hebrews call it, for they had come to love it, and looked back to it as to a paradise. "In our time," says Isaac Arama at the end of the 15th century, "the smoky column ascends to heaven in all the Spanish kingdoms and islands. A third of the new Christians (the nominally converted Jews) have perished by fire—a third wander as fugitives trying to hide, in continual fear of arrest. Beautiful Spain has become a flaming Tophet whose fiery tongue is all-devouring."

Two hundred years later the spirit of Spain was unchanged. I find in a Jewish writer an account of an *auto-da-fe* celebrated in 1680, in honor of the marriage of Charles II. with Marie Louise, niece of Louis XIV. Upon the great square in Madrid an amphitheatre was reared, with a box for the royal family upon one side, opposite to which was a dais

* This is the statement of Graetz: "Geschichte des Judenthums," volume VIII., the Spanish chapter. It can hardly be said, however, that Spain showed symptoms of decline until one hundred years later, at the time of the revolt of the Netherlands and rise of the Dutch Republic.

for the grand inquisitor and his train. The court officials were present in gala uniforms, the trade guilds in their state dresses, the orders of monks, an immense concourse of the populace. From the church towers pealed the bells, among whose sounds, were heard the chants of the monks. At 8 o'clock entered the procession. Before the grand inquisitor was borne the green cross of the Holy Office, while the bystanders shouted: "Long live the Catholic faith!" First marched a hundred charcoal burners, dressed in black and armed with pikes. It was their prescriptive right to lead the procession, as having furnished the fuel for the sacrifice. A troop of Dominican monks followed, then a duke of the bluest blood, hereditary standard-bearer of the Holy Office. After friars and nobles carrying banners and crosses came thirty-five effigies of life size, with names attached, borne by familiars of the Inquisition, representing condemned men who had died in prison or escaped. Other Dominicans appeared, a ghastly row carrying coffins containing the bones of those convicted of heresy after death; then fifty-four penitents with the dress and badge of victims, bearing lighted tapers. In turn came a company of Jews and Jewesses (in the interval since Ferdinand and Isabella a portion of the Jews had returned from banishment), mostly persons of humble rank, in whom the interest of the ceremony chiefly centred; these were to be burned as obstinate in their refusal of the faith. Each wore a cloak of coarse serge, yellow in color, covered with representations, in crimson, of flames, demons, serpents, and crosses. Upon their heads were high-pointed caps, with placards in front bearing the name and offence of the wearer. Haggard they were through long endurance of dungeon damp and darkness, broken and torn from the torture chambers, glad, for the most part, that the end of their weary days had come.

As the procession moved past the station of the royal personages, a girl of seventeen, whose great beauty had not been destroyed, cried out aloud from among the condemned to the young queen: "Noble queen, cannot your royal presence save me from this? I sucked in my religion with my mother's milk; must I now die for it?" The queen's eyes filled with tears, and she turned away her face. She was unused to such sights. Even she, probably, could not have interceded without danger to herself. The supplicating girl passed on with her companions to her fate. High mass having been performed, the preliminaries to the terrible concluding scene are transacted. The sun descends, the Angelus is rung from the belfrys, the vespers are chanted, the multitude proceeds to the place of suffering. It is a square platform of stone in the outskirts of the city, at whose four corners stand mis-shapen statues of prophets. Those who repent at the last moment have the privilege of being strangled before burning. The effigies and bones of the dead are first given to the flames. Last perish the living victims, the king himself lighting the fagots; their constancy is so marked that they are believed to be sustained by the devil. Night deepens; the glare of the flames falls upon the cowl of the Capuchin, the cord of the

Franciscan—upon corselet and plume—everywhere upon faces fierce with fanaticism. In the background rises the gloomy city—all alight as if with the lurid fire of hell.

CHAPTER XI.

THE BLOODY HAND IN GERMANY.

IN one of the old towns on the Rhine,* I went to see a synagogue which, tradition says, was built before the Christian era. In Roman legions served certain Jews, who, stationed here on the frontier of Gaul, which had just been subdued, founded a temple of their faith. I felt that the low, blackened walls of time-defying masonry had at any rate an immense antiquity. The blocks of stone were beaten by the weather—the thresholds nearly worn through by the passing of feet; a deep hollow lay in a stone at the portal, where the multitude of generations had touched it with the finger in sacred observances. Within the low interior my Jewish guide told me a sorrowful legend, which was, no doubt, in part true, relating to a lamp burning with a double flame before the shrine. Once, in the old cruel days, that hatred might be excited against the Jews of the city, a dead child was secretly thrown by the Christians into the cellar of one of that faith. Straightway an accusation was brought by the contrivers of the trick; the child was found, and the innocent Hebrews accused of the murder. The authorities of the city

* See the author's " Short History of German Literature."

threatened at once to throw the chief men of the congregation into a caldron of boiling oil if the murderers were not produced. Time pressed; the rabbi and elders were bound, and heard already, close at hand, the simmering of the preparing torture. There appeared two strangers, who gave themselves into the hands of the magistrates, voluntarily accusing themselves of the crime. Into the caldrons they were at once thrown, from which, as they died, ascended two milk-white doves. Innocent, with a pious lie upon their lips, they sacrificed themselves to save others. To commemorate their deed, the lamp with the double flame had been kept forever burning within the low arch.

I walked one day through the Juden-gasse at Frankfort. The modern world is ashamed of the cruelty and prejudice of the past, and would like to hide from sight the things that bear witness to it. The low, strong wall, however, was still standing, within whose narrow confine the Jews were crowded, never safe from violence or even death if they were found outside at times not permitted. Many of the ancient houses still remained, the fronts discolored, channelled, rising in mutilation and decay that were pathetic. The Hebrews of to-day seem to take pleasure in contrasting their present condition with their past misery. They have chosen to erect their stately synagogue among the old roofs,—upon the foundations even of the wall with which the past tried to fence them off from all Christian contact. Among such surroundings, how does the story, so long and so tragic, come home to us!

The persecution of the Jews in Germany, a chapter ages long, culminated * at the time of the Black Death, 1348-1350. This scourge, which carried off a quarter of the population of Europe, afflicted the Jews but lightly, on account of their isolation, and their simple and wholesome way of life. This comparative exemption from the pest was enough to make them suspected. The Jews poison the wells and the springs, it was said. The rabbis of Toledo were believed to have formed a plot to destroy all Christendom. The composition of the poison, the color of the packages in which it was transported, the emissaries who conveyed them, were all declared to have been discovered. Confirmations of these reports, extracted by torture from certain poor creatures, were forthcoming, and the people flew upon the Jews until entire communities were destroyed. The "Flagellants," fanatical sectaries, half naked and scourging themselves, swarmed through Germany, preaching extermination to all unbelievers. Basle expelled its Jews, Fribourg burned them, Spires drowned them. The entire community at Strassbourg, 2,000 souls, was dragged upon an immense scaffold, which was set on fire. At Worms, Frankfort, and Mainz, the Israelites anticipated their fate, setting their homes on fire and throwing themselves into the flames.

A picture, derived from Jewish authorities,† shall make vivid for us the condition of the Israelites in mediæval Germany.

* Reinach : " Histoire des Israélites."
† Based upon the incomplete novel of Heine, "The Rabbi of Bacharach," and accounts contained in the history of Graetz.

The little community of Hebrews which already in the time of the Romans had settled in the town of Woistes, on the Rhine, was a body isolated, crowded out of all civil rights, and weak in numbers, notwithstanding that it had received in times of persecution many fugitives. The suffering had begun with the Crusades. Familiar accusations that were made at an early day, were that the Jews stole the consecrated Host to pierce it with knives, and also that they killed Christian children at their Passover, for the sake of using their blood in the service at night. The Jews, hated for their faith, and because they held the world to such an extent in their debt, were on that festival entirely in the hands of their enemies, who could easily bring about their destruction by some false accusation. Not infrequently through some contrivance a dead child was secretly introduced into a Jewish house, to be afterwards found and made a pretext for attack. Great miracles were sometimes reported and believed, as having happened over such a corpse, and there are cases in which the Pope canonized such supposed victims. St. Werner in this way reached his honors, to whom was dedicated the magnificent abbey at Oberwesel, now a picturesque ruin, whose carved and towering pillars and long-pointed windows are such a delight to the tourists who pass on pleasant summer days, and do not think of their origin.

The more outside hate oppressed them, however, so much the closer did the bond become, in these times, among the Jews themselves; so much the deeper did their piety take root. The Rabbi Abraham at Woistes was an example of excellence, a man still young, but famed far and wide for his learning. His father had also been rabbi of the little synagogue, and had left to his son as his only bequest, a chest of rare books, and the command never to leave Woistes, unless his life were in danger. Rabbi Abraham had acquired wealth through marriage with his beautiful cousin Sarah, daughter of a rich jeweller. He practised conscientiously, however, the smallest usages of the faith; he fasted each Monday and Thursday, enjoyed meat and wine only on Sundays and holidays, explained by day to his pupils the divine Law, and studied by night the courses of the stars. The marriage was childless, but there was abundant life about him; for the great hall of his house by the synagogue stood open to the congregation, who went in and out without formality, offered hasty prayers, and took counsel in times of distress. Here the children played on the Sabbath morning while the weekly lesson was read in the synagogue; here the people collected at weddings and funerals, quarrelled and became reconciled; here the freezing found warmth and the hungry food. A crowd of kinsmen moved also about the rabbi who celebrated with him, as head of the family, the great festivals.

Such meetings of the kindred took place especially at the Passover time, when the Jews celebrate their escape from Egyptian bondage. As soon as it is night the mistress of the house lights the lamps, spreads the table-cloth, and lays upon it three flat unleavened loaves; then covering these with a napkin, she places on the little mound six little plates, in which is contained symbolical food—namely, an egg, lettuce, a radish, a lamb's bone, and a brown mixture of oranges, cinnamon, and nuts. Then the master of the house, seating himself at the table with all his guests, reads aloud out of the Talmud a mixture of legends of the forefathers, miraculous stories out of Egypt, controversial questions, prayers, and festal songs. The symbolical dishes are tasted at set times during the reading, pieces of the unleavened bread are eaten, and cups of red wine are drunk. Pensively cheerful, seriously sportive is this evening festival, full also of mystery; and the traditional intonation with which the Talmud is read by the father of the house, and sometimes repeated after him by the hearers, in a chorus, sounds so strangely intimate, so like a mother's lullaby, and at the same time so stimulating, that even those Jews who have long since apostatized and sought friends and honors among strangers, are affected in their deepest hearts, if by chance the old Passover songs come to their ears.

Rabbi Abraham was once celebrating, in the great hall of his house, the Passover, with kindred, pupils, and guests. All was polished to an unusual brilliancy; on the table lay the covering of silk, variously embroidered, with fringes of gold hanging to the earth. The plates with the symbolical food gleamed brightly, as did also the tall wine-filled beakers, on which were embossed sacred scenes. The men sat in black mantles, black flat hats, and white ruffs. The women, in glistening attire of material brought from Lombardy, wore on head and neck ornaments of pearl. The silver Sabbath lamp poured its festal light over the pleased and devout faces of old and young. On the purple velvet cushion of a seat raised above the rest, and leaning as the usage requires, Rabbi Abraham intoned the Talmud, and the contrasting voices of the chorus answered or joined in unison at the prescribed places. The rabbi wore also his black festival garment; his noble, somewhat severely formed features were milder than usual. His beautiful wife sat upon a raised velvet seat at his side, wearing, as hostess, no ornament, while simple white linen alone wrapped her form and face. Her countenance was touchingly fair, of that beauty which Jewesses have often possessed; for the consciousness of the deep misery, the bitter contempt, and appalling dangers in which they and their kindred are forced to live, spreads often over their features a trace of suffering and loving anxiety which strangely entrances the heart. She looked into her husband's eyes, with now and then a glance at the copy of the Talmud lying before her, a parchment volume bound in gold and velvet, an heirloom from the time of her grandfather, marked with ancient wine stains. The gay pictures which it contained, to look at which had been part of her amusement as a child, at the Passover time, presented various Biblical stories: Abraham with a hammer, dashed in pieces the stone idols of his fathers; Moses struck dead the Egyptian; Pharaoh sat magnificent upon his throne; again, the plague of frogs left him no quiet, and finally he was drowned in the Red Sea; the children of Israel stood open-mouthed in their wonder before Sinai; pious King David played the harp; and finally Jerusalem with the towers and pinnacles of the Temple was illuminated by the sun.

The second cup was already poured out. The faces and voices of the guests were becoming always clearer, and the Rabbi, seizing one of the unleavened loaves, and holding it up with a cheerful greeting, read the following words: "Lo, this is the food of which our fathers in Egypt partook! every one who is hungry let him come and eat; let the afflicted share our Passover joy; for the present we celebrate the festival here, but in the coming years in the land of Israel; we celebrate now as bondmen, but hereafter as sons of freedom." Just here the door of the long hall opened, and two tall, pale figures entered, wrapt in broad cloaks, one of whom said: "Peace be with you. We are your companions in the faith, who now are journeying, and we wish to celebrate the Passover with you." The Rabbi answered quickly and kindly: "Peace be with you; sit here by me." The strangers seated themselves at the table, and Abraham continued his reading. Often, while the by-standers were still occupied with the responses, he addressed sportively caressing words to his wife, then again took up his part, how "Rabbi Eleazar, Rabbi Asaria, Rabbi Akiba, and Rabbi Tarphen, sat in Bona-brak and talked together the whole night of the Exodus, until their scholars came and called out to them that it was day, and in the synagogue great morning-prayer was already being read," or some similar passage from the quaint disjointed record.

As the Hebrew woman reverently listened with eyes fixed on her husband, she saw that his face suddenly became distorted with horror, the blood fled from his cheeks and lips, and his eyes stood out in dreadful astonishment. Instantly, however, he recovered himself. The agitation passed off like a momentary spasm, his features resuming their former quiet cheerfulness. Presently a mad humor, quite foreign to him, seemed to take possession of him. The wife was terrified, less on account of the signs of astonished fear than on account of the insane merriment. Abraham pushed his cap in wild sport from one ear to the other, plucked and curled the locks of his beard like a buffoon, sang the text of the Talmud like a street minstrel; and in counting up the Egyptian plagues, when the index-finger is dipped several times into the full beaker, and the drop hanging from it thrown to the ground, the Rabbi spattered the younger girls with red wine, and there was loud complaint over destroyed ruffles, and resounding laughter. This convulsive levity on the part of her husband seemed constantly stranger to Sarah, and she looked on with nameless anxiety, as the guests, incited by Abraham, danced back and forth, tasted the Passover bread, sipped the wine, and sang aloud.

At length came the time of the evening meal, and all prepared to wash themselves. The wife brought the great silver laver, adorned with figures of beaten gold, and held it before each guest, who poured water over his hands. While she was performing this service, her husband made a significant sign to her, and during the preparations slipped unnoticed from the room. As she followed him immediately, he seized her hand with a hasty clutch, drew her quickly forth through the dark lanes of the town, and passed at length out of the gate to the highroad along the Rhine. It was one of those quiet nights of spring which, indeed, is mild and bright, but fills the soul with a strange thrill. The flowers exhaled an oppressive odor, the birds filled the air with a kind of anxious twitter, the moon threw white streaks of light uncannily over the dark, murmuring stream. The lofty cliffs of the bank seemed like heads of giants threateningly nodding; the watchman on the tower of a lonely castle opposite blew from his bugle a melancholy note, and now sounded forth the death-bell from the abbey of St. Werner, quickly pealing. The wife still carried in her right hand the silver basin, while Abraham kept fast his clutch upon her left wrist. She felt that his fingers were icy cold and that his arm trembled, but she followed in silence, foreboding she knew not what, while the sights and sounds of the night seemed to her, in her mood, pervaded with such strange terror. Reaching at length a rock which overhung the rivershore, the Rabbi mounted with his wife, looked warily in all directions, then stared upward at the stars. The moon illuminated his pale face in a ghastly way, showing a mingled expression of pain, fear, and devotion. As he suddenly snatched the laver from her hand and flung it down into the river she could no longer bear it, but throwing herself at his feet, begged him to reveal the mystery. The lips of Abraham moved, but at first no sound came forth. At length he stammered: "Do you see the angel of death there hovering over Woistes? We, however, have escaped his sword, praised be the Lord!" With voice still trembling with horror he then related, his spirit growing calmer gradually as it found utterance, how, while in pleasant frame he sat chanting from the Talmud, he had happened to look under the table, and had beheld there at his feet the bloody corpse of a child. "Then I saw," he went on, "that the two tall strangers were not of the congregation of Israel, but of the assembly of the godless, who had taken council to accuse us of child-murder, and afterwards excite the people to plunder and slay us. I dared not let it be seen that I had discovered the work of darkness. I should have hastened our destruction by doing so, and only cunning and promptness have saved us. Be not anxious, Sarah. Our friends and kindred will be saved. The ruthless men coveted my death alone. Since I have escaped them, they will satisfy themselves with our silver and gold. Let us depart to another land, leaving misfortune behind us; and in order that misfortune may not pursue us, I have thrown away in atonement the last of our possessions, the basin of silver. The God of our fathers will not abandon us. Come down, thou art tired. Wilhelm, the dumb boy, waits with his boat there at the shore; he will carry us down the Rhine."

Speechless and as if with broken limbs, the beautiful Sarah had sunk away into the arms of Abraham, who bore her slowly down toward the shore. There stood Wilhelm, who, the support of his old mother, the Rabbi's neighbor, followed the calling of a fisherman, and had here fastened his boat. He seemed to have already guessed the intention of the Rabbi, and to be waiting for him. About his closed lips played an expression of gentle pity, his great blue eyes, full of feeling, rested upon the fainting woman, whom he carried tenderly to the little boat. The look of the dumb boy aroused her from her stupefaction. She felt suddenly that all which her husband had told her was no mere dream, and streams of bitter tears poured down her cheeks, which were now as white as her robe. There she sat in the middle of the boat, a weeping form of marble,—by her side her husband and Wilhelm, who plied the oars vigorously.

Whether it is the monotonous stroke of the oars, or the rocking of the craft, or the fragrance of those mountainous shores, upon which grow the clusters that inspire man with joy, it always happens that the most afflicted man is strangely calmed, when on a spring night, in a light skiff, he sails upon the beautiful Rhine. Old good-hearted father Rhine cannot bear, indeed, to have his children weep. He rocks them in his faithful arms, stilling their sobbing, relates to them his finest tales, promises them his richest treasures, perhaps the hoard of the Nibelungen, sunk so long ago. Sarah's tears flowed at last less passionately. The whispering waves charmed away her sorrows, the night lost its gloom, and the mountains about her home wished her, as it were, a tender farewell. As she mused, at length it seemed to her as if she, a child, were once more seated upon the little stool before her father's velvet chair, who stroked her long hair, laughed at her pleasantly, and rocked back and forth in his ample Sabbath dressing-gown of blue silk. It must have been the Sabbath, for the flower-embroidered covering was laid on the table. All the utensils in the room shone brightly polished, the white-bearded servant of the congregation sat at her father's side and talked Hebrew. Abraham too came in, as in his boyhood, bearing a great book, and wished to expound a passage of Holy Writ in order that his uncle might be convinced that he had learned much the past week. The little fellow laid the book on the arm of the broad chair, and gave the story of Jacob and Rachel, how Jacob had lifted up his voice and wept aloud, when he first beheld his cousin Rachel, how he had spoken to her intimately at the well, how he had been obliged to serve for Rachel seven years, how quickly they had passed, and how he had married Rachel and had loved her forever. Sarah remembered that her father suddenly cried out in merry tones: "Wilt thou not marry just so?" Whereupon the little Abraham answered earnestly: "That will I, and she shall wait seven years."

As the figures passed vaguely through the fancy of the fugitive, they became strangely confused. The Rhine seemed at length to murmur the monotonous melodies of the Talmud, and the pictures she had known in her childhood appeared to rise large as life, and distorted. Old Abraham dashed in pieces the forms of the idols, which grew quickly together again; Mt. Sinai lightened and flamed;

King Pharaoh swam in the Red Sea, holding fast in his teeth his crown of gold with its points; frogs with human countenances swam behind, the waves foamed and roared, and a dark, gigantic hand was thrust threateningly forth. Coming to herself for a moment, Sarah looked up to the mountains of the shore, upon whose summits the lights of the castles flickered and at whose foot the moonlit mist was spread. Suddenly she seemed to see there her friends and kindred, hurrying along the Rhine full of terror, with corpse-like faces and white, waving shrouds. A blackness passed before her eyes, a stream of ice was poured into her soul, and vaguely into her half swoon came the voice of the Rabbi, saying his evening prayer slowly and anxiously, as by the bedside of people sick unto death. But suddenly the gloomy curtain was drawn away. Above the Hebrew woman appeared the holy city of Jerusalem with its towers and gates. The Temple shone in golden splendor; in its court she beheld her father, in his Sabbath attire, and with joyful countenance. From the windows her friends and kindred treated her joyfully; in the Holy of Holies knelt pious King David, with purple mantle and sparkling crown, sending forth afar the music of psalm and harp. Peacefully smiling at length, as if comforted by the vision, she slept.

When she opened her eyes again upon the world, she was almost blinded by the bright beams of the morning sun. The lofty towers of a great city rose close at hand, and Wilhelm, standing upright with his boat-hook, guided the boat through a thick press of gay-pennoned craft. "This is Niegeschenburg," said Abraham. "There you see the great bridge, with its thirteen arches, and in the midst the little cabin, where, they say, dwells a certain baptized Jew. He acts for the Israelite congregation, and pays to whomsoever shall bring him a dead rat six farthings; for the Jews must deliver yearly to the city council five thousand rat-tails." Presently they landed, and the Rabbi conducted his wife through the great crowd on the bank, where now, because it was Easter, a crowd of wooden booths had been built.

What a various throng! For the most part they were trades-people, bargaining with one another aloud, or talking to themselves while they reckoned on their fingers; often heavy-laden porters ran behind them in a dog-trot to carry their purchases to their warehouses. Other faces gave evidence that only curiosity had attracted them. The stout city councillor could be recognized by his red cloak and golden neck-chain; the iron-spiked helmet, the yellow leather doublet, and the clinking spurs announced the man-at-arms. Under the black-velvet cap, which came together in a point on the forehead, a rosy girl's face was concealed, and the young fellows who followed her appeared like fops, with their plumed caps, their peaked shoes, and their silken parti-colored dress. In this the right side was green, and the left side red; or on one side streaked rainbow-like, the other checkered, so that the foolish fellows looked as if they were split in the middle. Drawn on by the crowd, the Rabbi, with his wife, reached the great market-place of the town, surrounded by high-gabled houses, chief among them the great Rath-haus. In this building the emperors of Germany had been sometimes entertained, and knightly sports were often held before it. King Maximilian, who loved such things passionately, was then present in the city, and the day before, in his honor, a great tournament had taken place before the Rath-haus. About the lists which the carpenters were now taking away many idlers were standing, telling one another how yesterday the Duke of Brunswick and the Margrave of Brandenburg had charged against each other amid the sound of trumpets and drums; and how Sir Walter had thrust the Knight of the Bear so violently out of the saddle that the splinters of his lance flew into the air, the tall, fair King Max standing meanwhile among his courtiers on the balcony, and rubbing his hands with joy. The covering of golden material still lay upon the balcony and in the arched windows of the Rath-haus; the rest of the houses of the market-place were still in festal dress.

What a crowd of every station and age were assembled here! People laughed, rejoiced, played practical jokes. Sometimes the trumpet of the mountebank pealed sharply, who, in a red cloak, with his clown and ape, stood on a lofty scaffold, proclaimed aloud his own skill, and praised his miraculous tinctures and salves. Two fencing-masters, swinging their rapiers, with ribbons fluttering, met here as if by chance, and thrust at one another in apparent anger; after a long battle, each declared the other invincible, and collected a few pennies. With drum and fife, the newly-constituted guilds of archers marched past. The sound was at last lost, and the long-drawn chanting of an approaching procession was heard. It was a solemn train of tonsured and bare-footed monks, carrying burning tapers, banners with images of the saints, or great silver crucifixes. At their head went acolytes in robes of red and white, with smoking censers; in the midst, under a beautiful canopy, priests were seen in white robes of costly lace, or in stoles of variegated silk, one of whom bore in his hand a golden vessel, shaped like the sun, which he held on high before the shrine of a saint in the market-place, while he half shouted and half sang Latin words. At the same time a little bell sounded, and all the people fell upon their knees and crossed themselves.

The Rabbi drew his wife away by a narrow lane, then through a labyrinth of contracted, crooked streets, to the Jewish quarter. This was provided with strong walls, with chains of iron before the gates, to bar them against the pressure of the rabble. Here the Jews lived, oppressed and anxious in the recollection of previous calamity. When the Flagellants, in passing through, had set the city on fire, and accused the Jews of doing it, many of the latter had been murdered by the frenzied populace, or found death in the flames of their own houses. Since then the Jews had often been threatened with similar destruction, and in the internal dissensions of the city, the Christian rabble had always stood ready to storm the Jewish quarter. The great wall which enclosed it had two gates, which on Catholic holidays were closed from the outside, and on Jewish holidays from within.

The keys rattled, the gate opened with a jar, as the Rabbi and his wife stepped into the Judengasse, which was quite empty of people. "Don't be surprised," said the Jewish gatekeeper, "that the street is so quiet. An our people are now in the synagogue, and you come just at the right time to hear the story read of the sacrifice of Isaac." The pair wandered slowly through the long, empty street, and approached at length the synagogue. Even at a distance they heard the loud confusion of voices. In the court the Rabbi separated from his wife, and after he had washed his hands at the spring which flowed there, he stepped into the lower part of the synagogue, where the men pray. Sarah, on the other hand, ascended the staircase, and reached the place of the women above. This was a gallery, with three rows of wooden seats, dull red in color, whose rail was provided above with a hanging shelf, which could be propped up for the support of the prayer-book. Here women were sitting, talking, or standing erect as they earnestly prayed. Often they approached with curiosity the great lattice in the East, through whose green slats they could look down into the lower part of the synagogue. There, behind tall prayer desks, stood the men in their black cloaks, their pointed beards falling over their white collars, and their heads more or less veiled by a square cloth of white wool or silk, and now and then decorated with golden tassels.

The walls of the synagogue were whitened uniformly, and no other adornment could be seen than the gilded iron lattice about the square platform where the passages from the Law were read, and the sacred shrine. This was a chest handsomely wrought, apparently borne on marble columns with luxuriant capitals, whose flowers and foliage were beautifully entwined. On the velvet curtain which covered it a pious inscription was embroidered with gold, pearls, and many-colored stones. Here hung the silver memorial lamp, near a raised stage with a lattice, on whose rail were various sacred vessels, among others the seven-branched candlestick. Before this, his countenance toward the shrine, stood the precentor, whose chant was accompanied by the voice of his two assistants, a bass and a treble singer. The Jews have banished from their worship all instrumental music, thinking that the praise of God ascends more edifyingly out of the warm human breast than out of cold organ pipes. Sarah took a child-like pleasure, when now the precentor, an excellent tenor, raised his voice, and the ancient, solemn melodies which she knew so well rang out with a beauty such as she had never imagined. While the bass in contrast poured forth his deep, heavy tones, in the intervals the soprano trilled with delicate sweetness.

Sarah had never heard such music in the synagogue of Woistes. A pious pleasure, mingled with feminine curiosity, drew her to the lattice, where she could look down into the lower compartment. She had never as yet seen so large a number of fellow believers as she beheld there below, and her heart was cheered in the midst of so many people so nearly allied to her through common descent, belief, and suffering. But the woman's soul was still more moved when three old men reverently approached the sacred shrine, pushed the curtain to one side, opened the chest, and carefully took out that book which God had written with his own sacred hand, and for whose preservation the Jews had suffered so much misery and hate, insult and death, a martyrdom of a thousand years.

This book, a great roll of parchment, was wrapped, like a prince's child, in a richly embroidered mantle of velvet, and wound about a pin set off with bells and pomegranates. The precentor took the book, and as if it were a real child, a child for whom great pangs had been endured, and whom on that account one loves all the more, he rocked it in his arms pressed it to his breast, and as if thrilled by such contact, raised his voice in joyful thanksgiving. It seemed to the woman as if the columns of the holy shrine must begin to bloom, and the wonderful flowers of the capitals grow constantly higher. At the same time, the tones of the more delicate voice became like those of a nightingale, while the vaulted ceiling of the synagogue threw back the powerful notes of the bass.

It was a beautiful psalm. The congregation repeated the concluding verse in chorus. To the elevated platform in the midst of the synagogue strode slowly the precentor, with the sacred book, while men and boys hastily pressed forward to kiss, or, indeed, only to touch the velvet covering. The wrapping at last was drawn off from the sacred book; also the swathings in which it was enveloped, written over with variegated letters, and out of the opened parchment roll, in that intonation, which at the Passover is strangely modulated, was read the edifying tale of the temptation of Abraham. At last a prayer of especial solemnity was intoned, which no one is permitted to neglect. It was performed while the congregation stood with faces turned toward the East, where lies Jerusalem.

It is customary in the synagogue for any one who has escaped great danger to step publicly forward after the reading of the Law, and thank God for his salvation. When now Rabbi Abraham arose in the synagogue for such a thanksgiving, and Sarah recognized the voice of her husband, she noticed that his tone gradually dropped into the solemn murmur of the prayer for the dead. She heard the names of her familiar friends, and the conviction took possession of her that their kindred and loved ones at Woistes had not, after all, escaped the sword. She felt that some dread tidings must have reached Abraham, and hope vanished from her soul.

But now from without the walls resounded a heavy tumult. While the congregation had been gathered in the synagogue, a friar proceeding through the streets, carrying in a monstrance the Host to a dying man, had come upon a group of Jewish boys, throwing sand at one another in sport. Gravel-stones had hit the robes of the monk, and those that followed him had become so enraged that they pursued and maltreated the boys. The parents of the children had interfered to free them from the excessive punishment, upon which the friar had run to the marketplace, and cried with a loud voice that the Host, and his own office, as priest, had been desecrated by Jews. The rabble had attacked the Hebrew quarter, and the ominous sounds, at first not understood, that were heard within the synagogue, were the tumult of their frenzied onset. The Hebrews were overpowered wherever they could be seized—as they rushed from their houses, or made their way from the temple,—and given the alternative of death or baptism. The persecuted were, with few exceptions, steadfast, and destruction fell upon them. In their desperation they laid hands upon themselves. Fathers slew first their families, then took their own lives. The details are too dreadful to be dwelt upon. Rabbi Abraham and Sarah had escaped death the night before, only to find it now in a form not less terrible. The synagogue was burned, and the holy Law torn and trampled under foot. Thousands perished that day and the night following, only here and there a fugitive escaping.

As the tidings spread in Germany, the venerable Rabbi whose authority had become greatest among his people, counselled them as follows: " I have been told of the sufferings which have befallen our brethren—of the tyrannical laws, the compulsory baptisms, the exiles, and now at length of the massacres. There is woe within, and woe without. I hear an insolent people raise its raging voice over the faithful; I see it swing its hand against them. The

187. JEWS' PLACE OF WAILING, JERUSALEM.

priests and the monks rise against them and say: 'We will persecute them to extermination; the name of Israel shall no longer be named.' How the holy German brotherhood is handled! We are driven from place to place. We are smitten with the sharp sword, flung into flaming fire, into raging floods, or poisonous swamps. Brethren and friends! I cry to you that the land of the Turks is a land where nothing is wanting. If you consent to go thither, it may still be well with you. You can safely proceed thence to the promised land. Israel, why dost thou sleep! Up, and depart from this accursed soil!" The Hebrews obeyed in multitudes. They sought the far East, and found in the dominions of the Sultan a sway which, as contrasted with that of the sovereigns of Christendom, was merciful, even benignant.

What wonder that those who found their way back to Jerusalem established among the fragments of the ancient glory of their fathers, a wailing-place!

CHAPTER XII.

THE FROWN AND THE CURSE IN ENGLAND, ITALY, AND FRANCE.

THE reader will have had a surfeit of tragedy in the details that have been given of Hebrew tribulations in Spain and Germany, but whoso tells the story faithfully must give yet more. The treatment accorded the Jews by Englishmen was no kinder, though the persecution was less colossal, from the fact that the number of victims was smaller. The Israelites probably came to Britain in the Roman day, antedating, therefore, in their occupation, the Saxon conquerors, by two or three centuries, and the Normans by perhaps a thousand years. With the beginnings of English history their presence can be traced, the inevitable proscription appearing as far back as the time of the Heptarchy. Saxon strove with Briton, and Dane with Saxon, and all alike were at enmity with the Jew. Canute banished them to the Continent, where they took refuge in Normandy, and were well received. With the conquering William they returned to England, and for a time were protected by a kindly policy. William Rufus, in particular, showed them indulgence. He appointed a public debate in London between rabbis and bishops, and swore by the face of St. Luke that if the churchmen were defeated, he would turn Jew himself. This favor, however, was transient; the Hebrews soon found themselves again under the harrow, their suffering culminating at the accession of Richard Cœur de Lion, in 1189.

The imprudent Israelites, over-anxious to win the favor of the new reign, thronged to the coronation in rich attire, and bearing costly gifts. The crusading spirit was rife; the presence of such infidel sorcerers at the ceremony was held to be of evil omen. An attempt was made to exclude them from Westminster Abbey, which many evaded, and the boldness of the intruders cost the Jews dear throughout the entire kingdom. Not a Hebrew household in London escaped robbery and murder, and outrage proceeding through the land wreaked enormities in the provinces that exceeded those of the capital. The preaching friars, omnipresent, taught that the rescue of the Holy Sepulchre could well begin with a harrying of infidels at home; and at York, at last, occurred a tragedy which only in Israelite history can find a parallel.

The great body of the Jews sought refuge in the castle, whence they defied the fanatics. The people, fired by the exhortations of the monks, who promised salvation to such as should shed the blood of an unbeliever, and who themselves, cross in hand, in their cowls, led the attacks, soon made it plain that resistance was hopeless. As in the old days of the Maccabees, a priest was at the head of the Jews. The chief rabbi of York, a man of great learning and virtue, thus addressed them: "Men of Israel, this day the God of our fathers commands us to die for his Law—the Law which the people have cherished from the first hour it was given, which we have preserved through our captivity in all nations, and for which can we do less than die? Death is before our eyes; let us escape the tortures of the Christians, who prowl about us like wolves athirst for our blood, by surrendering, as our fathers have done before us, our lives with our own hands to our Creator. God seems to call for us; let us not be unworthy!"

The old man wept as he spoke, but the people said he had uttered words of wisdom. As the council closed, night descended, and while the besiegers watched upon their arms, lo, within the stronghold flared the blaze of a furious conflagration. In the morning an entrance was easily forced, for the walls were no longer defended. The fathers had slain with the sword their wives and children, then fallen by the hands of one another, the less distinguished yielding up their lives to the elders. These in turn had fallen by the hand of the chief rabbi. He at last stood alone; upon the congregation about him, man and maid, child and graybeard, had descended the everlasting silence. The flames that had been kindled devoured not only the possessions, but consumed the people like the sacrifice upon an altar. A final stroke and the old man lay with his fellows, leaving to the persecutors an ash-heap which entombed five hundred skeletons.

For a century longer a remnant of the Israelites maintained themselves in England; but Edward I., the " English Justinian," though in so many ways a great and good prince, drove them forth, 16,500 in number, and from that time for nearly four centuries, there is no evidence that British soil felt a Hebrew footprint. At length sat in the place of power a man mightier than Plantagenet or Tudor or Stuart, —Cromwell, the plain squire, lifted to the rulership by the uprisen people. With him pleaded for tolerance Menasseh ben Israel, a Hebrew of the synagogue of Amsterdam, wise and gentle, and the pleading was not in vain. The heart of the ruler was softened, the gates of the land swung open to admit the descendants of the banished. At first it was the barest sufferance, limited by every kind of disability; but the chain has fallen from the limbs of the children of those men. Just as this record is completed, a son of Jacob is made a peer of the realm.

Near one of the arches of London Bridge, the " bridge of sighs," beneath which the sullen current pours so gloomily seaward, there is a spot in the river where at a certain stage of the tide the waters whirl in a strange, uncanny agitation. There, says tradition, in far off, terrible days, a company of Jews were thrown in and drowned. Men once believed, and it is said there are men who still believe, that the mysterious, uneasy bubbling and rush of the flood dates from the day when it coldly stifled the death-cries of those perishing victims. It is as if that stream of tragedy, which has helped and hidden so much of ghastly crime, had somewhere a conscience of its own, and, remorseful through the ages for having been the accomplice in wickedness so terrible, betrayed its secret trouble even to the present hour.

In Italy, the hardships which the Jews were forced to suffer were somewhat less terrible than elsewhere. The land had no political unity: the great trading republics, Venice, Florence, Genoa, dominated the northern portion; the power of the Church held the centre; the influence of Spain made itself balefully felt in Sicily and at the south. There was no harmonious policy in the great peninsula, thus disintegrated. Each little state was, as regardeed the Hebrews, sometimes oppressive, sometimes favorable; when in any city or district the skies grew dark for them, the Jews could often find more easily in the principalities than in the great kingdoms a convenient refuge. In the commercial states no prejudice, of course, was felt toward the Israelites from the fact that they were traders and money-lenders. What else were Venetian, Florentine, Lombard, and Cahorsin?* They were the Jew's rivals, not his contemners, and there is good reason for thinking that these Christian usurers were harsher and more extortionate than the sons of Jacob, whose calling they had appropriated. The attitude of the mercantile cities toward the Hebrews was generally that of surly tolerance, that brought, however, no exemption from insult, or indeed, bodily ill-treatment, if caprice turned that way.

In Rome, the fate of the Jews hung upon the personal character of the Popes, who sometimes bravely

* Money-lenders who probably came from Piedmont. See Depping, 175.

and humanely protected them; sometimes threw over them a shield from the selfish advantage they might reap from their presence; sometimes drove against them with fagot and sword as bitter persecutors. A little company of Hebrews had dwelt in Rome even from ante-Christian days, suffered to remain, it has been said,* as a monumental symbol, presenting the Old-Testament root of Christianity. Unmixed with Romans or barbarians, they had transmitted their blood. The community had seen the ancient Roman republic, after Brutus and Cassius had fallen at Philippi, tumble about them into dust; the immeasurable marble city of the imperial time had held them in its circuit; when the maces of the Goths had dashed this into ruins they lived on in the desolation. More indestructible than a column of brass, the little troop survived the fearful Nemesis of the ages. In the days of papal splendor they prayed—yes, in our own day they pray—to the God of Abraham and Moses in the same lanes, on the bank of the Tiber, in which their fathers dwelt in the times of Consul and Cæsar.

Whenever, in mediæval times, a pope was consecrated, the Hebrew congregation were among the attendants, standing with slavish gestures, full of fear or timid hope, while the chief rabbi at their head carried on his shoulder the mysterious veiled roll of the holy Law. They were accustomed to read their fate in the gloomy or genial countenance of the new pope. Was it to be toleration or oppression? While

* Güdemann: "Die Juden in Italian während des Mittelalters," p. 73.

the rabbi handed the vicar of Christ the scroll for
confirmation, their eyes scanned keenly the face that
turned toward him. As the scroll was handed back,
this was the formula which the pope was accustomed
to utter : " We recognize the Law, but we condemn
the view of Judaism ; for the Law is fulfilled through
Christ, whom the blind people of Judah still expect
as the Messiah." Sometimes shielded, sometimes
hounded, they drove their bargains, exercised many
a profession,—in particular, as physicians, attended
peasant and prince, monk and nun, even the popes
themselves; but for them, as they went and came,
the frown was never far from the Christian's brow,
or the curse from his lip.

In Southern Italy the Jews had an especial note as
artisans. They were the principal dyers, raisers and
manufacturers of silk, blacksmiths, locksmiths, silver-
smiths. Ferdinand the Catholic forbade them to
carry on noisy labors upon Christian holidays. They
were also builders and miners. When the mournful
banishment of the Jews from the dominions of Spain
came about, the story of which has been related,
Sicily, as a country subject to Ferdinand, suffered
with the rest. The foremost magistrates and officials
of the island, however, interposed a protest, an eloquent testimony to the character of the exiles, a few
words of which it will be well to quote :

" A difficulty arises from the circumstance that in
this land almost all the handicraftsmen are Jews.
If, then, all depart at once, there will be a want of
workmen for the Christians—especially of workmen
able to carry on the iron industry,—the shoeing of

horses, the manufacturing of farming-tools, the making of vehicles, of ships and galleys." The document continues in the same strain, illustrating convincingly, as a Jewish scholar urges, how the Hebrews have labored with eagerness wherever narrow-minded guilds and a spirit of envy did not forbid them to do so. If we may trust Sicilian testimony, relations of unusual friendliness existed between the island population and the Israelites thus suddenly banished. " It was an entire race which went into banishment. Another race with which it had lived for centuries, stood dumb, astonished, weeping, upon the city walls, the galleries, and roofs of the neighboring buildings, to give and receive a last greeting. The Jews abandoned Sicily—the land which had beheld so many successive generations of their forefathers, holding their ashes in its bosom. The despot who thus punished and drove forth the innocent, could not measure the infinite bitterness of such a separation. The catastrophe of 1492 remains indelibly inscribed among the saddest memories which the rule of Spain has left in this island." *

It is worth while to dwell for a moment upon the spectacle of this compassionate Christian multitude, gathered there upon the shore of the summer sea, weeping as they watched in the distance the departing sails of the exiled Hebrews. Rarely indeed did the dark world of those times afford such a scene. In a night of tempest the clouds will sometimes divide for a moment and suffer to fall a gentle beam

* La Lumia: " The Sicilian Hebrews," quoted by Güdemann, p. 291.

of moonlight. For the Jews it was everywhere storm and thick darkness—and how seldom came any parting of those wrath-charged shadows!

For some time after the Jews of England and Germany had found themselves oppressed, the situation of their brethren in France, was an enviable one. They were spread abroad even among the villages— on the farms, and in the vineyards, as well as in the towns, devoting themselves to agriculture, to medicine, to the mechanic arts, to study; traders and money-changers, however, they were for the most part. The skies were usually favorable, a fitful hail of persecution beating upon them only now and then ; not until the accession of Philip Augustus, in 1180, did prince and populace, the upper and the nether millstone, begin their pitiless grinding. For a time it was less the fanatical hatred of the people, than the avarice of the king and lords, that bore hard. The treasures of the Hebrews were wrung from them in all cruel ways; where torture was unavailing, massacre was brought to bear, and at last a plundered remnant were cast as off-scourings beyond the frontiers. The term of exile was short. The rejected crept once more to their homes, to find they were henceforth to be held as the serfs of the king— themselves and their havings utterly subject to his disposal. The blessed St. Louis,* whom history and legend have so exalted, could sell his Jews like a troop of cattle, while he did so tearing from them, as a work of blasphemy, the beloved book, which in

* Reinach : " Histoire des Juifs," p. 160.

the midst of sufferings was their supreme consolation, the safeguard of their morality, and the bond of their religious unity—the Talmud. St. Louis burned the books of the Jews; Philip the Fair burned the Jews themselves. In 1306, on the morrow of the fast commemorating the destruction of Jerusalem, all the Jews of France, men, women, and children, to the number of 100,000, stripped of every possession for the benefit of the royal treasury, were cast naked out of the land. As in the case of the proscription of Philip Augustus, this, too, did not endure. The kingdom languished for want of them, and in ten years such as survived were recalled. They were scarcely re-established when there was a new experience of steel and fire; the "Pastoureaux," bands of fanatical shepherds and malefactors, swept them away by thousands. Soon the "Black Pest" was upon the land; the Israelites protected in a measure by observing the hygienic prescriptions of their law, felt the sickness somewhat less; that the pestilence spared them caused them to be suspected; the spear, the caldron, and the devouring flame were again at work until victims failed and exhaustion fell upon the persecutors. The cold extortions of heartless princes, enforced by dungeons and the rack—the anathemas of bishop and monk—the whirling cyclones of popular fury—how among them all could a single one be saved! From these times a tragic Hebrew lay has been handed down to us, which affords a glimpse into the souls of those who thus suffered. It describes the immolation upon the funeral pile of a rabbi and his family,—a chant characteristically Jewish, pathetic, tenderly affectionate, but bitterly scornful to the last, and audacious in its imprecations. A few passages from this follow *:

"Israel is in mourning, bewailing its brave martyred saints. Thou, O God, dost behold our flowing tears. Without thy help we perish!

"O Sage, who day and night grew pale over the Bible, for the Bible you have died.

"When his noble wife saw the flames burst forth, 'My love calls me,' she cried. 'As he died, I would die.' His youngest child trembled and wept. 'Courage!' said the elder. 'In this hour Paradise will open.' And the rabbi's daughter, the gentle maid! 'Abjure your creed,' they cry. 'A faithful knight stands here who dies for love of thee.' 'Death by fire rather than renounce my God! it is God whom I desire for my spouse.'

"'Choose,' said the priest, 'the cross or the torture'; but the rabbi said: 'Priest, I owe my body to God, who now requires it,' and tranquilly he mounts the pile.

"Together in the midst of the unchained flames, like cheerful friends at a festival, they raise high and clear the hymn of deliverance, and their feet would move in dances were they not bound in fetters.

"God of vengeance, chastise the impious!
Doth thy wrath sleep?
What are the crimes which I am forced to expiate under the torch of these felons?
Answer, O Lord, for long have we suffered; answer, for we count the hours!"

* Reinach, 163.

We need look no further in that lurid mediæval world. The Hebrew story is everywhere the same substantially—a constant moan as it were, with variations indeed, but seldom a note in which we miss the quality of agony. In their best estate, the Jews were but chattels of the sovereign, who sometimes followed his interest in protecting them. The king kept his Jews as the farmer keeps his bees, creatures whose power for mischief is to be feared, but tolerated for their marvellous faculty of storing up something held to be of value. As the price of his protection, the prince helped himself from the Jew's hoard, sometimes leaving the Jew enough for a livelihood,—enough sometimes, indeed, to maintain a rich state. If they increased, however, the potentate did not scruple to sell them, as the farmer sells his superfluous swarms; and if fanaticism drove out in the royal mind the sense of greed, as in the case of Richard Cœur de Lion, St. Louis, and Isabella, the Jew had no defence against a world in arms before him. If sickness prevailed, it was because the Jews had poisoned the wells; if a Christian child were lost, it had been crucified at a Jewish ceremony; if a church sacristan was careless, it was the Jews who had stolen the Host from the altar, to stab it with knives at the time of the Passover. In many periods in almost all lands, whoever sinned or suffered, the Jew was accused, and the occasion straightway made use of for attacks in which hundreds or thousands might perish. The wild cry of the rabble, "Hep! hep!" said to be derived from the Latin formula, "*Hierosolyma est perdita*," might break out at any time. The Jew was made conspicuous, sometimes by a badge in the shape of a wheel, red, yellow, or parti-colored, fixed upon the breast. In some lands the mark was square and placed upon the shoulder or hat. At Avignon the sign was a pointed yellow cap; at Prague, a sleeve of the same color; in Italy and Germany, a horn-shaped head-dress, red or green. This distinguishing mark or dress the Jew was forced to wear, and when the "Hep, Hep!" was heard, he might well raise his hands in despair. He might indeed flee to the Turk; but the tender mercies of the Turk, tolerant as he was as compared with the Christian, were often very cruel.

As time advanced, the spirit of early Protestantism was often no milder toward them than that of the old faith, though it may have refrained from fagots and the rack. Men wise before their age have not been able to rise to the height of charity for the Jew.

Said Luther: "Know, dear Christian, and doubt it not, that next to the Devil himself, thou hast no more bitter, poisonous, violent enemy than a Jew, who is set upon being a Jew,"—a judgment of the great reformer perhaps not far wrong, for the Jew is, indeed, the best of haters. Luther's means, however, for opposing Hebrew enmity was not the law of kindness, but to set against it a more energetic enmity. In a similar spirit, the great Puritan body, which in Cromwell's day lifted England into glory, through their representative men, the ministers, set their faces steadily against all tolerance of the Jew; and it should be counted among the great Protector's chief titles to a noble fame, that he bore down, with all the weight of his tremendous personality, the stubborn prejudice of his friends and upholders, insisted that the decree of Edward I. should be abrogated, and that the Israelite should once more have a place in England.

Men standing quite aloof from Christianity, even in times close to our own, have had regard scarcely kinder. To Gibbon they stand as an obstinate and sullen company who merit only his much-celebrated sneer. Voltaire could speak of them as "an ignorant and barbarous people, who for a long time have joined the foulest creed to the most frightful superstition, and most unconquerable hate against all who endure and enrich them." Even Buckle can say nothing kinder than to call them "that ignorant and obstinate race."

CHAPTER XIII.

SHYLOCK—THE WANDERING JEW.

ONE cannot study this many-volumed record of bloody outrage without feeling almost a sense of satisfaction, when sometimes the writhing victim turns and strikes a dagger into the persecutor who crushes him so cruelly. The Jews have not been, since the dispersion, a martial, combative race, but their history shows in them abundant power to smite when they have chosen to do so. When the Visigothic king, Sisebut, opened for them the chapter of persecution in the Spanish peninsula, they revenged themselves by smoothing energetically the path of the invading Moors. On Palm-Sunday at Toledo, while the people went in procession to church outside the walls, the Jews secretly admitted the Saracens into the city, joined their host, and fell upon the Christians with the sword as they were returning home.

One reads almost with pleasure of the conduct of a Jew at Oxford, in 1272. The university was going in procession to visit the shrine of St. Frideswide, when an audacious figure started from the Jewish quarter, wrested the cross from the hands of the bearer, and, to the horror of the pious, trampled it, with loud execrations, into the mire.

Among the portrayals of Shakespeare stands one figure,—a figure which perhaps has affected us with aversion, but which as we view him with minds thrilled by the story I have tried to make vivid, beholding him, as he towers from this mediæval landscape, whose features are torture-chambers, massacre, and the flame-encircled stake, is characterized not only by fierce barbaric grandeur, but almost by a certain sublime virtue,—the figure of Shylock.

Cast as our lot is in a humane age, as we go from all our softened circumstances to sit for an evening before the stage where the great magician reflects for us a scene from one of those dreadful times of blood and iron which we have left behind us, we have, perhaps, felt the flesh fairly creep as that arrogant hater, cringing so stealthily, darting so tiger-like, reaches with intense greed for the heart of the Christian. "What news upon the Rialto?" Ah, what news might he have heard, indeed! We are told only in part how bad match came upon bad match—the Goodwin sands breaking to pieces the argosies of Antonio,—his treacherous daughter squandering the stolen ducats, and bartering for monkeys the relics of her dead mother. That was all bad enough; but there was other news, of which the poet has told us nothing, which must have come to those outcasts in the Italian trading-cities, clinging, as it were, precariously to the gunwale, with cruel clubs raised everywhere to beat off their hold, in the midst of the raging sea of persecution and death which tossed all around them. Tubal could have told him more from Genoa than of the heartlessness of Jessica—for instance, of a fleet of his countrymen, driven from Spain, who arrived starving off the harbor; of their being allowed to land only upon the bleak mole—men, women, and tender children, beaten by the sea-wind, swept by the waves, so pale and emaciated that if they had not moved a little they would have passed for corpses; there they were allowed to lie with the dear land at hand, till hunger and drowning brought the bitter end. This half-crazed Jewess just arrived in a Lisbon caravel that has brought a cargo to the Rialto—what tale has she to tell? That she was cast out of the city; that seven children were torn from her to be carried to the Lost Islands—remote places to the West, on the verge of the world, believed to be alive with serpents and dragons; that when she flung herself at the feet of the king and begged that she might keep the youngest—the babe at her breast,—the king spurned her, and the babe's cries grew faint on her ear as ruffians carried it away. This young man whose eyes can scarcely meet the gaze of men, as if he were weighed down by some unutterable humiliation,—what story does Shylock hear from him? "Under pain of being burned at the stake, I was forced to go to the Dominicans of a distant city; to ask that the bones of my father, buried there, might be dug up and outraged, as having died an infidel; then bring back from them a certificate, that at the request of me, the son, the dead father had been insulted."

To some group of fugitives we may imagine

Shylock exclaiming: "And you, poor wanderers of our household, so bruised and maimed, whence come ye with your rags, your broken bodies, your hollow eyes?" "We are from the four quarters of Christendom, from the Elbe, the Seine, the Thames, the Danube; from the dungeons of nobles; from galleys where we were fettered to the oars until the chains ate through the bone, and from the edge of cauldrons of boiling oil. We poor remnant have escaped. Ask not how many perished!" In a sordid pursuit the soul of the Venetian usurer has become contaminated, but he is not without the nobler affections. He loves his dead wife Leah, his lost Jessica,—above all, his sacred nation, so cruelly ground,—with passion fervid as the Syrian sun which has given to his cheek its swarthy color. The simoom of the desert is not so fierce as the hatred in his strong heart, which he has been forced to smother. He has read well the law of Moses: "An eye for an eye, and a tooth for a tooth." Amid the humiliations of a lifetime he, for a moment, by a strange chance, has a persecutor within his grasp. As he crouches for an instant before the attack to whet upon his shoe-sole that merciless blade, cannot one see in the flash of his dark eye a light that is not utterly devilish! It is the lightning of revenge—but then revenge may be a distorted justice.

Is there not something moving in this portraiture of Shylock by his fellow Jew, Heinrich Heine?*
"When I saw the 'Merchant of Venice' given at Drury Lane, there stood behind me a beautiful, pale

---

* Shakespeare's "Mädchen und Frauen."

English lady, who at the end of the fourth act wept earnestly, and cried out several times : ' The poor man is wronged. The poor man is wronged.' It was a face of the noblest Grecian cast, and the eyes were large and black. I have never been able to forget them, those great black eyes which wept for Shylock ! Truly, with the exception of Portia, Shylock is the most respectable personage in the whole play. The domestic affections appear in him most touchingly."

Far more than all historic personalities does one remember in Venice, Shakespeare's Shylock. If you go over the Rialto, your eye seeks him everywhere, and you think he must be concealed there behind some pillar or other, with his Jewish gaberdine, with his mistrustful, calculating face, and you think you hear even his grating voice: " Three thousands ducats, well!"—I, at least, wandering dreamer as I am, looked everywhere on the Rialto trying whether I could find Shylock. Seeing him nowhere, I determined to seek him in the synagogue. The Jews were just celebrating here their holy day of reconciliation, and stood, wrapped in their white robes, with uncanny bowings of their heads, appearing almost like an assembly of ghosts. But although I looked everywhere, I could not behold the countenance of Shylock. And yet it seemed to me as if he stood concealed there, behind one of those white robes, praying more fervently than the rest of his fellow believers, with tempestuous wildness even, at the throne of Jehovah. I saw him not ! But toward evening, when, according to the belief of the Jews, the gates of heaven are shut, and no prayer finds admission, I heard a voice in which the tears were trickling as they were never wept with eyes. It was a sobbing which might move a stone to pity; they were tones of pain such as could come only from a breast that held shut up within itself all the martyrdom which a tortured race has endured for eighteen hundred years. It was the panting of a soul which sinks down, tired to death, before the gates of heaven. And this voice seemed well known to me. I felt as if I had heard it once, when it lamented in such despair, " Jessica, my child."

The terrible tale of the Jews' humiliation is completed as far as I dare unfold it, and the effect of it must be to leave the mind in a fit state to dwell upon the pathetic legend of "The Wandering Jew." Of all the old superstitions there is scarcely one so sad and picturesque as that of the human being who cannot die, but must suffer on through the centuries, until the day of judgment. The mediæval chroniclers, from the thirteenth century downwards, report with undoubting faith the appearances of the poor fury-scourged pilgrim, and there are men in the world to-day who think the story not impossible.

According to one version, Cartaphilus, gatekeeper of the house of Pilate, as Jesus descended from the judgment-hall, pushed the Saviour, bidding him go quicker; and Jesus looking back on him with a severe countenance said to him: "I am going and you shall wait till I return."

According to the more common tale, Ahasuerus, a

shoemaker, had done his best to compass the destruction of Jesus, believing him to be a misleader of the people. When Christ was condemned and about to be dragged past the house of Ahasuerus on his way to crucifixion, the shoemaker ran home and called together his household that they might have a look at the one about to suffer. He stood in his doorway when the troop ascended Calvary. As then Christ was led by, bowed under the weight of the heavy cross, he tried to rest a little and stood still a moment; but the shoemaker, in zeal and rage, and for the sake of obtaining credit among the other Jews, drove him forward and told him to hasten on his way. Jesus, obeying, looked at him and said: " I shall stand and rest, but thou shalt go till the last day." At these words the man left his house and went forward to behold the crucifixion. As soon as it had taken place, it came upon him that he could no more return to Jerusalem, nor see again his wife and child, but must go forth into foreign lands one after another, a mournful pilgrim.

So the broken, impenitent figure has been seen— sometimes in the throngs of cities, sometimes in deserts, sometimes in mountain solitudes, the tragedy of Calvary ever haunting him in rock, in forest, in the clouds of heaven, passing ever onward with no rest for the sole of his foot, every corner of the earth again and again visited. Whenever a hundred years have passed, his manhood is renewed for him, so that he stands again at thirty, the age at which he committed the sin whose expiation is so terrible. The accounts are so detailed and circumstantial, we are forced to believe that many a half-crazed man has actually made himself and others believe that he was the Wandering Jew, and that many an impostor, seeking to affect men with the deepest awe, has assumed the character. How striking and picturesque are some of the developments of the conception; for instance, where it becomes combined with the myth of the god Odin, and appears as the Wild Huntsman!

One of the most philosophic students of modern times, Jacob Grimm, has taught the world that many a fairy tale and many a peasant superstition are nothing more or less than the remains of the great legends of the old heathen religious faiths, softened down, but still living in the souls of the people. Grimm and his school would have us believe that the phantoms of the mighty Norse gods still haunt the modern generations of the Teutonic stock, refusing to be exorcised from the popular mind. "Balder the beautiful is dead, is dead," sings the Swedish poet Tegner, after the old saga ; and in like manner with Balder, we have believed that Odin and Thor and Freya were utterly gone, with the men that paid them worship. These students would have us believe that the ghosts of the gods, at any rate, refuse to be laid. Sometimes in blithe and merry guise they continue to appear in the souls of men belonging to the great races whose forefathers worshipped them; sometimes the grim circumstance that attended them in their former pre-eminence is not laid aside. What wonderful grandeur in the thought that these rough hands of the old gods

THE WANDERING JEW.

refuse to become decrepit through time, or beaten off by culture! How they reach round the new altars that have crowded out their own simple fanes, because the all-conquering Jew has willed it should be so! How they cross the widest oceans to the homes of the farthest wanderers, still haunting, phantom-like, the hearts of men whose barbarian sires held them dear!

The superstition of the Wild Huntsman, still cherished by many a simple peasant soul, can be thus traced back through the centuries to an origin in the stormy faith professed by the vikings. The fierce rider who presses unsatisfied, attended by his troop of deathless hounds, 'mid the roar of the winter's blast, through the heavens torn with the tempest, in pursuit of the stag that forever flies before him, was really the god Odin. As we think how the Wandering Jew has become connected with this stormy Northern myth, it might seem as if the old dispossessed chief of the Norse deities, wrathful at the usurpation that had reared the new temples in place of his own ancient fanes, had caught the Jew into the heavens in a spirit of weird revenge, compelling him to a companionship with himself in his desolate and fruitless quest.

In this elaboration of the legend of the Wandering Jew, Christ asked permission to drink at a horse trough in his agony, but was refused—the Jew pointing at the same time to the track of a horse's hoof, which was filled with water, as a place where his thirst might be slaked. At this point the heathen and Christian myth become confused. The Wandering

Jew, as the Wild Huntsman, must drive forever with his train through the fury of the tempest. The moaning of the wind at night through the forest—about the dwellings of men,—will cause the souls of the most unsuperstitious to thrill, as if it were filled in some way with the voices of spirits! Imagine the tumult in the breast of the peasant child of the Harz, or the Black Forest, or the rude districts in France, who, as the November blast at midnight wails and hurtles through the hills, believes it the dreary hunt of the everlasting Jew, and sees in the torn clouds, by the fitful moonlight, the tails of his phantom horses, the forms of his dogs, the streaming of his own white beard, careering forward in this eternal chase!

There is a tale current among the simple people of Switzerland which, to my mind, is as weird and thrilling as this. Whoever has climbed from Zermatt to the Gorner Grat, and stood with the snowy mass of Monte Rosa on the left, the Weisshorn on the right, and directly in front the bleakest and boldest of the Alpine peaks, the Matterhorn—its sublimity deepened and made dreadful by the story with which it is associated, of the men who have fallen from its precipices, four thousand feet to the ice below,—whoever has done this will well believe that there are few spots on earth more full of dreary grandeur. There is a bald, lonely mountain-spur confronting all the awful desolation, upon which the Wandering Jew was once seen standing, solitary, his haggard figure relieved against the heavens, before the abashed eyes of the dwellers in the vale who looked up. He had been there before far back in the dim centuries; again in the fulness of time he will be seen standing there, his tattered garments and dishevelled beard given to the winds, his battered staff in hands shrivelled and wrinkled till they seem like talons, bent and furrowed by his thousand-fold accumulated woes. It will be on the judgment-day; on that bleak summit he is to receive release from his exceptional doom.

We shall best interpret the myth if we understand the Wandering Jew to be the Hebrew race typified— its deathless course, its transgression, its centuries of expiating agony, in this way made for us concrete and vivid.

CHAPTER XIV.

THE CASTING OUT OF A PROPHET.

THE writer who aims at a fair presentation of the sorrowful subject that has occupied us, must take pains to bring into a clear light the palliations which most certainly can be urged in mitigation of this horrible, widespread ruthlessness. The Christian world was just emerging from the barbarism of the dark ages: utter intolerance of all other creeds than that which it professed itself appeared to be a paramount duty. Without doubt, nothing could be more exasperating than the attitude of the Hebrews toward the surrounding Gentiles, whenever, for a moment the clutch was taken from his throat, and he was in a measure free to follow his own impulses. The heart of the Jew can be very unamiable; from the mountain of his scorn, the Gentile has seemed to him worthy of contempt more often than of any softer feeling. Toward the brethren of his own household indeed, the Jew has not seldom been unkind. Until the army of Titus could be descried from the pinnacles of the Temple, the factions in Jerusalem wrangled and slew one another. We are about to see how the synagogue excluded a most noble spirit with blasting anathemas. In all ages, in fact, the grandest prophets of Israel have been too often cast out and stoned, for of no other race of men is the utterance of the disheartened Faust any truer:

> "The few by whom high truth was recognized,
> Who foolishly their full hearts left unguarded,
> Revealing to the crowd their noble vision,
> Have always banished been, and crucified."*

One's wrath at the mediæval Christian is somewhat lessened, on reading the story of the treatment accorded by his own brethren to the illustrious Spinoza.

But before we take up the tale of the great teacher whom his people persisted in rejecting, let us glance at a false prophet, whom in the same age they seemed very willing to accept. Their blindness is as plainly shown, perhaps, by exhibiting the leader they were ready to follow, as the leader whom they reviled and cast off. Throughout their history, the Jews have constantly maintained the ancient Messianic hope— a hope again and again disappointed. The twelfth, the thirteenth, and the sixteenth centuries produced impostors who claimed to be the Prince of the House of David, destined to restore the glory of Zion; such too in the more ancient time was Bar Cocheba, the champion of the reign of Hadrian. No false Messiah, however, has been so successful as Sabbatäi Zevi,† a

---

* "Die wenigen die was davon erkannt,
  Die thöricht g'nug ihr volles Herz nicht wahrten,
  Dem Pöbel ihr Gefühl, ihr Schauen offenbarten,
  Hat man von je gekreuzigt und verbannt."
† Reinach, p. 270, etc.

Jew of Smyrna, born in 1626. He was the son of a commercial agent employed by an English house; his person was attractive, his manner austere and reticent; by fasts, ablutions, and zealous attention to the rites in general, he early made himself marked. At the age of twenty-five he announced himself as Messiah, and followed by a troop of disciples which constantly grew larger, he travelled from city to city through Greece, Syria, and Egypt. A mad fanatic, Nathan of Gaza, went before him to announce his coming. At Cairo, meeting a young Polish Jewess of rare beauty, who had escaped by miracle from the massacres of the Cossacks, and afterwards from a Catholic cloister in which she had taken refuge, Sabbatäi married her, declaring that she had been destined for him from all eternity. Returning to Smyrna, he took openly, in full synagogue, the title of Messiah, exciting transports of enthusiasm. The feeble protestations of a few rabbis of good sense were smothered in the popular clamor. The renown of the new prophet spread everywhere; he soon counted ardent adherents at Amsterdam, at Hamburg, even at London. Zealots in many places destroyed their dwellings, collected their wealth, and prepared to set out for the East, where at length Israel was to be restored to glory. In Persia, the Jewish laborers refused to cultivate longer the earth. A mad inspiration seemed to have seized upon the whole Hebrew race.

The audacity of Sabbatäi became stimulated by his success. He made daring changes in the Jewish ritual, abrogating and transferring fasts and feasts ancient as the race itself; he divided the crowns of the earth among his brothers and friends, reserving for himself the title of King of Kings. At length he set out for Constantinople, where, he declared, his mission was to be accomplished. The Turkish Government, which left him unmolested while the excitement which he created was distant, now seized upon him, threw him into chains, and imprisoned him at the Castle of the Dardanelles.

The fidelity of the proselytes was not at all disturbed by this misfortune. The cunning Turks saw their chance. The captivity of Sabbatäi came at last to resemble a sumptuous hospitality. He lived in state in the castle, whither Jews hastened by thousands to contemplate his divine features, taxed heavily meantime by the Mussulmans, who managed shrewdly to reap advantages. A rabbi from Poland finally denounced him as an impostor and disturber of the peace. The Sultan, Mahomet IV., had Sabbatäi brought before him, caused him to be fastened naked to a post, and commanded archers to shoot at him. At the same time he promised to become a Jew, if the "Son of God," by a miracle which ought to be easy to him, should render his body invulnerable to the arrows. Sabbatäi immediately quailed. The alternative being offered him of becoming a Mussulman or being instantly driven forth, he adopted the turban without hesitation, adored the prophet of Medina, and received the name of Mahomet Effendi.

The stupor of his followers may be imagined. The rabbis, undeceived at last, hurried to excommunicate his partisans. Faithful adherents even now remained to him in Africa, Italy, Germany, and Poland. Some declared he had not turned Turk, that his shadow only remained upon the earth, while his body had ascended to heaven. Others maintained that his passage through Islamism, as well as his preceding trials and experiences, were part of his mission. This view Sabbatäi encouraged, conforming externally to Mussulman rites, but secretly returning to the synagogue and posing anew as a fervent Israelite. The hypocrite was unmasked: the Sultan contemptuously gave him his life, and he died at last in obscurity.

At the very hour when infatuated Israel had abused herself most deeply, pouring out her veneration at the feet of the wretched charlatan of Smyrna, she cast forth from herself one of the most illustrious of her sons, a spirit capable of the highest leadership, wise, and of the purest beauty.

It was Holland, just set free by the heroism of its people from the bigot grip of Spain, which led the way among the countries of Europe in the new path of toleration. Hither flocked in the seventeenth century the oppressed and the outcasts of all nations,—the Puritan from England, sore from the persecution of the Stuarts,—the free-thinker and Huguenot from France, just escaped from the stake in the Catholic reaction,—the bolder and finer spirits of Italy, Germany, Poland, whom neither bribe nor brow-beating could reduce to conformity. Hither, too, came the foot-sore and down-hearted Jew, making at length shrines for the sacred rolls of the Law which were not to be desecrated, and taking breath from the scourge in the noble cities whose atmosphere was sweet and bracing with liberty. The Israelitish aristocracy are the "Sephardim," the band that in Spain and Portugal contributed so much to the greatness of those countries in their golden period. Of this Hebrew aristocracy among the Spanish Jews, in Amsterdam, early in the seventeenth century, was born Baruch or Benedict Spinoza.

The name of Spinoza is one burdened long with undeserved reproach. He was falsely accused of atheism, whereas, as his vindicators justly claim, he should rather be called a God-intoxicated man. Lewes, a writer who has no sympathy with his philosophical system, but a great admiration for his vast intellectual power and noble character, gives in a picture full of brilliant lights the story of his career. He describes him as "a little Jewish boy playing with his sisters on the Burgwal of Amsterdam, close to the Portuguese synagogue. His face is mild and ingenuous; his eyes small, but bright, quick, and penetrative, his dark hair flowing in luxuriant curls over his neck and shoulders. Amsterdam is noisy with the creaking of cordage, the bawling of sailors, and the busy trafficking of traders. The Zuyder Zee is crowded with vessels laden with precious stores from all quarters of the globe. The canals which ramify that city, like a great arterial system, are blocked up with boats and barges, the whole scene vivid with the greatness and the littleness of commerce. The parents of Spinoza were from mercantile families, among the fugitives from Spain.

SPINOZA.

having their part in all this commercial bustle; and the lively boy would, it was supposed, like his ancestors, play a part upon the market and exchange." His passion for study, however, and the brightness of his mind induced his parents to educate him as a rabbi. Upon the study of Talmud and Old Testament Spinoza entered with zeal, and at fourteen, even, is said to have rivalled almost all the doctors in the exactitude and extent of his knowledge.

Great hopes were entertained of the youth, hopes which gave way to fears when the rabbis discovered that the boy was developing a questioning spirit whose pertinacity they were unable to satisfy. He was summoned before the synagogue, and at length threatened with excommunication.* An offer of an annual pension of a thousand florins was made to him, if he would only consent to be silent and assist from time to time in the services of the synagogue, which, however, was refused with scorn.

In truth, the learning which the boy was set to master was excessively intricate and fantastic. Vast respect was paid at that time among the Hebrews to the "Cabala," about which a word must be said. The pious Jew of that day believed that, aside from its obvious signification, every tittle of Scripture had its symbolical meaning, and a strange collection of rhapsodies and wild imaginings had been growing up from the thirteenth century, which were generally received as an authentic interpretation of this secondary sense. From this source all Jewry was overrun with demonology, thaumaturgy, and other

* " Life of Spinoza," by Colerus.

strange fancies.* In Spinoza's generation this had its most extravagant development. It was, indeed, unmitigated nonsense, whose puerilities, if not disgusting, were ludicrous. The clear-brained youth, as he matured, rejected it all, withdrew from the synagogue, and made ready to win his bread by learning the trade of polishing lenses for optical instruments, a craft in which he became dexterous.

The discipline of the rabbis was severe. Shortly before, a Jew, who had incurred the displeasure of the elders, had been forced to lie across the threshold of the synagogue, presenting his body to the feet of the congregation as it passed out. In some such way they would have been glad to humiliate Spinoza. No penance could, however, be imposed upon him, for he had withdrawn himself. But fanaticism felt justified in trying another means. One evening as Spinoza was coming out of the theatre, he was startled by the fierce expression of a dark face, thrust eagerly before his. A knife gleamed in the air, and he had barely time to parry the blow. It fell upon his chest, but fortunately, deadened in its force, only tore his coat. Thus he escaped assassination, but he could still be excommunicated and cursed.

"The day of excommunication at length arrived, and a vast concourse assembled to witness the awful ceremony. It began by the solemn and silent lighting of a quantity of black wax-candles, and by opening the tabernacle wherein were deposited the books of the law of Moses. Thus were the dim

* Pollock: "Life of Spinoza,"

imaginations of the faithful prepared for all the horror of the scene. The chief-rabbi, the ancient friend and master, now the fiercest enemy, of the condemned, was to order the execution. He stood there pained, but implacable; the people fixed their eager eyes upon him. High above the chanter rose and chanted forth in loud, lugubrious tones the words of execration; while from the opposite side another mingled with these curses the thrilling sounds of the trumpet. And now the black candles were reversed, and were made to melt drop by drop into a huge tub filled with blood." *

Then came the final anathema. " With the judgment of the angels and of the saints, we excommunicate, cut off, curse, and anathematize Baruch de Espinoza, with the consent of the elders and of all this holy congregation, in the presence of the holy books: by the 613 precepts which are written therein, with the anathema wherewith Joshua cursed Jericho, with the curse which Elisha laid upon the children, and with all the curses which are written in the law. Cursed be he by day, and cursed be he by night. Cursed be he in sleeping, and cursed be he in waking, cursed in going out, and cursed in coming in. The Lord shall not pardon him, the wrath and fury of the Lord shall henceforth be kindled against this man, and shall lay upon him all the curses which are written in the book of the Law. The Lord shall destroy his name under the sun, and cut him off for his undoing from all the tribes of Israel, with all the curses of the firmament

* Lewes : " Biog. Hist. of Philosophy."

which are written in the book of the Law. But ye that cleave unto the Lord your God, live all of you this day. And we warn you that none may speak with him by word of mouth nor by writing, nor show any favor to him, nor be under one roof with him, nor come within four cubits of him, nor read any paper composed or written by him."*

As the blasting words were uttered, the lights were all suddenly immersed in the blood, a cry of religious horror and execration burst from all; and in that solemn darkness, and to those solemn curses, they shouted Amen, Amen! Thus the blinded race cast forth the noblest man of his generation, as it had done in ages before—a man whom, as in the preceding time, the Gentile world was to adopt and love, to set upon a pinnacle indeed as a guide and benefactor.

There is a singular elevation about the life of Spinoza henceforth. His legal right to inherit a portion of his father's estate was denied. He established it, but handed the share over to his sisters, who had disputed his claim, magnanimously overlooking their enmity. The handsome fortune which a friend desired to leave him he refused to receive; he declined an ample pension from Louis XIV.; he refused a position at the University of Heidelberg, as compromising his independence. By polishing his crystals he was able to keep soul and body together, while he devoted his main strength to speculations as profound as have ever occupied the brain of man. He was serenely brave. The great Condé having

* Pollock : "Life of Spinoza."

invaded Holland with a French army, sent for Spinoza, whose reputation had interested him, to visit him in his camp. The mob, hearing of the intercourse, suspected the philosopher of being a spy, and were about to tear him in pieces. He showed himself ready to face their rage with a heart undaunted. His character was made up of generous simplicity and heroic forbearance. He taught the learned world the doctrines he had elaborated with endless toil; but he taught children to be regular in their attendance on divine service. He had no unwise proselytism which would destroy old convictions in minds unfitted to receive others. One day his hostess, a simple unlettered Christian, asked him if he believed she could be saved by her religion. He answered: "Your religion is a good one, you ought not to seek another, nor doubt that yours will procure your salvation, provided you add to your piety the tranquil virtues of domestic life." *

He died when but forty-five, the peer of the sublimest leaders of the human race. It would be out of place here to attempt to outline the vast system which forms his title to immortal fame. He was persecuted in life and in death. The charge of atheism, with which his fame has long been burdened, he regarded as the grossest and most wicked of calumnies, and great champions at last arose to vindicate his memory. It was, indeed, his teaching that there was but one infinite substance, and that is God. Whatever is, is in God; and without Him nothing can be conceived. He is the universal being,

* Colerus.

of which all things are the manifestations. He is the sole substance; every thing else is a mode; yet without substance, mode cannot exist. God, viewed under the attributes of infinite substance, is the *natura naturans*, that which forever creates; God, viewed as a manifestation, as the modes under which his attributes appear, is the *natura naturata*, that which is created. He is the cause of all things, and that immanently, not transiently. This, according to G. H. Lewes, is the heart and pith of the system of Spinoza,—certainly not atheism,—certainly not materialism, for though God is called substance (*substans*), it is only in a high spiritual sense which the thinker is careful to make clear. If the scheme deserves to be called pantheism, the destroying of the creation while God is made all in all, a few citations will show that the entertaining of these ideas was not inconsistent in Spinoza, with an active and beautiful spirit of humanity.

"He who lives according to reason endeavors to the utmost of his power to outweigh another man's hate, anger, or despite against him with love or highmindedness. * * * He who chooses to avenge wrong by requiting it with hatred is assuredly miserable. But he who strives to cast out hatred by love, may fight his fight in joy and confidence. As for those he doth conquer, they yield to him joyfully, and that not because their strength faileth, but because it is increased.

"A man who desires to help others by counsel or deeds, so that they may together enjoy the chief good, will be very forward to win their love to him, but not to draw them into admiration of him. In common talk he will eschew telling of men's faults, and will speak but sparingly of human weakness. But he will speak at large of man's virtue and power, and the means of perfecting the same, that thus men may endeavor, not from fear and disgust, but wholly in joyfulness, to live, so far as in them lies, after the commandment of reason." *

The biographer of Spinoza calls this "a lofty refinement of the fundamental duty of good-will to men, which is not to be found, so far as I know, in any other moralist." The tone of the passage is declared to be like that of Marcus Aurelius, but there is no exact parallel.

Very lofty too is the teaching of this pure sage as regards the motive which should influence man in the pursuit of virtue. Good must be done not through any hope of reward or fear of punishment, for the reward of virtue is virtue itself. As we should expect, Spinoza was a firm and consistent supporter of political liberty, disposed to go much farther in allowing individual thought, habits, and enterprise to have free scope, than the statesmen of his time. Rising above the Jewish prejudices in which he had been nurtured, he regarded Jesus as a man indeed, but a man of unique and transcendent moral genius, above Moses and the prophets. With broad-minded tolerance he declares: "For Turks and heathen, if they worship God by justice and charity to their neighbors, I believe they have the spirit of Christ and are saved."

* Pollock.

If we trace for a moment the history of Spinoza's fame we find him at first hated and denounced, but never forgotten. The unlearned held him in holy horror, and the learned refused to do him justice. Leibnitz, his contemporary, and at one time his correspondent, depreciated him; Locke speaks of him as "justly decried"; and Bishop Berkeley refers to his "wild imaginations." It was the great Lessing, in the middle of the eighteenth century, who first elevated Spinoza to a lofty position; he declared that there was no philosophy but his. Goethe accepted with no less enthusiasm the outcast Jew, being drawn especially by his boundless unselfishness. He finds the saying marvellous: "Whoso truly loves God must not expect that God will love him in return." In our own century he has held the hearts of the most gifted of the world. It was Novalis who called him the God-intoxicated man. Heine and Fichte were penetrated by his influence. Hegel declared that "to be a philosopher one must first be a Spinozist." Auerbach, who translated him, believed that "Spinoza's mind had fed the thought of two centuries." Coleridge brought it to pass that he received at last a fair appreciation from English thinkers, and in connection with this introduction an amusing story is told by Coleridge himself.

It was the troublous time of the French Revolution, and as the young Englishman returned from the Continent, and with little reticence proceeded to pour out wild ideas into the ear of his friend Wordsworth, who was also known to entertain extravagant opinions, a worthy magistrate of Somersetshire, felt it to be his duty as an Englishman to cause these mad-brained men to be watched. A spy was set upon them, who, after a careful investigation, reported Coleridge and Wordsworth as after all loyal men. " He had repeatedly hid himself for hours together behind a bank at the seaside (our favorite seat), and overheard our conversation. At first he fancied that we were aware of our danger, for he often heard me talk of our ' Spy Nozy ' which he was inclined to interpret of himself, and of a remarkable feature belonging to him, but he was speedily convinced it was the name of a man who had made a book, and lived long ago."

The best England of Coleridge's day was as densely ignorant of the high-souled philosopher, as was the worthy spy. But appreciation came. Shelley drew from him inspiration ; Maurice, Froude, and Matthew Arnold, in our time, have done him justice. Not less so Taine and Renan in France. At the present time there is no more honored name among all the heroes of abstract thought. Says the pious Schleiermacher: "Sacrifice with me to the manes of the holy but repudiated Spinoza. The great spirit of the world penetrated him ; the Infinite was his beginning and his end ; the universe his only and eternal love. He was filled with religion and religious feeling, and therefore it is that he stands alone, unapproachable—the master in his art, but elevated above the profane world, without adherents, and without even citizenship." Says G. H. Lewes: " He was a brave and simple man, earnestly meditating on the deepest subjects that can occupy the human race. He produced a system which will ever remain as one of the most astounding efforts of abstract speculation—a system that has been decried for nearly two centuries as the most iniquitous and blasphemous of human invention; and which has now, within the last sixty years, become the acknowledged parent of a whole nation's philosophy, ranking among its admirers some of the most pious and illustrious intellects of the age."

PART III.

THE BREAKING OF THE CHAIN.

CHAPTER XV.

ISRAEL'S NEW MOSES.

THE total Jewish population of the world, at the present time, according to the latest estimates,* is 6,300,000, distributed as follows: To Europe 5,400,-000, to Asia 300,000, to Africa 350,000, to America 250,000, to Oceanica 12,000. Of the different countries of Europe, Russia has a Hebrew population of 2,552,000; Austria with Hungary, 1,644,000; Germany, 562,000; France, 63,000; and Great Britain, 60,000. Of the portion assigned to America, the United States contains 230,000.

It appears from these figures that there are no lands in which the Jews form a large element of the population; but for some reason an astonishing change from their old abasement is to be noticed in the position they have come to occupy. The mediæval outcast is everywhere climbing into places of power, until it begins to seem possible that he may attain in the future an ascendancy as remarkable as his past abjectness. Cries, sometimes of admiration, but more often of dislike and alarm, are uttered over this fact in all parts of the civilized world,—all, however, whether laudatory or ill-natured, giving evidence of

* Reinach: " Histoire des Israélites," 1885.

a deep-seated conviction, that this strange tribe, forever with us but never of us, is at any rate of quality most masterful.

Let us survey for a moment the various departments of human energy, and obtain some comprehensive idea of what the Hebrew is accomplishing.

In military life, we find that although in antiquity Israel fought many a stern fight under valiant champions, it can claim since the dispersion no great note in war. Jews have fought, however, in the ranks of various armies, and have furnished good generals to various standards and causes. The most distinguished soldier of Hebrew descent that can be mentioned is probably Marshal Massena, whose real name is said to have been Manasseh,—the warrior whom Napoleon called " the favorite child of victory," one of the most scientific as well as one of the most brave and tenacious of the great chieftains whom the fateful Corsican summoned to fight at his side.

Turning to the employments of peace, the record of Hebrew achievements in agriculture and the handicrafts will also be a short one. We have seen that there have been times when the Jew has figured as farmer and mechanic; it is not so at present, and the fact that he so seldom works with his hands, really earns his bread by the sweat of his brow, is often made the basis of a harsh judgment against him. But really do we not find here an evidence of Israelitish power? We should all prefer, if we could, to get on by our wits, rather than by labor of the hands; hence the crowding up everywhere into trade and the professions, away from the soil and the tool.

We feel that the tendency ought to be discouraged; and in the case of the Jew, we should like him better, if now and then he put to the wheel of life actual muscle, instead of, forever, that subtle power of his brain. But when a whole race undertakes to live by its wits, and succeeds so remarkably, what ability it must possess!

It is indeed a brilliant success. In the world of trade, it has in some way come about that a preeminence is everywhere conceded to the Jew. He is omnipresent and everywhere dreaded. It is of competition with him that the pedlar who deals in sixpence-worths stands most in fear; the same aggressive elbows are crowding cavalierly the millionaire in the transactions of *la haute finance.* Keen indeed must the man be who can match him in the high or low places; and as for Gentile accusations of meanness and knavery, shall the pot call the kettle black? There are exchanges in great cities of the world practically abandoned to all but Jews. In our new Western and Southern towns, there are sometimes scarce any but Hebrew signs on the business streets. In trade, the Hebrew is ubiquitous and always at the front.

Turning to the fine arts, the Hebrews have rarely become famed as painters and sculptors, a result to which perhaps the ancient Semitic repugnance to the representation of the forms of living creatures has helped. In music, however, their glory is of the highest. Mendelssohn, Halévy, Moscheles, Meyerbeer, Rubinstein, Joachim, as composers and performers, are among the greatest. Wagner, indeed, wrote a diatribe against Jewish influence in music, and there is a story that he prepared a composition especially to vindicate against the Hebrews the superiority of a pure Teutonic taste; but when it came to the performance, lo, the patriotic master beheld the first violins all in the hands of the aliens, whose dark eyes were scanning serenely the tangled score that was to bring them to confusion! The fact was that none but Jews could be found skilful enough to take the burden of the performance. As actors, the Israelites have also been very illustrious. With Rachel and Bernhardt at the summit, it would be easy to mention a long and most distinguished list.

If we follow graver paths we encounter, among philosophers, the great Spinoza, at whose work we have just glanced, and we shall presently consider still another most illustrious name. Franke is great in medicine, Bernays, of Bonn, is noted for erudition in Greek, Benfey the first of Sanscrit scholars, Auerbach at the head of German novelists, Heine the chief of German poets since the death of Goethe,—all men of the ancient Israelitish strain, though in the case of some of them the ancient faith was forsaken. When we look at the field of statesmanship, as we shall presently do, what men of Jewish blood have done is as astonishing as their achievements elsewhere.

How is it that the wonderful transformation has been brought about? We have seen the poor Hebrew under the heel—a hundred nations trying to stamp the life out of him as if he were a venomous reptile. He makes the claim at the present hour that he has conquered the world,* and many are ready, with fear and dread, to concede it. Let us study certain great figures in various departments of effort, men whose genius and energy are thoroughly Jewish, so that they can well be regarded as types. In reviewing these careers, the change will soon become explicable.

As we enter the eighteenth century, though the harshness of men has become somewhat modified, the chain that binds the Jew, nevertheless, throughout the civilized world is firmly fastened. The massacres and fierce bodily tortures are indeed for the most part things of the past, except perhaps in Spain, or in outlying regions where barbarism yields slowly. In many a city, however, the Jew's presence in the streets is scarcely suffered, and with every night he is barred pitilessly into the dirt and discomfort of Ghetto and Juden-gasse. Germany was especially narrow and cruel toward the Israelites. In many towns they could not live upon the street corners; in others only a certain small number could be married in the course of a year. In Berlin, the Hebrews, to whom, through their creed, swine's flesh was accursed, were forced to buy the wild boars slain in the king's hunts. Thus exposed to insult and hardship, the Jews of Germany, the "Askenazim," as they were called, were sunk among their co-religionists into an especial degradation; progress was stopped, and wide views became lost. They had a language of their own, a jargon of Hebrew and Ger-

* Beaconsfield's assertion : see p. 2.

man. Their religion became corrupted through superstitions; their rabbis came largely from among the Polish Jews, who were usually ignorant and debased. Under these teachers efforts to become enlightened were repressed; to speak German correctly, or to read a German book, was heresy. The handicrafts were forbidden them,—to a large extent even trade; the professions were of course closed avenues; to sell old clothes, to wander about as pedlars, and to lend money at interest were almost the only occupations that remained.

From the midst of the German Jews, however, sprang at this time a man, who, if of less wonderful intellect than Spinoza, was yet of spirit most keen and enlightened. In magnanimity and broad charity he was not surpassed by the great outcast of Holland. In the story which we are following his figure has even a greater significance than that of Spinoza, from the fact that though persecuted he remained among his people, beneficently setting in motion reforms which have been felt by Jews in every land, and which in times following those in which we live, will bring about for Jews a happy future. As has been urged, the intolerance with which the Hebrew has been treated must not be ascribed solely to Christian narrowness. The persecutor has been provoked to clench his fist by the stern pride with which the victim has asserted his superiority and held himself aloof. Such modifications of prejudice in the oppressor as can be now seen, would be much less marked than they are had not a more conciliatory spirit begun to manifest itself in the oppressed.

In the year 1729, in the town of Dessau, was born the benign and far-seeing genius, Moses the son of Mendel, who, like Moses of old, the son of Amram, was to lead Israel to better things.

Moses Mendelssohn was a precocious child, devouring with passionate appetite the rabbinical husks upon which alone his mind was permitted to feed, until at length his premature labor brought upon him curvature of the spine, from which he never recovered. As a boy of thirteen he followed to Berlin the rabbi who had been his teacher, his parents disapproving his course and withdrawing their support. The little humpback faced starvation with unshrinking persistence while he followed his bent, until, after much suffering, he won over friends who could help him. As the youth approached manhood he broadened his acquirements, adding almost by stealth German, Latin, mathematics, French, and English to his Talmudic lore, soon beginning also to seize upon the thoughts of the great philosophers. As his culture widened his old friends became cold; as in Spinoza's case his former teachers feared his heresies, and soon began to frown and threaten.

When he had reached twenty-one, however, a rich silk-manufacturer of Berlin became his patron, made him the tutor of his children, also his business assistant, and at last his partner; henceforth, then, Mendelssohn was free to follow his own path, unannoyed by the wolf of hunger, and, later, even in affluence. The young man became a member of a circle of brilliant minds, among whom ruled as chief one of the mightiest gods of the German Olympus, Gotthold Ephraim Lessing, and henceforth, to the day of Lessing's death, Mendelssohn was held in the heart of hearts of that courageous striver. The slender silk-merchant, while with Hebrew thrift he managed to seize upon gold in the ways of commerce, possessed at the same time strength for the sublimest flights. He early became known as an able writer for the literary periodicals, and at length found himself growing famous. One day the frank and hearty Lessing came with a laugh to Mendelssohn's desk in the counting-room, holding in his hand a volume fresh from printer and binder. To the amazement of Mendelssohn, it was a manuscript of his own, which he had modestly withheld from the press; his friend, however, had taken it without his knowledge, and was spreading it far and wide in an ample edition. Its success was so marked that he was henceforth a maker of books. In literature he was fruitful and always beneficent, doing much toward the spread in Germany of an elegant culture and taste, in the years immediately preceding the glorious sun-burst, when with Goethe and Schiller the great day of German letters begins.

At first known as a writer upon æsthetic subjects, the excellence of his thoughts was scarcely more remarkable than the beauty of his style; but at length in his forty-second year came the book which has given him a note of a far grander kind, and placed his name among the chief helpers of his age and country. This was his "Phædo," a work upon the immortality of the soul. In this book Mendelssohn translated the dialogue of Plato, of the same name, but enlarged and developed the consideration in the spirit of the later philosophy. As an introduction to the work, a picture of the life and character of Socrates was given, full of the highest love and veneration for the master-sage. The tone of the "Phædo" of Mendelssohn is most exalted, and soon excited in the world general admiration. Edition followed edition; it was translated into most European languages. Inasmuch as so many German thinkers have hidden their speculations within a thorny and forbidding entanglement which renders them quite inaccessible except to minds of exceptional power of penetration, it is worth while to speak of the admirable clearness and beauty of Mendelssohn's method of presentment. The work is a series of the sublimest thoughts, fitly framed, pervaded with the broadest and noblest spirit.*

Like Maimonides, the grand Hebrew of the thirteenth century,—like Spinoza,—in the spirit, too, of that higher and holier soul that came forth from Zion, the supernal Christ,—Mendelssohn, looked and worked toward the broadest tolerance and human brotherhood. In the truest spirit of charity he labored with his people, trying to raise them from their ignorance, and to smooth away from the Jewish countenance the arrogant frown and lifting of the eyelid with which through the ages they have stubbornly faced the Gentile. Of one of his books written for his co-religionists, called "Jerusalem," Immanuel Kant wrote in such terms as these: "With

* Kurz. "Geschicte der deutschen Literatur."

what admiration I have read your 'Jerusalem'! I regard this book as the announcement of a great though slow-coming reform, which will affect not only your nation, but also others. You have managed to unite with your religion such a spirit of freedom and tolerance as it has not had credit for, and such as no other faith can boast. You have so powerfully presented the necessity of an unlimited freedom of conscience for every faith, that at length on our side, too, the church must think about it. The Christians must study whether in their creeds there are not things which burden and oppress the spirit, and look toward a union which, as regards essential religious points, shall bring together all."

As Judaism spurned forth its nobler spirits in the earlier time, so the effort was made to put under ban this later liberalizing genius. He, however, though looked at askance by all the stricter members of the synagogue, who to this day have not ceased to oppose the fruitful influence that proceeded from him, clung tenaciously until his death to his Jewish birthright. One finds something most pathetic in the story of a certain grave embarrassment into which he was thrown by an over-zealous Christian friend. Lavater, the Swiss clergyman, well known in the world for his writings upon physiognomy, was a most earnest upholder of the faith. Having translated from the French a work upon the Christian evidences which he felt to be unanswerable, he dedicated it to Mendelssohn, summoning him, as he did so, either to show that the positions of the work were groundless, or to renounce the Jewish creed.

Circumstances forced Mendelssohn to take some notice of the challenge. To renounce Judaism of course he was not ready, believing, as he did, that it was capable of expansion into a faith most beneficent. On the other hand, he was scarcely more ready to controvert Christianity; for he hated strife, felt no desire to proselyte, and hoped for some reconciliation of the jarring creeds by other than polemic means. In his trouble he wrote and published a letter to Lavater, in which was unfolded all the beauty of his soul, and which gained for him the approval of all intelligent men. Without transgressing moderation, he convinced all fair-minded readers, overcoming even the proselyter himself.

A passage from this famous letter of Mendelssohn will be interesting*:

"For all I cared Judaism might have been hurled down in every polemical compendium, and triumphantly sneered at in every academic exercise, and I would not have entered into a dispute about it. Rabbinical scholars and rabbinical smatterers might have grubbed in obsolete scribblings, which no sensible Jew reads or knows of, and have amused the public with the most fantastic ideas of Judaism, without so much as a contradiction on my part. It is by virtue that I wish to shame the opprobrious opinion commonly entertained of a Jew, and not by controversial writings.

"Pursuant to the principles of my religion, I am not to seek to convert any one who is not born according to our laws. This proneness to conversion, the

* From "Memoirs of M. Mendelssohn," by M. Samuels, p. 54, etc.

origin of which some would fain tack on the Jewish religion, is, nevertheless, diametrically opposed to it. Our rabbis unanimously teach that the written and oral laws which form conjointly our revealed religion, are obligatory on our nation only. 'Moses commanded us a Law, even the inheritance of the congregation of Jacob.' We believe that all other nations of the earth have been directed by God to adhere to the laws of nature. Those who regulate their conduct according to this religion of nature and of reason, are called *virtuous men of other nations*, and are the children of eternal salvation.

"Our rabbis are so remote from desiring to make proselytes, that they enjoin us to dissuade by forcible remonstrances, every one who comes forward to be converted. We are to lead him to reflect that by such a step he is subjecting himself needlessly to a most onerous burden; that in his present condition he has only to observe the precepts of nature and reason, to be saved; but the moment he embraces the religion of the Israelites, he subscribes gratuitously to all the rigid rules of that faith, to which he must then strictly conform, or await the punishment which the legislator has denounced on their infraction. Finally, we are to hold up to him a faithful picture of the misery, tribulation, and obloquy in which our nation is now living, in order to guard him from a rash act which he might ultimately repent.

"Thus you see the religion of my fathers *does not wish* to be extended. We are not to send abroad missions. Whoever is not born conformable to our laws has no occasion to live according to them. We alone consider ourselves bound to acknowledge their authority; and this can give no offence to our neighbors. Suppose there were amongst my neighbors a Confucius or a Solon. I could, consistently with my religious principles, love and admire the great man; but I should never hit on the extravagant idea of converting a Confucius or a Solon. What should I convert him for? As he does not belong to the *Congregation of Jacob*, my religious laws were not legislated for him; and on *doctrines* we should soon come to an understanding. 'Do I think there is a chance of his being saved?' I certainly believe that he who leads mankind on to virtue in this world cannot be damned in the next.

"I am so fortunate as to count among my friends many a worthy man who is not of my faith. We love each other sincerely, notwithstanding we presume, or take for granted, that in matters of belief we differ widely in opinion. I enjoy the delight of their society, which both improves and solaces me. Never has my heart whispered: 'Alas, for this excellent man's soul!' He who believes that no salvation is to be found out of the pale of his own church must often feel such sighs rise in his bosom."

The candid Lavater wrote Mendelssohn a public letter, acknowledging that he had been thoughtless and indelicate, and begging his pardon. This trial, however, and another, in which he was obliged to defend the fame of Lessing, as he thought, unjustly aspersed, proved, for his sensitive nature, too severe a strain. He fell ill, and at length, in 1786, came death.

Moses Mendelssohn was undersized and always badly deformed. A habit of stammering, also, made conversation difficult. He possessed, however, a personal charm, which overcame all impediments. Lavater, who so disquieted him, was an enthusiastic friend, and has left a description of his face, which, as coming from the famous physiognomist, has great interest. " I rejoice to see these outlines. My glance descends from the noble curve of the forehead to the prominent bones of the eye. In the depth of this eye resides a Socratic soul. The decided shape of the nose, the magnificent transition from the nose to the upper lip, the prominence of both lips, neither projecting beyond the other,—oh! how all this harmonizes and makes sensible and visible the divine truth of physiognomy ! "

A pleasant story is told by Auerbach of the wooing of Moses Mendelssohn.

" He was at the baths of Pyrmont where he became acquainted with Gugenheim, a merchant of Hamburg. 'Rabbi Moses,' said Gugenheim one day, ' we all admire you, but my daughter most of all. It would be the greatest happiness to me to have you for a son-in-law. Come and see us in Hamburg.' "

Mendelssohn was very shy in consequence of his sad deformity, but at last he resolved upon the journey. He arrived in Hamburg and called upon Gugenheim at his office. The latter said : " Go up-stairs and see my daughter ; she will be pleased to see you, I have told her so much about you."

He saw the daughter, and the next day came to

see Gugenheim, and presently asked him what his daughter, who was a very charming girl, had said of him.

"Ah, most honored rabbi," said Gugenheim, "shall I candidly tell you?"

"Of course."

"Well, as you are a philosopher, a wise and great man, you will not be angry with the girl. She said she was frightened on seeing you, because you——"

"Because I have a hump?"

Gugenheim nodded.

"I thought so; but I will still go and take leave of your daughter."

He went up-stairs and sat down by the young lady, who was sewing. They conversed in the most friendly manner, but the girl never raised her eyes from her work, and avoided looking at him. At last, when he had cleverly turned the conversation in that direction, she asked him:

"Do you believe that marriages are made in heaven?"

"Yes, indeed," said he; "and something especially wonderful happened to me. At the birth of a child, proclamation is made in heaven: He or she shall marry such or such a one. When I was born, my future wife was also named, but at the same time it was said: 'Alas! she will have a dreadful humpback.' 'O God,' I said then, 'a deformed girl will become embittered and unhappy, whereas she should be beautiful. Dear Lord, give me the hump-back, and let the maiden be well formed and agreeable.'"

Scarcely had Moses Mendelssohn finished speaking when the girl threw herself upon his neck: she afterwards became his wife; they lived happily together, and had good and handsome children."

Pleasant pictures of the life of Mendelssohn with his wife and children have been drawn. But the shadow of their origin was always about them. "I sometimes go out in the evening," he once wrote, "with my wife and children. 'Papa,' inquires one of them, in innocent simplicity, 'what is it that those lads call out after us? Why do they throw stones at us? What have we done to them?' 'Yes, dear papa,' says another, 'they always run after us in the streets and shout, "Jew-boy! Jew-boy." Is it a disgrace in the eyes of the people to be a Jew? What is that to them?' I cast down my eyes and sigh to myself: 'Poor humanity? To what point have things come!'"

The data for this sketch have been derived from Mendelssohn's great-grandson, Sebastian Hensel, from the literary historian Kurz, and other biographers. We have also a beautiful and graphic portrait, drawn by the man who perhaps possessed as sharp powers of discrimination as any mind which the world has known. Mendelssohn, as we have seen, early became the friend of Lessing, and it was under the influence of that benign atmosphere that the latter created his "Nathan the Wise," in the conception of the Syrian Jew, establishing a memorial of the reforming genius which the world will never forget.

When Lessing * selected a Jew to be the hero of

* See the writer's "Short History of German Literature."

his grandest play, the innovation was so unheard of as to mark his courage more strikingly perhaps than any act he ever performed—and he was the most intrepid of men. "Nathan the Wise" was written late in life, when Lessing's philosophy had ripened, and when his spirit, sorely tried in every way, had gained from sad experience only sweeter humanity. Judged by rules of art, it is easy to find fault with it, but one is impatient at any attempt to measure it by such a trivial standard. It is thrilled from first to last by a glowing God-sent fire—such as has appeared rarely in the literature of the world. It teaches love to God and man, tolerance, the beauty of peace.

In Nathan, a Jew who has suffered at the hands of the Crusaders the extremest affliction—the loss of his wife and seven children—is not embittered by the experience. He, with the two other leading figures, Saladin and the Templar, are bound together in a close intimacy. They are all examples of nobleness, though individualized. In Nathan, severe chastening has brought to pass the finest gentleness and love. Saladin is the perfect type of chivalry, though impetuous and over-lavish, through the possession of great power. The Templar is full of the vehemence of youth. So they stand, side by side, patterns of admirable manhood, yet representatives of creeds most deeply hostile. Thus, in concrete presentment, Lessing teaches impressively, what he had often elsewhere inculcated in a less varied way, one of the grandest lessons, that nobleness is bound to no confession of faith.

It was his thought—and here many will think he

went too far—that every historic religion is in some sense divine, a necessary evolution, from the conditions under which it originates. What a man believes is a matter of utter indifference if his life is not good.

Goldwin Smith, in a paper in the *Nineteenth Century*, in which some injustice is done to the Jewish character and the facts of Jewish history, declares that Nathan the Wise is an impossible personage, the pure creation of the brain of the dramatist. Lessing, however, as is well known, found the suggestion for his superb figure in Moses Mendelssohn, and as I have given with some detail the facts of the life of the grand Israelite, it must have appeared that there are abundant data for concluding that Lessing's Jew was no mere fancy sketch. It may be said, in truth, that the character is exceptional, and that Jews, as the world knows them, are something quite different. But among the votaries of what creed, pray, would not such a character be exceptional! If exceptional, it is not unparalleled, as we shall hereafter see. Judaism is capable of giving birth to humane and tolerant spirits, even in our time, and such spirits are not at all unknown in its past annals.

CHAPTER XVI.

THE MONEY KINGS.

IN no department at the present day will, the conspicuous ability of the Jew be so readily conceded as in that of business. Whether as great practical operators, or as political economists, like Ricardo, no class of men have so close a hold of both theory and practice. It seems strange enough to us that trade, in all its various forms, than which no human transactions are now considered more honorable and legitimate, was once held to be disgraceful, to a large extent unlawful. It was indispensable to the ongoing of society, and therefore, of necessity, tolerated. The agents of business, however, have, for the most part, been held in ill-repute, or at least in low regard, from antiquity almost to the present day.

Says Cicero: "Those sources of emolument are condemned that incur the public hatred; such as those of tax-gatherers and usurers. We are likewise to account as ungenteel and mean the gains of all hired workmen, whose source of profit is not their art, but their labor; for their very wages are the consideration of their servitude. We are also to despise all who retail from merchants goods for prompt sale, for they never can succeed unless they lie most abominably. All mechanical laborers are by their profession mean, for a workshop can contain nothing befitting a gentleman." Toward commerce on a large scale, indeed, Cicero is somewhat more lenient : " As to merchandizing, if on a small scale it is mean, but if it is extensive and rich, bringing numerous commodities from all parts of the world, and giving bread to numbers without fraud, it is not so despicable." Still the moralist thinks it is in a measure despicable, for he straightway proceeds to commend the course of the merchant who, in good time, abandons his calling: "If, satiated with his profits, he shall from the harbor step into an estate and lands, such a man seems most justly deserving of praise ; for of all gainful professions, nothing better becomes a well-bred man than agriculture." *

This view of trade, held by one of the wisest of the ancients, has prevailed almost to our own time. The ill-repute accorded to the agents of commerce has of course fallen abundantly upon the Jews. Accusations of exceptional sordidness and avarice brought against them we may be sure are often unfounded. How different from the view of our predecessors has come to be modern judgment with respect to taking interest for money? To take interest is the unquestioned right of every lender, and whether this interest be large or small, four per cent. or forty per cent., is a matter, as most sensible men now believe, which should be left to take care of itself, unrestricted by law. If the risk is great the borrower expects to pay correspondingly ; if the risk is small,

* Offices, 1, 42.

the lender contents himself with a trifle. The picture which has been drawn of Jewish avarice is far from being an entire fiction, but let the circumstances be always remembered. If the Jew grew greedy in his money-lending, the world often closed to him every avenue of effort except the one narrow, sordid channel. The Christian set himself against him like flint. Can the Jew be blamed that he skinned the flint?

In some ways, men who in the past have been regarded with abhorrence, are seen by our fuller light to have been benefactors. The cautious creditor who looks narrowly at the borrower, who forecloses the mortgage promptly and firmly when the due payment fails, and who exacts to the last cent the principal and interest,—has not the time gone by for calling such men only hard-souled money-getters, and for accusing them of grinding the faces of the poor? Ought we not rather to look upon them as agents of the greatest value in the discipline and education of society? What lessons they enforce upon the idle, the unpunctual, the improvident! The thrifty and industrious have nothing to fear from them; the influence of such lenders in a community is to drive out shiftlessness—to make all careful and diligent. It may be affirmed that the Jews, through the long ages when they have been vilified as so sordid and covetous, administered to the world a most important schooling. No doubt they have been sometimes rapacious, but it could not well have been otherwise. While all other avenues were closed to the Jew, the jealousy of artisans on the one hand excluding them from the handicrafts much more strictly than American mechanics shut out negroes and Chinese,—on the other hand the higher professions and public life being quite inaccessible, there was no path for them but in the one despised direction. What wonder that there was sometimes overreaching, and that a habit of taking the largest advantage of the hard world which maltreated them so cruelly, should have sprung up and become hereditary? When his prejudices have not acted, the Jew has been charitable and generous. Among themselves there has not usually been mean withholding of aid. Even where his prejudices have stood in the way, the number of instances is not small where the Jew has nobly surmounted them. rising into a charity extended even toward his persecutors.

In trade and exchange, the Jew in the darkest times has had sufficient vigor and shrewdness to flourish; as society has become humane and established,—as the rights of property have been recognized and made secure, straightway the children of Jacob step to the front, become the kings of market and bourse, and by the might of money make a way for themselves. Men like Spinoza and Moses Mendelssohn, with their great intellectual power and beautiful spirit, have caused the world to respect their race. Israel, however, has brought to bear coarser instruments, which have been more effective, perhaps, in breaking for her a path to a better place. And now let us glance at the career of a remarkable family.

The streets in the Juden-gasse at Frankfort are dark even by day; the worn thresholds are still in place that have been stained with blood in the old massacres; the houses are furrowed and decrepit as if they had shared in the scourgings which their owners have undergone. A picturesque, gabled dwelling rises not far from the spot where once stood the gate within which the Jews were barred at nightfall, and behind which they sometimes sought to shelter themselves when the wolves of persecution were upon their track. Here lived one hundred years ago Meyer Anselm, whose surname, derived from the sign above his door, was Rothschild. The money-changer had raised himself from a low position by unusual dexterity.* By a touch of the finger he could tell the value of any strange coin; at the same time he had won a name as an honest man. At length into the Rhine region, in the year 1793, came pouring the legions of the red republicans from France. The princes fled in terror from the invasion, and the landgrave of Hesse Cassel, driving up to the door of the Jew, in the confusion, surprised him with this address: "I know of old your trustiness. I confide all I have in the world to you. Here is my treasure; here are the jewels of my family. Save the jewels if you can, and do with the money as you choose." The landgrave became a fugitive, and within an hour or two the *sans culottes*, taking possession of the city, were plundering high and low. Neither Jew nor Christian escaped, Meyer Anselm suffering with the rest.

* Several interesting facts in this sketch are derived from a letter of "Junot's" in the *Philadelphia Press*.

IN THE FRANKFORT JUDEN-GASSE.

Ten years later, with the coming of Napoleon into power, stability was again restored. The landgrave, returning, called at the Red Shield in the Juden-gasse of Frankfort, with small hope of receiving a good report. "Well, here I am, friend Meyer, escaped with nothing but life." To his astonishment, the faithful trustee had been able through all the trouble of the time to conduct affairs prosperously. While his own means had been plundered, he had saved in some hiding-place in the cellar-wall the treasure of the prince. The heirloom jewels were untouched; with the money he had made a million; and he now restored all to the wondering landgrave, principal and interest. This was the beginning of the marvellous career of the great house of Rothschild. The prince spread far and wide the story of his rescue from ruin. One may well suspect that the shrewd old hawk of the Juden-gasse had had all along a careful eye toward the comfortable feathering of his own nest. At any rate, no better policy for the advancement of his interests could have been hit upon than this honesty in the affairs of the distressed prince. In ten years he was the money king of Europe, transmitting to his able sons, when he himself died in 1812, a proud inheritance which they well knew how to improve.

Heinrich Heine has left an interesting account of being conducted by Ludwig Börne through the Juden-gasse of Frankfort, both of them at the time poor Jewish boys, but destined in after years to become the most famous writers of Germany. It was the evening of the "Hanoukhah," the feast of lamps. The story has been told how Judas Maccabæus, after a victory over the oppressor of his race, had caused the altar of the true God to be reconstructed. It was necessary that the lamps in the sacred porches should be rekindled, to the sound of instruments and the chant of the Levites. Only one vial of oil, however, could be found in the Temple, but, miraculously, the one poor vial sufficed to feed the golden candlestick for a week. This wonder it is which the children of Jacob commemorate in the feast of lamps. Meyer Anselm had gone to his account, but his wife survived, a personality as marked as the old money-changer himself. "Here," said Börne to Heine, pointing to the weather-beaten house, " dwells the old woman, mother of the Rothschilds, the Letitia who has borne so many financial Bonapartes. In spite of the magnificence of her kingly sons, rulers of the world, she will never leave her little castle in the Juden-gasse. To-day she has adorned her windows with white curtains in honor of the great feast of joy. How pleasantly sparkle the little lights which she has kindled, with her own hands, to celebrate a day of victory! While the old lady looks at these lamps, the tears start in her eyes, and she remembers with a sad delight that younger time when her dear husband celebrated the Hanoukhah with her. Her sons then were yet little children, who planted their silver-branched lamps upon the floor, and, as is the custom in Israel, jumped over them in childish ecstasy."

On his death-bed Meyer Anselm made his five sons bind themselves by an oath that they would remain faithful Jews, that they would always carry on business in company, that they would increase money as much as possible, but never divide it, and that they would consult their mother on all affairs of importance. The old mother long survived her husband. She had a singular reason for never sleeping away from her poor home in the Juden-gasse; she felt that her remaining there was in some way connected with the fortune of her sons. H. C. Andersen draws a picturesque scene, the open door of the house of one of her sons at Frankfort, when he had become a financial prince, rows of servants with lighted candles on heavy silver candlesticks, between them the old mother carried down stairs in an armchair. The son kisses reverently the mother's hand as she nods genially right and left, and they bear her to the poor lodging in the despised quarter. The luxury of sovereigns was prepared for her, but that the good fortune of her sons depended upon her remaining where she had borne them was her superstition.

The wish of the father was conscientiously fulfilled. The house abounded in wealth, and in children and grandchildren. The five sons, Anselm, Solomon, Nathan, Charles, and James, divided among themselves the principal exchanges of the world, were diplomatically represented in foreign lands, regulating all their affairs, their dowries, marriages, and inheritances, by their own family laws. Nathan Meyer, the third son of Anselm, who became head of the London house early in the present century, was the leader of the family. He went to England a youth of twenty-one, with a portion of about $100,000. Establishing himself in Manchester as manufacturer, merchant, and banker, he became a millionaire in six years. Removing then to London, his famous career in connection with the government began. In every move he was adroit as a fox, and yet full of audacity. He managed in surprising ways to obtain news, breeding carrier-pigeons, employing the fastest vessels, discovering short routes for uniting the great capitals, using his superior information often with too little scruple, but in ways which few business men would question. On the memorable 18th of June, 1815, the sharp eyes of Nathan Meyer watched the fortunes of Waterloo as eagerly as those of Napoleon or Wellington. He found some shot-proof nook near Hougomont, whence he peered over the field,—saw the charge before which Picton fell, the countercharge of the Enniskilleners and Scotch Grays, the immolation of the French Cuirassiers, the seizure of La Haye Sainte at the English centre, the gradual gathering of the Prussians, and at last the catastrophe, as the sunset light threw the shadow of the poplars on the Nivelles road across the awful wreck, and the "*sauve qui peut*" of the panic-stricken wretches arose, who fled in the dusk before the implacable sabres of Blücher. When the decision came, the alert observer cried, exultingly: "The house of Rothschild has won this battle!" Then, mounting a swift horse which all day had stood saddled and bridled, he rode through the short June night at a gallop, reaching, with daybreak, the shore of the German ocean. The waters were tossing stormily, and no vessel would venture forth. The eager Jew, hurrying restlessly along the shore, found a bold fisherman at last, who, for a great bribe, was induced to risk his craft and himself. In the cockle-shell, drenched and in danger of foundering, but driving forward, the English shore was at length gained, and immediately after, through whip and spur, London.

It was early morning of June 20th when he dropped upon the capital, as if borne thither upon the enchanted mantle of the Arabian Nights. Only gloomy rumors, so far, had reached the British world. The hearts of men were depressed, and stocks had sunk to the lowest. No hint of the truth fell from the lips of the travel-worn but vigilant banker, so suddenly at his post in St. Swithin's Lane. Simply, he was ready to buy consols as others were to sell. With due calculation, all appearance of suspicious eagerness was avoided. He moved among the bankers and brokers, shaking his head lugubriously. "It is a sad state of affairs," his forlorn face seemed to say; "what hope is there for England?" and so his head went on shaking solemnly, and those who met him felt confirmed in their impression that England had gone by the board, and that it was perhaps best to get away in time, before the French advanced guard took possession of the city. But he bought consols, for some unaccountable reason, and his agents were in secret everywhere, ready to buy, though a panic seemed to be impending. So passed June 20th—so passed June 21st. On the evening of that day the exchange closed, and the chests of Nathan

Meyer were crammed with paper. An hour later, came galloping into the city the government courier, with the first clear news of victory. London flashed into bonfires and illuminations. The exchange opened next day with every thing advanced to fabulous prices. In the south corner, under a pillar which

NATHAN MEYER ROTHSCHILD.

was known as his place, leaned the operator so matchless in swiftness and audacity. His face was pale, his eye somewhat jaded; but his head, for some reason, had lost its unsteadiness. His face, too, had lost its lugubriousness, but had a dreamy, happy expression, as if he beheld some beatific vision. The little gentleman had made ten millions of dollars.

The house of Rothschild, it has been said, was rapacious, as well as bold and full of tact, often showing toward the hard world the ancient Hebrew implacability, and stripping it without mercy. When England in the struggle with Napoleon was sore pressed to supply its fleets and armies, the Rothschilds, buying up all the available food and clothing, are accused of having caused prices to advance largely; at the same time they possessed themselves of all the gold. Supplies must be purchased of the house, and when the settlement came, gold must also be purchased at a great premium. The treasury bought gold of the Rothschilds to pay its obligations to the Rothschilds, and so the child of Jacob flayed the Gentile with a two-edged sword. Wellington, it is said, could never afterward endure the family, and put many a slight upon them, even while they held between thumb and finger the princes of Europe. The famous martinet was familiar with military, but not with business, expedients. It is not probable that the financiers of any bourse in the world, at the present time, could condemn the methods of the able Hebrews without condemning themselves.

So grew great the house of Rothschild. Its whole course was a marvel of enterprise. Its boldness brought it sometimes to the brink of ruin, but more often the Jews' shekels were breeding like rabbits. Now it acquired the monopoly of supplying the world with quicksilver, now it saved a bankrupt monarchy from destruction, now it turned aside the march of armies. The five sons of the wrinkled old money-changer of the red shield in the Frankfort

Juden-gasse, who had played as little children on the Maccabæan festival with their seven-branched silver candlesticks, held court as money kings in London, Paris, Vienna, Berlin, and Naples. They were financial agents of all the important governments, conductors of every money transaction upon a large scale. Meantime the oath sworn to the dying father was respected. The brothers were bound by the strongest ties, their children intermarried, they got all they could, and kept all they got, until men scarcely dared to name their wealth. It was a giddy and harassing eminence. One day in 1836, Nathan Meyer, a man scarcely past middle age, left London to attend the marriage of his eldest son in a distant city of the continent. Weeks passed; at length a little incident happened at Brighton, exciting at first slight wonder, but afterward gaining more fully the world's attention. An idle marksman, catching sight of a bird which, after breasting the breeze of the English channel, was flying somewhat heavily over the town, its wings drooping as if from a long passage, brought it down by a lucky shot. It proved to be a carrier-pigeon, about whose neck was tied a slip of paper, dated only the day before in a far-away part of Europe. It contained only the three French words: "Il est mort." The marksman wondered who the mysterious dead man could be, and speculated with his neighbors over the slip. At length it was made plain. The bird whose flight was interrupted was carrying to St. Swithin's Lane news of the great banker's death,—a timely message, that sail might be reefed and all be tight and trim for the shock, when perhaps after a fortnight's time, by slow-moving coach and bark, the news should reach the world that the money king no longer lived.

Lionel Rothschild, eldest son of Nathan Meyer, and his successor as head of the London house, was, in a different way, not less famous than his father. He was of agreeable person and manners, the friend of royalty and the nobility, himself at last ennobled, and of great political influence, even before he sat in Parliament. He became the central figure in the struggle for the abrogation of Jewish disabilities. He was elected to Parliament in 1847, the first son of his race so honored; but for ten years, as he stood before the bar of the House of Commons to take the oath, he was each year rejected, because his uplifted hand, upon the enunciation of the words "on the faith of a Christian," fell promptly to his side. The Israelite yielded by no jot, but the Christian at last gave way. Baron Lionel's palace in London adjoined Apsley House, the mansion of Wellington, and bore on its front the arms of the German empire, the consul-generalship of which was handed down through the generations of the family. Great statesmen were his guests, the princes of the royal family made a point of being present at the weddings and christenings of his children, ambassadors of the highest powers came to sign as witnesses, and the sovereign sent gifts.

The career of James, the son of Anselm Meyer who became head of the Paris house, is no less extraordinary than that of Nathan Meyer in London.

After the overthrow of Napoleon, the allies required from the restored Bourbon, Louis XVIII., the immense sum of 200,000,000 francs, as an indemnity for their sacrifices in bringing about the consummation. James Rothschild first became a great power in France, through his successful conduct of this immense operation. With soul as haughty as the royal line to whose relief he had come, he demanded social recognition for himself and wife. "What!" cried the Duchesse d' Angoulême, daughter of the king, " the chair of a Jew in the royal circle! They forget the ruler of France is the most Christian king." The demand was refused; but Baron James, for he had acquired a title, established in the magnificent palace presented by Napoleon I. to his step-daughter Queen Hortense de Beauharnais, waited for his opportunity. When at length, at the revolution of 1830, the house of Orleans supplanted the Bourbons, it was the Hebrew parvenu who made it possible for Louis Philippe to mount the throne. The social barrier was now surmounted. The monarchy itself only existed at the Baron's pleasure. His family were as splendidly lodged as royalty itself at the Tuileries. Madame la Baronne gave the law to the social world. Paris followed her beck, and at the fashionable watering-places, in magnificence of raiment, in ornaments and equipages, she outdazzled the sovereigns. But the ambition of the Israelite was insatiable. He used his high position for further money-making, and was accused of showing little loyalty except to his own faith and race. The sons of the various houses of Rothschild in general, with

the exception of the branch in England, even while
deciding the fate of nations hold themselves, as it
were, above politics. Parties and governments shift,
revolutions come and go, dynasty succeeding dynasty; but every turn of the political wheel drops
gold into their ever-hungry coffers.

Often they have cared little to respect the feelings,
reasonable or otherwise, of the world which they have
substantially swayed. In the time of Baron James
at Paris, the journals were full of hits at the alleged
meanness and vulgarity which, it was insisted, the
house of Rothschild coupled with their magnificence.
Millions, it was charged, went in luxurious display,
but rarely a sou for art or public improvements. One
finds such stories as follow: One day, at a festival,
Rothschild was approached by a lady who asked
from him a contribution for a charitable object. The
baron dropped a gold piece into her box, which the
lady, whose attention at the moment was attracted
elsewhere, did not perceive. She repeated her request, whereupon the rich man curtly declared he
had already given. "Pardon," said the lady, "I
did not see you, but I believe you." "And I,"
said a witty princess who stood near, "saw it, but I
do not believe it." Some one once related before
Scribe, the dramatist, that Rothschild had the evening before lost ten napoleons at play, without an
expression of regret. "Nothing surprising in that,"
was the quick remark; "great griefs are always voiceless." But Plutus elbowed his way cavalierly forward, caring little for gibes or harsher criticism.
"How is Madame la Baronne?" politely inquired a

man of high rank, who met the Jew at the opera. "What's that to you," was the rejoinder, as he turned his back. To Prince Paul of Würtemberg, who was once his guest at dinner, the baron took pleasure in being roughly familiar. "Paul, let me help you to some of this Johannisberg," at length he began. As the prince did not reply, the presuming host repeated the remark; upon which his highness, with his feathers well ruffled, beckoning to the steward, said: "Do you not hear? the baron is addressing you," and left the house.

Baron James could snub a duke, or even a sovereign, with perfect self-possession, but there was one man by whom he seemed to be cowed and mastered, the brilliant Heinrich Heine, one of his own race, already more than once mentioned in these pages, and whom we shall hereafter attentively consider. Heine was often at the banker's palace, maintaining his intimacy, not through any obsequiousness, but by a kind of spell which his bitter tongue exercised over the host. As Heine declared, he was received "*famillionairement*," because the poor banker wished to be the first to hear the evil which his reckless guest was going to say about him. One day, as the baron was drinking a glass of the Neapolitan wine called "Lacrimæ Christi," he remarked on the strangeness of the name, and wondered how it could have originated. "That's easy enough," said Heine; "it means, translated, that Christ shed tears to have such good wine wasted on Jews like you.

As Baron Lionel, in London, was more courtly and gracious than his pushing father, so Baron

Alphonse, the son of James, showed to the world a less brusque exterior than might have been expected from the atmosphere in which he had been educated. Napoleon III. received him almost as a member of the imperial family. A palace of the Orleans house, in the Rue St. Honoré, became his Paris home, while for a country-seat he bought the magnificent ducal estate of Ferrières, thirty miles from the city. Here the display was profuse and ostentatious beyond all example. A great fête, given to the court in 1869, cost a million francs, and the gold and silver plate which the sovereign had used was melted down after the dinner that it might serve no humbler guests. It was a proper fate that the ruler who could countenance such coarse wastefulness, should be driven within a twelvemonth from his power. The house of Rothschild, however, floated buoyant on the waves of the stormy upheaval, saw the Prussians enter with little regret, and was even spared by the Commune, when all else was subjected to destruction or pillage.

CHAPTER XVII.

SIR MOSES MONTEFIORE.

IN a worldly sense, nothing can be more brilliant than the career of the great family of Rothschild. Before their time there have been rich Hebrews; but, whether from the extraordinary ability of the men, or whether because now circumstances have made such a thing possible, as never before, such an aggregation of wealth has never before been known in the hands of a few individuals. The power they have wielded in consequence of it has been enormous, and has contributed essentially to lift their whole race into a prominent position before the world. Can the career of the family be called an honorable one? Before many a transaction of theirs the moralist will shake his head dubiously, as perplexed as poor Nathan Meyer seemed to be on the London Exchange on those June days in 1815. Let us refer for a moment to an old-fashioned way of looking at these things. To cite once more Cicero, we are told in his "De Officiis," a story of certain vessels which, in a time of great scarcity at Rhodes, set sail thither in company from Alexandria, in Egypt, loaded with corn. One ship, swifter than the rest, and with a more skilful captain, outsailed its companions, and arrived at its anchorage near the Colossus, while the remainder of the fleet was several hours distant. The newly arrived captain is straightway surrounded by a hungry crowd, who, quite ignorant of the abundance close at hand, are willing to give him an enormous price for his cargo. "What now does right require?" asks the old moralist. Is the captain justified in keeping quiet, letting the people find out for themselves, and taking the immense price,—or is he in duty bound to tell the Rhodians there is provision enough three hours away to feed them all? Put the case to a crowd on 'Change in any modern city, what would the reply be likely to be? Cicero was in no doubt. In his view, there was no right course but for the captain to tell the people frankly that the other ships were coming; to conceal the fact was to take an unfair advantage. Ought Nathan Meyer to have told the Londoners of Wellington's victory, or did he do right to keep quiet and pocket his ten millions? and in a thousand other instances in the history of the great house, do we find the dealing fair and above-board; or is it rather sharp practice that trenches all along upon dishonesty?

That the old heathen would have condemned much of the cunning scheming and adroit manipulation, there can be no manner of doubt. For our modern day, let our preachers and moralists speak for themselves. It would be ludicrous, however, to hear criticisms upon such a course from the American business world. You inquire as you ride with a friend through some great city: "Who is building this magnificent palace here on the bon-ton boulevard?" "That belongs to A, so famous for his corner in butter last fall. To be sure a hundred weaker operators came to the ground, and many a poor family went with their bread dry, but it was capitally managed, and perhaps he will be president of the Board of Trade." "Who drives yonder superb horses and equipage?" That is B, so lucky the other day at the 'bucket-shop'; and he is about to dine at the club with C, who makes the world pay five prices for that indispensable commodity which he is shrewd enough to control." Now who are A and B and C? "Hebrew sharpers"? Far from it. The first is a Vermonter, whose ancestor held the torch while Ethan Allen broke down the gate at Ticonderoga. The line of the second goes back to the "Mayflower"; and as to the third, his great-grandfather, in the heart of old Virginia, sold George Washington the very hatchet which Truth, as we all know, bears for an emblem, as Hope carries the anchor, and Faith the cross, and Justice the scales,— Americans all, unmixed, and of the finest strains. It may be suggested to Americans inclined to find fault with "Jew sharpers," that their house is of glass from which it is not wise to throw stones.

 Over-harsh judgment of the ways of modern commerce are perhaps possible. The Israelite businessman sometimes trades in old clothes, and sometimes is finance minister of an empire; his Yankee counterpart sometimes peddles pop-corn on a railroad train, or as a railroad king brings now prosperity, now ruin, to whole States by a nod of his head. Much that goes for rapacity, over-reaching, criminal indifference to human welfare, possibly deserves far milder characterization. With what genius, at any rate, does the son of Jacob move in this tangled world of affairs—so energetic, so persistent, so adroit,—springing to the leadership so dexterously, whoever may be his competitors! As he invented banking in the middle ages, so now in our more complex modern life, it is the Jew who leads the way in the devising of expedients, in the planning of adjustments, by which order can be brought out of the perplexity— new methods of manipulation coming to pass under his dexterous hand, the financial domain spun across with bewildering devices, until the plain man finds it all unintelligible, however necessary it may be in the confusion of immense and intricate relations.

Good types of this strange Semitic ingenuity, often blameless, often beneficent, but on the other hand often unscrupulous,—in ways, however, which it is not always easy to find fault with,—full of audacity, full also of cunning,—which sees to it narrowly that the bold bound shall not overleap or fall short of the precise aim, one may find in the great French operators Isaac and Emile Pereire. Natives of Bordeaux, they began their careers in Paris as brokers. Growing in wealth, they were the first Frenchmen to build railroads, managing to obtain for them money and credit when they were looked upon askance as disturbing, perhaps dangerous, innovations. Their enterprises became colossal, until, from being the railroad kings of France, they grasped at power over the whole continent of Europe, organizing and controlling companies by the score, buying up, for instance, at a stroke, all the government railroads of Austria. It is said the Pereires are to be looked upon as the originators of all those intricacies of modern railroad-finance, whose nomenclature is so constantly in the mouths of the men on 'Change, but before which the plain citizen despairs as having a meaning quite impenetrable,—common stock, preferred stock, first, second, third, perhaps thirteenth mortgage-bonds, floating-debt, watering, credit mobilier, and what not. The practice of founding joint-stock corporations for the sole purpose of negotiating the stock and realizing on it, is said to be strictly their own invention, copied to a calamitous extent throughout the entire civilized world. The Pereires, the elder brother in particular, were zealous philanthropists, combining in a most incongruous way heartless selfishness in business matters with universal charity. The account which is given of them declares: " They illustrate the quaint mixture of virtue and vice in human nature. They thought themselves honestly virtuous, while stern moralists may think them simply vicious. In reality they were a novel mixture of good hearts and egregious business habits which made them rich while others were impoverished."*

It is pleasant to be able to show, after the consideration of careers somewhat questionable, such as have just been detailed, that the Hebrew businessman is by no means necessarily rapacious. One of

* Boston *Advertiser*.

the noblest and most picturesque types of modern philanthropy has come forth directly from the inner circle of these great financial princes, a man whose labors, journeys, and benefactions, prompted by a wise and generous spirit, are as unparalleled as the shrewdness, audacity, and persistence through which his kindred and partners succeeded in winning the world.

Sir Moses Montefiore,* whose death is announced just as this book goes to press, as full of honors as of years, received the homage of the whole civilized world, October 24, 1884, upon his hundredth birthday. He united in himself all that is most characteristic of his race in mental and physical respects. A close observer of the old Mosaic law, he showed in his body the astonishing vigor which a faithful following of the sanitary provisions of Pentateuch and Talmud may bring to pass. In mind he had the characteristic Jewish sharpness which won for him on the exchange a colossal fortune ; in spirit he had the Jewish intensity, manifested in his case not in any narrow or selfish way, but in a humanity broad as the world ; at the same time he cherished with perfect devotion the traditions and faith of his forefathers, and anticipated with enthusiasm the day when the throne of David should be again established on the holy mountain at Jerusalem. Few biographies can be cited which offer so much that is extraordinary as the varied story of this elder of the Hebrews, from his youth to his retirement in his quiet home by the sea, in Kent.

* "Life of Sir Moses Montefiore," by Simon Wolfe.

SIR MOSES MONTEFIORE.

His blood was of the best Israelite strain. An ancestor of his was the bold sailor, Lamego, that captain of Vasco de Gama, who brought back to Europe the first intelligence that his admiral had found the passage about the Cape of Good Hope. Of his particular family, whose Italian origin is made plain by the name, Montefiore, the earliest memorial preserved is a silk ritual curtain in the synagogue at Ancona, magnificently embroidered and fringed with gold; this was the work of an ancestress as far back as 1630, and is suspended before the ark on the great festivals. Like the Disraelis, the Montefiores came to England, when at length, through Cromwell, the bars had been removed, and with the present century reached fame and wealth. Moses Montefiore's way to fortune was smoothed by his marriage with the sister-in-law of Nathan Meyer Rothschild. His brother, also, was married to a sister of Nathan Meyer; still a third link bound the families together, for the second son of Nathan Meyer married his first cousin, the niece of Moses Montefiore. With the strong Jewish feeling of clanship, one can understand how close the connection must have become with the great house which possessed such power. Moses Montefiore was, in fact, the broker of the Rothschilds during the most heroic period of the great operators. No suspicion, however, has ever attached to him, of the sharp practice which has sometimes hurt the repute of the famous bankers. Free from all overweening greed, he withdrew early from active business, with a fine fortune indeed, but untainted by the spirit of covetousness, and through constant beneficent activity, has won for himself the best possible renown.

He set on foot among his people the movement which resulted in the doing away of Jewish disabilities, and at length brought it about that his nephew, Baron Lionel Rothschild, sat in the British Parliament. But most memorable have been his journeys, —one should rather say his lordly progresses,—again and again undertaken, to Africa, to Asia, and throughout the whole of Europe, in behalf of his suffering co-religionists, whose bonds he has broken and whose poverty he has relieved, rather as if he were a magnificent potentate than a simple British citizen. Side by side with his wife, of spirit and energy resembling his own, in a kind of princely state, with a coach and six, or a special train, upon land, and upon sea in French or British frigates placed at his disposal, he discharged his self-imposed missions with a curious pomp. Nothing can be more picturesque than the scenes described as attending these expeditions. Barbaric princes yield humbly to the demand that humanity shall be respected. Sultan, Czar, and Pope, no less than petty princeling and robber captain, give him honor and promise amendment. The Jew's urging, it is felt, is backed by immense power, and his hands scatter largesses such as the coffers of few monarchs could afford.

It is scarcely credible that within fifty years civilized men should have aided and abetted in such enormities as occurred in Damascus and Rhodes in 1840. A Jewish persecution sprang up in those towns, scarcely less terrible than the dark deeds of those mediæval zealots to which certain of these pages have referred. The inveterate blood-accusation, that Jews had committed murder to obtain human blood for use in their sacrifices, was again made, and fanaticism once more expressed itself in torture and slaughter. Men were scourged to death, as of old; others were blinded and maimed for life; sixty little children, from three to ten years old, were taken from their mothers and shut up without food; by their starvation, the parents were to be forced, through anguish of soul, into confession. Damascus and Rhodes are, to be sure, Turkish cities, but the French Consul of the former town was one of the most active persecutors, and in the latter, the representatives of several civilized powers connived at the cruelties.

Montefiore, living retired in his beautiful Kentish villa, felt his heart stirred at the sufferings of the faithful. He roused civilized Europe to indignation, proceeding himself to the spot where the persecutions were taking place. The French statesman Crémieux, himself of Hebrew race, was at the same time active at the court of Louis Philippe, and elsewhere were heard influential Hebrew voices. It was the British Jew, however, whose hands and tongue were most helpful. He was presently on the spot, backed by all the power of enormous wealth and the might of England. The dead could not be brought back to life, nor could the blinded and crippled regain their lost members, but so far as human means could avail, the wrongs were righted. Out of the agitation grew the powerful "Alliance Israélite Universelle," an organization through which the well-placed Hebrews of civilized lands have sought to make impossible hereafter the renewal of mediæval barbarities.

Sir Moses Montefiore has felt keenly the taunt of Cobbett, that the "Israelite is never seen to take a spade in his hand, but waits, like the voracious slug, to devour what has been produced by labor in which he has no share." In Palestine and elsewhere, he has sought to make the Jews agricultural and industrial, and in his records seems never more pleased than when he can describe Hebrew farmers and artisans. Great though his might has everywhere been through his personal force and the power always behind him, he has met with his rebuffs. Said Prince Paskievitch, the Russian governor of Poland, to him, when he was urging upon that official the propriety of doing something for the education of his people: "God forbid! the Jews are already too clever for us. How would it be if they got good schooling!"

The pictures are touching and dramatic which are given in the accounts of Sir Moses Montefiore's journeys, and none are finer than those drawn by his wife, Judith, his frequent companion, a devoted Hebrew like her husband. Both believed in the restoration of Israel to the Holy Land, the soil of which they loved as if they were native to it, with all the wondrous Hebrew patriotism. On one occasion, as they arrive, she breaks out: "Anchor was cast in the Bay of Beyrout, and magnificent was the scene presented to our view. Immediately before us rose the lofty mountains of Lebanon, precipitous and crowned with snow, in strange contrast with the yellow, barren shore, and, stranger still, the glowing sky, and the dazzling rays of the sun, wrapping the town of Sidon itself in a blaze of morning splendor."

"At the ancient Gilead, how many solemn though pleasurable thoughts floated through our minds! Oh, how does the heart of the pilgrim cling to and yearn over the words of the prophet! 'I will bring Israel again to his habitation, and he shall feed on Carmel and Bashan, and his soul shall be satisfied upon Mount Ephraim and Gilead. In those days and in that time, saith the Lord, the iniquity of Israel shall be sought for and there shall be none; and the sins of Judah, and they shall not be found, for I will pardon them whom I reserve.'"

The strain of the writer rises into solemn rapture as Jerusalem is approached: "What the feelings of a traveller are, when among the mountains on which the awful power of the Almighty once visibly rested, and when approaching the city where he placed his name, whence his Law was to go forth to all the world, where the beauty of holiness shone in its morning splendor, and to which, even in its sorrow and captivity, even in its desolation, the very Gentiles, the people of all nations of the earth, as well as its own children, look with profound awe and admiration,—oh, what the feelings of the traveller are on such a spot, and when listening to the enraptured tones of Israel's own inspired king, none can imagine but those who have had the felicity to experience them!"

They approach, probably, by the same place "Scopus," whence Alexander saw in the distance

JERUSALEM FROM THE MOUNT OF OLIVES.

the vision of the Temple, and whence Titus caught sight of the mighty ramparts which his army must force. "Solemn as were the feelings excited by the melancholy desolateness of the rocky hills and valleys through which we were passing, they were suddenly lost in a sense of indescribable joy—for now the Holy City itself rose full into view, with all its cupolas and minarets reflecting the splendor of the heavens. Dismounting from our horses, we sat down and poured forth the sentiments which so strongly animated our hearts in devout praises to Him whose mercy and providence alone had thus brought us, in health and safety, to the city of our fathers." Passing on, the train encamps upon the Mount of Olives, separated from the town by the narrow ravine. "The pure air of the Mount breathed around us with the most refreshing fragrance; and as we directed our attention to the surrounding view, Jerusalem was seen in its entire extent at our feet, the Valley of Jehoshaphat to our left, and, in the distance, the dark, misty waves of the Dead Sea."

They drew near Jerusalem on the following day in a magnificent cavalcade. The Turkish governor led the way, attended by his officers, and an escort in costly and brilliant dress mounted upon the finest Arab steeds. It would have been impossible to pay more honor to a king. Through the Gate of the Tribes the city was entered, and, as the Jewish quarter was reached, bands of music and choirs of singers welcomed the arrival, while a vast crowd clapped their hands in joy. Montefiore paid his first visit

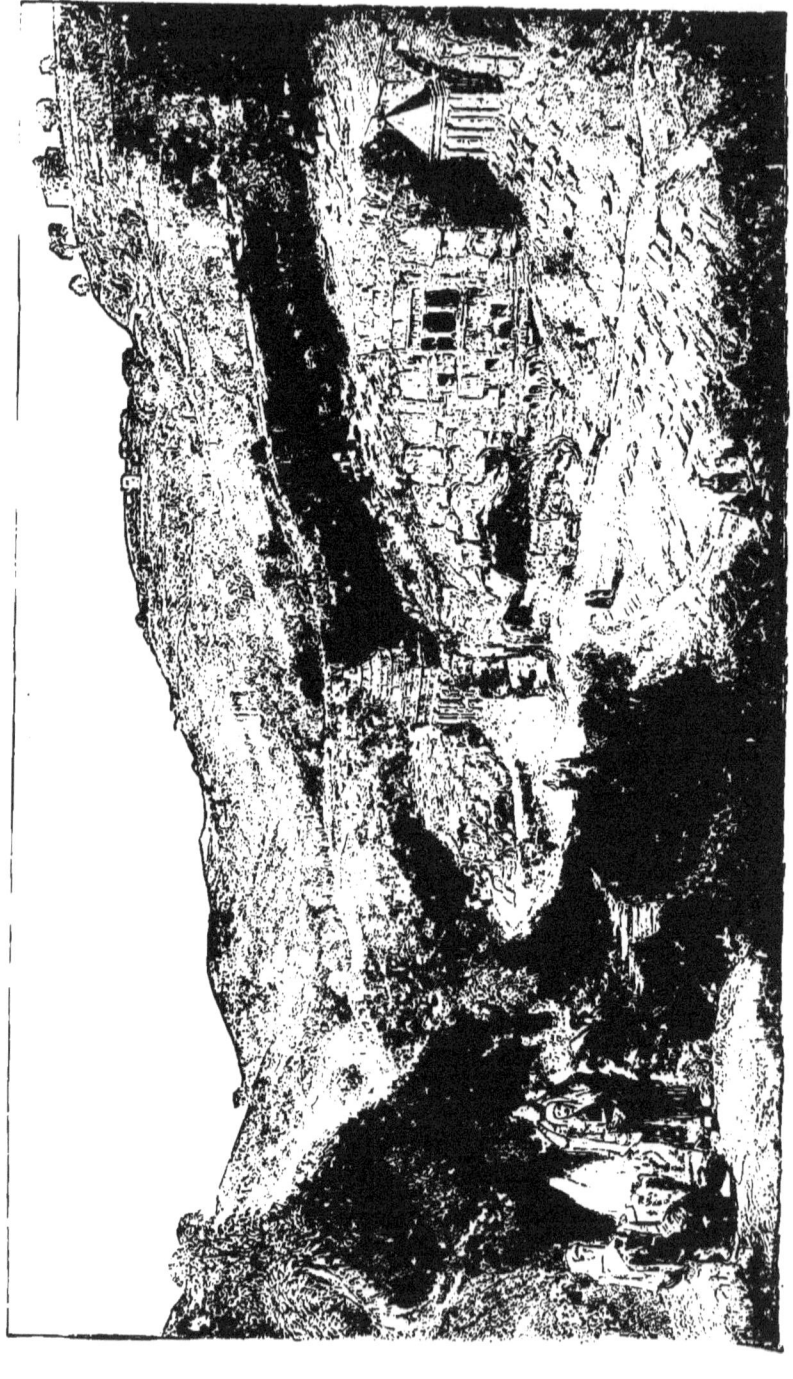

VALLEY OF JEHOSHAPHAT OR KIDRON.

to the synagogue, where, being called to the Sepher, or sacred book, he offered prayer in the Jewish manner for those present and also for English friends. Judith Montefiore was allowed the honor of lighting four lamps in front of the shrine, and putting the bells on the Sepher. During this sojourn, and also at other times, for Montefiore has repeatedly visited the Holy Land, charity was bestowed as wisely as profusely, oppression was made to relax its hold, and provision made for the education of the Jews in intelligence and habits of thrift. "Farewell, Holy City!" exclaims Judith Montefiore, at last. "Blessed be the Almighty who has protected us while contemplating the sacred scenes which environ thee! Thankful may we ever be for his manifold mercies! May the fountain of our feelings evermore run in the current of praise and entire devotion to his will and his truth, till the time shall arrive when the ransomed of the Lord shall return and come to Zion with songs and everlasting joy upon their heads!"

In reading the story of Montefiore's life, one feels transported back to the days of the patriarchs, so astonishing is his long-continued strength. After reaching eighty, he undertook four of his great philanthropic journeys—two to Jerusalem, one to Roumania, and one to Russia. Of the feats of his age, none is more interesting than his visit to the Sultan of Morocco, whose half million Jewish subjects had become exposed to persecution, largely, as in the Damascus case, through the incitement of the representatives of Christian powers resident among them.

A French frigate conveyed him from Gibraltar to Tangier, where his landing had a touch of the comic. "Our captain," writes one of his retinue, "had contrived a kind of car, in which, for want of a suitable landing-place, Sir Moses might be borne over a considerable extent of shallow water between the boat and the shore. His porters, and a great many of the laboring class of Israelites were wading, and his superior size thus conspicuously moving over the water, surrounded by a shabby amphibious group, appeared to me like a travestied representation of Neptune among the Tritons." When matters at Tangier had been put to rights, Sir Moses set out once more from Gibraltar, this time with an English frigate at his disposal, to make his way to the city of Morocco. Arriving with an imposing suite, he was received by the Sultan with the utmost honor. The barbaric prince, surrounded by the flower of his army, mounted upon a charger whose white color indicated that the highest deference was shown, met the strangers. An important edict was issued, granting all for which the guest had asked. Thus relief was afforded not only to Jews, but to Christians also, for the catholic intercessor had besought of the Mohammedan good treatment for men of all confessions.

Sir Moses stood in Jerusalem for the last time in his ninetieth year, on a mission for the improvement of the Palestinian Jews. Something of the fervor of the psalms pervades the pages of the old man's diary. On the night before reaching the sacred shore, "Myriads of celestial luminaries, each of them as large and bright almost as any of the radiant planets in the Western horizon, were now emitting their silvery rays of light in the spangled canopy over us. Sure and steady our ship steered towards the coast of the land so dearly beloved, summoning all to sleep; but few of the passengers retired that night. Every one of them appeared to be in meditation. It was silent all around us—silent, so that the palpitation of the heart might almost be heard. It was as if every one had the words on his lips: 'Ah, when will our eyes be gladdened by the first glance of the Holy Land! When shall we be able to set foot on the spot which was the long-wished for goal of our meditations!' Such were that night the feelings of every Gentile passenger on board. And what other thoughts, I ask, could have engrossed the mind of an Israelite? The words of Rabbi Jehuda Halevi, which he uttered when entering the gates of Jerusalem, now came into my mind: 'The kingdoms of idolatry will all change and disappear; thy glory alone, O Zion, will last forever; for the Eternal has chosen thee for his abode. Happy the man who is now waiting in confiding hope to behold the rising glory of thy light!'"

But while the heart of Sir Moses could thus rhapsodize, a cool and practical good sense was shown, as always, in his conduct. On the way to Jerusalem he inspected narrowly the farms which he had before set in operation, counted the fruit-trees that had been set out, saw to the efficiency of the machines for irrigation, with prudent thrift refused the steam-engines that were petitioned for, because he thought fuel too scarce and skilled labor too scanty; and

GOLDEN GATE.

when he reached at last Jerusalem, set all to work to clean the city to prevent the spread of cholera. Nothing so pleased him as the evidence he found that the Palestinian Jews could be made to work. In his appeal in their behalf he declares: "The Jews in Jerusalem, in every part of the Holy Land, I tell you, do work; are more industrious even than many men in Europe; otherwise none of them would remain alive. But, when the work does not sufficiently pay; when there is no market for the produce of the land; when famine, cholera, and other misfortunes befall the inhabitants, we Israelites, unto whom God revealed himself on Sinai more than any other nation, must step forward and render them help." Practical suggestions follow, which were at once acted upon. In late years the "Montefiore Testimonial Committee" has helped agricultural colonies, established and loaned money to building societies, and in particular made a beginning at Jerusalem of a new and beautiful city outside the Jaffa gate, in which there are already six hundred houses, wholesome and modern, accommodating a population of four thousand.

The generous hand of Sir Moses was a thousand times stretched out in aid of the Gentile as well as the Jew. He helped to build Protestant churches, to found hospitals for the Turk and the Catholic, to lift up the poor of all races and colors. Naturally and properly, however, it was upon his fellow-Jews that his beneficence was for the most part poured out. It is quite possible that at the time of his death, no man upon the face of the earth was more widely known. The civilized world celebrated his hundredth birthday, and many a barbarian city as well; for his influence has been powerfully felt in Bokhara and Samarcand, as well as in St. Petersburg and Rome,—in Timbuctoo and Pekin, as in New York and San Francisco; the Bedouin freebooter, the Turkoman sheik, the Dahoman savage, not less than Czar and Pope, have found their ruthless hands stayed by his powerful intervention.

In face and form the old Hebrew was not less striking than in his years and deeds. He was six feet three inches in height, and stooped but little even at the last. His attire was of the fashion of sixty years ago,—the high-collared coat, the huge white neckcloth and ample frill of the days of George IV. There exists a fine portrait of him, in which things incongruous strangely come together, but for him it is all happily conceived. On a hill overlooking Jerusalem, with its walls and the mosque of Omar in the background, stands his towering form in the costume of a deputy-lieutenant of an English county.

It helps to the picturesqueness of this curious and interesting figure of our times, that he remained a thoroughly orthodox Jew. No one was more constant at the synagogue until within a few years, and even at one hundred he read daily every word of the prescribed prayers. He fasted on the anniversary of the capture of Jerusalem by the Romans, and on the Day of Atonement. The dietary laws of the Pentateuch he obeyed rigorously, and never tasted the flesh of animals that divide not the hoof nor chew the cud. For each Jewish man-child he would have had the ancient rite of circumcision,—at the passover time must be the feast of unleavened bread,—upon occasion he wore the embroidered *tephillin*, the phylacteries upon his front ;—he discharged in the synagogue the functions of Gabay, Parnass, and long filled the office of Lavadore, washer of the dead, conductor of the solemn rites by which the bodies of the chosen people are carefully made ready for the sepulchre. The supporters on his arms hold aloft banners on which the word "Jerusalem" is inscribed in Hebrew characters, and Jerusalem has been the watchword of his life. When questioned as to his hope of a restoration of Israel, as expressed by the rabbis and prophets, his reply was : " I am quite certain of it ; it has been my constant dream ; Palestine must belong to the Jews, and Jerusalem is destined to become the seat of a Jewish empire." Of this man it may, indeed, be said, following the words of George Eliot, " he had Oriental sunlight in his blood."

CHAPTER XVIII.

HEBREW STATESMEN.

THE astonishing deeds of men of Hebrew blood as statesmen, partly because leadership here always impresses men powerfully, partly because it is not until recently that we have seen Jews in this eminence, affect the world more profoundly than the other distinctions. It is startling enough to see within one decade this remnant of a race, a small fraction of the population of Europe, so far forward that a few years ago George Eliot could say: "At this moment the leader of the liberal party in Germany is a Jew, the leader of the Republican party in France is a Jew, and the head of the Conservatives of England is a Jew"; while, as others assert, the foremost Spanish republican, Castelar, is of Jewish descent, and the diplomacy of Russia is guided by minds of the same race.

Upon the career of the eloquent and public-spirited Castelar we will not here dwell. The name of Lasker, though he died among us, is less well-known to American ears than that of Gambetta, and much less familiar than that of Disraeli. Lasker * was, in the German Reichstag, or Parliament, the recognized leader

* "German Political Leaders," Tuttle.

of the great national liberal party (the majority of the body), the ablest debater in Germany, a man with a brave following. It was he who, in company with his fellow-Hebrews, the Frankfort banker Bamberger, and Oppenheim, dared to put a hook into the jaws of leviathan himself, the haughty Prince Bismarck, in his too cavalier dealing with the liberties of the people. One reads with great satisfaction of the triumph of this able, high-minded champion, over the sneering, supercilious Junker party, the German Squirearchy, which makes it its special work to throw obstacles in the path of freedom. They, naturally, beyond the rest of the nation, have felt the traditional dislike of the Jews, and have been accustomed to ask, when any financial scandal came out, with elevated eyebrow and curled lip : " Well, who is it this time, Isaac, or Abraham, or Moses?" as if a swindler must of necessity be a Jew. It was a complete turning of the tables, when Lasker, with adroitness and boldness equally remarkable, brought home some most discreditable railroad delinquencies directly to the doors of Count Itzenplitz and Prince Puttbus, high-born functionaries in especial favor with the great chancellor and the emperor. With all their influence, there was no escape for them from the exposures of the fearless deputy ; they hung gibbeted in their fraud, and the scoffers were silenced. A peculiarity of Lasker's oratory was that in his enunciation the syllables were curiously detached, as his speech flowed on in its fluent course. When he rose in his place, a small unimpressive figure, with a high piercing voice pouring itself out in

HERR LASKER.

this singular staccato, all heads bent forward in respectful listening; there was not a man in the empire that could cope with the Hebrew in the intellectual wrestle.

If it excites alarm in Germany that the Jews, not two per cent. in the population, are elbowing themselves into all the best places, France perhaps has scarcely less reason for fear. Those spiders, the brothers Pereire, entangling France, then all Europe, in a web of railroads, then sucking out the life and forces of the ensnared in a revenue of millions, are representatives of a class of great bankers. Much of whatever success and glory the Second Empire can lay claim to is due to the work of Achille Fould, four times Finance Minister; and in the times since, how frequent upon the lips of men have been the names of the republican deputies Crémieux and Gambetta.

Gambetta!* A year or two since, there was perhaps in the world no more interesting name. In the humiliations of his country, in 1870, his efforts to save her were colossal. He was afterwards, as premier, virtual ruler of France, and was almost as certain to become the real ruler had he lived as if the unswerving primogeniture of the old régime were still in force. He was descended from Jews of the Italian city of Genoa. A curious story is told of him in boyhood, which is of interest as betraying in him that strange characteristic intensity of the children of Jacob, and which in Gambetta was manifested constantly afterward in his career. His father sent

*"Certain Men of Mark: Gambetta," Towle.

GAMBETTA.

him to a school which for some reason was distasteful to him. He wrote home that if he were not taken away he would put out one of his eyes. His father laughed at the threat and disregarded the request, and was presently shocked at hearing that the boy had actually put out one of his eyes, at the same time coolly writing that if he were not removed from the hated place he would put out the other. Only a Jewish boy could have resorted to such a measure, so *outré*, so grotesque in the midst of its horrors, for bringing his parent to terms. In 1868, the day came at last when Gambetta, then an active, ambitious young lawyer, was to take the first step toward a wide fame. In defence of newspapers arbitrarily handled by the censors of Napoleon III., he made a speech which, for vivacity, strength of invective, and beauty, is said to be almost without parallel in the French language. It was delivered on a dull afternoon in December, in a little police court of the city. Gambetta spoke for several hours with an audacity and earnestness that completely overawed the tribunal, and he was not interrupted. What he uttered was the rankest treason, a veritable thunderbolt upon the imperial head. If it had been delivered by an ordinary man in an ordinary way, imprisonment would have followed at once. As it was, judge and people sat spellbound. Rumors ran through the city that a great revolutionary address was in progress, till prudent tradesmen got their shutters ready, and called their children home from school, fearing there would be riots in the streets. Police were on the alert; the cavalry were held ready as on days of barricade. The daring advocate was, however, left untouched, and next morning was famous.

News of his speech was breathed mysteriously from town to town, though the government watched the telegraph, and within a week printed copies were in the hands of the electors of all France. He was then just thirty years old, always carelessly dressed, nervous, with olive complexion, and intense, brusque ways. A speech soon followed at Toulouse, in which hostility to the empire was more plainly shown, and at once the republicans took him up as their champion. He soon appeared in the Corps Législatif. As the central figure of a group of men sworn to oppose the empire, he pointed out unshrinkingly the follies and knaveries of the imperialist policy, not hesitating to declare his belief that a new order of things was at hand. He once cried out to the minister of Napoleon III., Olivier: "We accept you and your constitution as a bridge to the republic; that's all." When at length those days of 1870 came, so dark for France, like Frenchmen in general, he had no conception of the abyss upon the brink of which they stood. Not sympathizing with the cry for war with Germany, he yet made no vigorous opposition, and awoke overwhelmed with surprise at the afflictions which prostrated his country. As the forces of the empire were so dismally parried and beaten down, the olive-skinned, one-eyed young deputy sprang to the front with an astonishing vigor. Then first the world at large began to read in the crowding despatches that odd Italian name which afterwards became so familiar. He attained at once to prominence in the

Committee of National Defence, and presently was Minister of the Interior. For some time after the beginning of the Prussian siege, he was at his post in Paris, acute and bold, always crying out against inaction, lavishing upon his disheartened countrymen, as he lashed now the poltroons, now uttered words of hope, such an eloquence as the French chamber has seldom heard. The great Bossuet, in the seventeenth century, was called "the eagle of Meaux." In our time the eagle of France for soaring speech was this impetuous son of the Jew; and appropriately enough, when he had tried in vain by miracles in the forum to make good disasters in the field, there came that picturesque balloon flight of his, in which he sailed through the clouds above the hostile belt of fire about Paris, and from a new eyrie at Tours, while France lay for the most part beneath the foot of the German, faced the danger with voice and talon undismayed!

In those days there was such unheard of impotency in ruler, in generals, in troops, that we knew almost nothing of the few real heroes who fought against fate with gigantic vigor—an astonishing struggle, worthy of the best hearts in any age of that chivalrous nation, though they were borne down. The wrestle of Gambetta was prodigious. Paris for the time was blotted out of France by the Prussian *cordon*. Elsewhere Gambetta was dictator, minister of war and of peace. By wonderful speech and unfaltering courage in the face of the desperate circumstances, he concluded loans, raised armies, appointed generals, quelled dissensions and revolts, combining in himself, as has been said, the executive faculties of half a hundred officers. If he had known how to handle the sword, those who studied the struggle believe that even then, after Metz and Sedan, he might have saved France. Such armies and leaders as were still left, he tried to make receptacles of his own abounding enthusiasm. His voice was heard everywhere in the southern provinces always counselling advance. He hoped against hope that a little experience would make solid troops out of raw peasant levies, inspirited his colleagues with confident despatches, fired the disheartened soldiers with proclamations that were Napoleonic, to face again and again the iron Prussians. He was undaunted even to the end.

For a moment he retired, but was forced into public life in 1871, being elected deputy by ten departments. After the return of quieter times, Gambetta stood in the fore-front of the Republicans, with a power of moving the masses beyond that of any contemporary. He grew more moderate, passing from a revolutionary leader into a prudent statesman. In quiet times his eloquence is described* as "rich, sensuous, full of heats, showers, lightnings, perfumes of the south." He spoke with an infinity of gesture, a constant play of thought and fancy in his mobile face, leaving upon all an impression of reserved power. But when the occasion called, there was a wild passion in Gambetta absolutely indescribable. " His hollow and resounding voice was like that of some furious prophet of doom. His intense face would

* Towle.

sometimes fly out of the mass of listeners, the more timorous of his side would catch him by the clothing, but he could not be restrained. His arm would be outstretched, and he would cry defiant contradiction or hurl the lie in the teeth of those who ventured to oppose him."

In fact there is nothing reported of those great and burning spirits of the old Revolution, of Camille Desmoulins, of Vergniaud, the Girondin, of the golden-mouthed Mirabeau, indeed, which surpasses what we hear of this towering descendant of the Hebrew. Says a writer describing a stormy scene in the Assembly: "Gambetta was astonishing in the midst of the tumult. He went on with his hollow, resounding voice, with a retort for every aggression, his grand, powerful gestures knowing so well how to give such terrific explosion to anger, such comic force to irony. He went on in disorder, his hair falling over his brow, shaking his head, throwing taunts at his interrupters, distributing sledge-hammer blows, sowing apostrophes and sarcasms broadcast."

Americans in general know little of the politics of France. We have been inclined to belittle the nation, though less of late than in 1870, when the brave people were so strangely panic-struck and delivered over. But down the dark future the wise reader of the signs of the times seems to hear even now a new clash of arms, a sudden, overwhelming spring upon Alsace and Lorraine, an outpouring of molten zeal, as in the revolutionary days, consuming, as it consumed before, Teutonic power and prestige. There was the other day, in France, a man of burning soul and commanding intellect, fully determined, if occasion served, to attempt this. The idol of masses of his countrymen, with his hand already on the strings of power, a soul perhaps scarcely less potent than that of the other Italian, the earth-shaking man of destiny. Had he lived, the Genoese might have repeated the career of the Corsican.

And now we take up the most singular and fascinating of characters, the adventurer born among outcasts, who had the address to make himself the leader of the haughtiest and most conservative of aristocracies, the Tories of Great Britain.* Born a Jew of the "Sephardim," the *élite* of the race, of a family of Spanish derivation, which, after a sojourn in Venice, came in the last century to England, the Earl of Beaconsfield, Benjamin Disraeli, when twelve years old, through the instrumentality of Samuel Rogers, the poet, who felt that the bright boy ought to have a career, was baptized a Christian.† We shall, however, find no better type of the Jew than he. His descent was written in every trait of his character, as in every feature of his face. The persistency with which he fought his way upward, handicapped by limitations of every kind, by outward circumstances, by personal peculiarities which brought ridicule, his origin in the eyes of the world so contemptible—it is that extraordinary Jewish force. Without dwelling upon his lighter title to fame, his literary career, let us take up at once the

* Brandes : " Life of Beaconsfield."
† His father was Isaac Disraeli, an author of some reputation.

story of his first speech in Parliament, into which he at last pushed himself after disappointments and labors that can scarcely be measured. At length he stood there, the strange, fantastic figure, the olive skin, the thick Jewish nose, the black curl on his forehead, the Oriental passion for glitter and adornment in his blood manifesting itself in excess of jewelry, finical attire, curling and scented hair,—and presumed to call to account Daniel O'Connell, then in the very height of his influence. The great agitator, with his hat tipped on the back of his head, leaning back in an attitude of easy insolence, stared at him in surprise, presently shaking his burly figure as he laughed in his face. The whole House of Commons at length was roaring with mockery at the dandy upstart, who seemed to most of them like some intruding pawnbroker. Showing no pity to the untried and friendless speaker, they laughed him into silence, but before the silence came, there was a memorable manifestation. Raising his voice to a scream which pierced the uproar, and shaking his thin hand at the hostile house, he cried, " The time will come when you will be glad to hear me!"

Thence onward he runs in his marvellous Parliamentary career, speaking on every question, more often the mark of obloquy than eulogy, advocating often policies which few Americans can approve, but always with pluck and fire perfectly indomitable, rising slowly toward leadership, battered as his head became prominent, by every Parliamentary missile, mercilessly lampooned, written down by able editors, ever pushing his way undismayed, until one day the

ISAAC DISRAELI.

world gave in to him and knelt to kiss his feet. It is interesting to read how he was borne up by his noble wife, whom he loved with all his soul. Here is a slight incident, one of many similar ones. Disraeli was to speak in Parliament at an important crisis. He entered the carriage with his wife to drive to Westminster. The coachman, slamming the door violently, caught the lady's hand, injuring it severely. Fearing to disturb her husband, on the eve, as he was, of a great effort, she wrapped it in her handkerchief hastily, without uttering a sound or changing her face, drove, cheerfully chatting to the House, and not until the arrow had been sent with all his steady strength, did the great archer know the circumstance which might have impaired his aim.

Disraeli's public course furnishes points enough to which exception might be taken; perhaps his personal character may have been in many ways open to criticism. But certainly, if a tonic influence goes forth into the world from every man who boldly wrestles with difficulty, no one has done more in this way to brace his generation than this superbly strong and courageous champion, rising from the dust to guide the mightiest and haughtiest power upon the face of the earth, so that it was obedient not only to his deliberate will, but to his caprices. A Christian and an orthodox Christian he was throughout his career, but none the less the most arrogant of Jews. He feared, says his able biographer, Brandes, if he dropped the supernatural origin of Jesus, he would be depriving his race of the nimbus which encircles it, as the people among whom God

LORD BEACONSFIELD.

himself, as the Redeemer of the world, was born. To him Christianity was only Judaism completed, Judaism for the multitude. "He hate Christ! He is the fairest flower and eternal pride of the Jewish race, a son of the chosen royal family of the chosen people,—the people which in an intellectual sense has conquered Europe, and the quarters of the world peopled by Europeans. Northern Europe worships the son of a Jewish mother, and gives him a place at the right hand of the Creator; Southern Europe worships besides, as queen of heaven, a Jewish maiden." Commemorating the glories of Jerusalem, Disraeli bursts out in his "Tancred": "There might be counted heroes and sages who need shrink from no rivalry with the brightest and wisest of other lands,—a lawgiver of the time of the Pharaohs whose laws are still obeyed; a monarch whose reign has ceased three thousand years, but whose wisdom is still a proverb in all the nations of the earth; a teacher whose doctrines have modelled the whole civilized world. The greatest of legislators, the greatest of administrators, the greatest of reformers—what race, extinct or living, can produce such men as these?" "Suppose," exclaims the Jewess Eva, with an earnestness which we may be sure is the real feeling of the author, "Suppose the Jews had not prevailed on the Romans to crucify Christ, what would have become of the atonement? The holy race supplied the victim and the immolators. What other race could have been entrusted with such a consummation? Persecute us! if you believe what you profess you should kneel to us. You raise statues to the hero that saves a country.

We have saved the human race and you persecute us for doing it!"

Elsewhere Disraeli eloquently dwells upon the magnificent influence of Hebrew literature. "The most popular poet of England is and has been David, the sweet singer of Israel. There never has been a race that sang so often the odes of David, and its best achievements have been performed under their inspiration. It was the "sword of the Lord and of Gideon" that won the boasted liberties of England in Cromwell's days; chanting the same canticles that cheered the heart of Judah among the glens, the Scotch upon their hill-sides achieved their religious freedom." Staying their souls upon the same brace, he might have continued, the Pilgrim Fathers lifted into place the foundation pillars of America. There are no bounds to the exultation of the patriotic enthusiast. Men of other lands have been deified, he says,—Alexander the Greek, Cæsar the Roman—but only in the case of Jesus, the Hebrew, has the apotheosis endured.

For pride of race what can surpass such utterances! "Out of Zion, the perfection of beauty, God hath shined"; "The seed of Jacob the chosen people;" God himself stooping from heaven to command the Egyptian, "Let my people go!" What an echo do these soaring claims of the old biblical writers find far down the ages from the nineteenth century! one and the same exultant utterance from ancient David, who before the ark of the Lord wore the diadem of Hebrew sovereignty, and from him who in the supreme places of the world just now wore the coronet of an English earl!

CHAPTER XIX.

A SWEET SINGER IN ISRAEL.*

HAS the spirit of this race, so intense, so persistent, so trampled by persecution, ever found in modern times an adequate voice in poetry? Yes; a voice which is pervaded with all the melancholy that such long-continued suffering would cause, in which we seem to hear sometimes the saddest wailing; then again a terrible wit, sometimes indeed lightly playful, but more often resembling the laughter of a man mad through despair; in which, too, there is at times a gall and bitterness as of the waters of Marah, poured out too indiscriminately upon the innocent, as upon those worthy of scorn,—the voice of Heinrich Heine.

He was born of Jewish parents at Düsseldorf on the Rhine. "How old are you?" says a personage to him in one of his works. "Signora, I was born on New Year's Day, 1800." "'I have always told you,' said the marquise, 'that he was one of the first men of the century.'" The Heine family came from Bückeburg, a little principality whose insignificance Heine merrily hits off. Alluding to a saying of Danton, in the French Revolution, who, when he

* Adapted from the writer's "Short Hist. of Germ. Lit."

was urged to leave his country to save his life, exclaimed: "What! can a man carry his fatherland on the soles of his feet!" he says:

> "O Danton, thou must for thine error atone;
> Thou art not one of the true souls;
> For a man *can* carry his fatherland
> About with him on his shoe-soles.
> Of Bückeburg's principality
> Full half on my boots I carried.
> Such muddy roads I 've never beheld;
> Since here in the world I 've tarried."

When Heine was nineteen he was sent to Frankfort to learn business. Waterloo had come four years before, and in the restored order the Jews were thrust back into their old condition from which Napoleon had freed them. As one passes through the Juden-gasse in Frankfort, it is perhaps the most interesting reminiscence that can be recalled, that there, in the noisome lanes, moved the figure of the young poet, hearing with his fellows, at the stroke of the hour, the bolting of the harsh gates. Soon after we find him in Hamburg, where his uncle, Solomon Heine, was the money-prince of North Germany, and a man famous for his benefactions in all directions. Convinced at length that a business career would never be to his taste, he was for a time at the University of Göttingen, then in Berlin, where he became intimate with Varnhagen von Ense and his Hebrew wife Rahel, people of elegant culture and brilliant gifts; whose *salon* fills almost the place in the literary history of the northern capital that is filled by the Hotel Rambouillet in

France. His gifts grew ripe in this literary atmosphere, and he presently entered upon his poetic career. He hoped at this time for a government position or a university professorship, for either of which the abjuration of the faith of his ancestors was necessary. This was resolved upon, and he was baptized into the Lutheran Church. The change was made purely from motives of expediency; he had no faith in the doctrines of the Church into which he was received; in his attachment to his race he remained a genuine Jew. For years after, Heine's mind was ill-at-ease for this apostasy. "I will be a Japanese," he writes. "They hate nothing so much as the cross. I will be a Japanese." The advantage he sought he did not secure; his position, on the other hand, becoming more uncomfortable than before. In this period of his life Heine strikes into that mocking vein of writing which he preserved so constantly afterward, both in his prose and his poetry. Leaving Göttingen for a journey in the Harz, after having contracted a spite against the society of the town, he laughed mercilessly at his old associates.

"I have especial fault to find that the conception has not been sufficiently refuted that the ladies of Göttingen have large feet. I have busied myself from year's end to year's end with the earnest confutation of this opinion, and in the profound treatise which shall contain the results of these studies, I speak, 1, of feet generally; 2, of the feet of the ancients; 3, of the feet of elephants; 4, of the feet of the ladies of Göttingen; then if I can get

HEINRICH HEINE.

paper big enough, I will add thereto some copper-plate engravings, with portraits, life-size, of the ladies' feet of Göttingen." Again, to hit off the pedantry of the town, he says: "In front of the Weender gate two little school-boys met me, one of whom said to the other: 'I will not walk with Theodor any more ; he is a low fellow, for yesterday he did not know the genitive of *mensa.*'"

He soon arrived at fame. A multitude of readers followed his pen with delight. His songs were everywhere sung ; his witty and graphic prose commended itself no less. His nonchalant irreverence, which not infrequently runs into insolence and blasphemy, his disregard of proprieties, his outspoken scorn of the powers that ruled, brought down upon him, not unnaturally, fierce persecution. He travelled in various directions, not only in Germany, but visiting Italy, France, and England, his sparkling record keeping pace with his steps. At length, outlawed in Germany, he made his home in Paris. He was constantly writing, did much as a critic of art and literature, much in the field of politics. His poems are numberless ; sometimes simple and sweet throughout as an outgush from the heart of the most innocent of children ; sometimes with an uncanny or diabolic suggestion thrown in at the end, as the red mouse at length runs out of the mouth of the beauty with whom Faust dances on the Brocken in the Walpurgis-nacht ; sometimes, again, full of a very vitriol of acrid denunciation.

The story of Heine's last years is one of almost unparalleled sadness. He was attacked with a softening of the spinal marrow; it stretched him upon his bed where he lingered eight years, enduring great agony. He wore out the weary time on his "mattress-grave," as he called it, nursed by his wife, an ignorant but good-hearted grisette. The terrible chastening brought no change to his spirit. It is a dark life almost everywhere; but as he lay stretched upon his mattress-grave, there was a bitterness in his mocking, an audacity in his blasphemies, which the wildest declarations of his preceding years had not possessed. No moanings from an Æolian harp were ever sweeter than the utterances which occasionally came as the tempestuous agony swept down upon him. We see, too, a better side in his will: "I die in the belief of one only God, the eternal creator of the world, whose pity I implore for my immortal soul. I lament that I have sometimes spoken of sacred things without due reverence, but I was carried away more by the spirit of my time than by my own inclinations. I pray both God and man for pardon." At length came Feb. 16, 1856. A friend bending over him asked him if he were on good terms with God. "Let your mind rest," said Heine. "God will pardon me; that's what he's for." And so with a devil-may-care mock upon his lips, the child of the Jew, in whom the spirit of the race, cruelly beset through so many slow-moving centuries, at length found utterance for its sorrow, its yearnings, its implacable spite, went forth to his account.

That Heine was the most unaccountable of men will hardly need further illustration. In one breath he writes "The Pilgrimage to Kevlaar," a poem which one would say must have come from the heart of an artless, ignorant peasant, full of unquestioning Catholic piety; in another, it is the grotesque satire Atta Troll, in which the Catholic conception of heaven is burlesqued with unshrinking, Mephistophelean audacity.

The difficulties of rendering in Heine's case are perhaps quite insurmountable. Nothing was ever so airy and volatile as his wit, nothing ever so delicate as his sentiment. In the process of translation the aroma half exhales. What, as Heine has distilled it, is most searchingly pungent, becomes insipid in a foreign phrase; what causes tears, as it flows on in the German rhythm in pathetic, child-like artlessness, in English words sinks to commonplace. Let us, however, attempt it. There has not lived in our time such a master of brilliant, graphic description. Here are passages from his child-life at Düsseldorf, quoted from the "Book Le Grand." The book is named from an old drummer who fills the child with Napoleonic inspirations.

"As I woke the sun appeared, as usual, through the windows, and a drum was beating below; and as I stepped into our parlor and bade my father, who still sat in the white gown in which the barber had been powdering him, good-morning, I heard the light-footed hair-dresser tell, while he was plying the curling-tongs, that that day, at the Town Hall, homage was to be rendered to the new Grand Duke, Joachim Murat. As he spoke, drums were beating once more; and I stepped to the house-door and saw in full march the French troops, the lighthearted sons of glory, who went singing and clinking through the world, the grave and gay grenadier guards, the tall bear-skin caps, the tricolored cockades, the glancing bayonets, the voltigeurs full of jollity and *point d'honneur*, and the great silver-sticked drum-major, who could reach with his stick up to the first story, and with his eyes up to the second, where the pretty girls sat at the windows."

At length Napoleon appears. "The emperor wore his unpretending green uniform, and the little world-historic hat. He rode a white pony; negligent, almost hanging, he sat, one hand holding high the reins, the other patting good-naturedly the pony's neck. His face had that color which we see in marble heads of Greek and Roman sculpture; its features were nobly impressed, like those of antiques; and on this countenance it stood written: 'Thou shalt have no other gods before me.' A smile— which warmed and quieted every heart hovered about the lips; and yet we know that those lips had only to whistle, and Prussia would no longer exist; those lips needed only to whistle, and all the clergy would be rung out; those lips needed only to whistle, and the whole Holy Roman Empire would dance; and those lips smiled, and the eye, too, smiled. It was an eye clear as the heavens; it could read in the heart of man; it saw with sudden quickness all the things of this world, while the rest of us only looked at one another and over colored shadows. The brow was not so clear; the ghosts of future battles haunted it; sometimes it moved convulsively, and those were the creating thoughts—the great seven-mile-boots thoughts—with which the emperor's spirit invisibly strode over the world. The emperor rode quietly through the avenue ; behind him, proud on snorting horses, and loaded with gold and ornaments, rode his suite; the drums rolled, the trumpets sounded and the people cried with a thousand voices: ' Vive l'empereur ! ' "

The Germans have been accused of wanting greatly in wit and humor,[*] but certain it is that this German Jew, more than any man probably of the present century in the civilized world possessed these gifts ; we must regard him as a genius coördinate with Aristophanes, Cervantes, and Montaigne. His conversation was full of wit, even when he lay in the greatest misery on his " mattress-grave." He was asked if he had read one of the shorter pieces of a certain dull writer. " No," said he, " I never read any but the great works of our friend. I like best his three-, four-, or five-volume books. Water on a large scale—a lake, a sea, an ocean—is a fine thing ; but I can't endure water in a spoon."

Once at a time of great distress, the physician who was examining his chest, asked : " Pouvez-vous siffler ? " " Hélas, non ! " was the reply. " Pas même les piéces de M. Scribe."

In many of his poems he rattles on in the merriest, most nonchalant carelessness, shooting out, now and then, the sharpest darts of spite. Poor Germany was forever his butt, as in the following:

> From Cologne, at quarter to eight in the morn,
> My journey's course I followed ;

[*] J. R. Lowell : Essay on Lessing.

Toward three of the clock to Hagen we came,
And there our dinner we swallowed.

The table was spread, and here I found
The real old German cooking.
I greet thee, dear old "sauer-kraut,"
With thy delicate perfume smoking!

Mother's stuffed chestnuts in cabbage green!
They set my heart in a flutter.
Codfish of my country, I greet ye fine
As ye cunningly swim in your butter!

How the sausage revelled in sputtering fat!
And field-fares, small angels pious,
All roasted and swaddled in apple-sauce,
Twittered out to me, " Only try us!"

" Welcome, countryman," twittered they,
" To us at length reverting.
How long, alas! in foreign parts,
With poultry strange you 've been flirting!"

A goose, a quiet and genial soul,
Was on the table extended.
Perhaps she loved me once, in the days
Before our youth was ended.

She threw at me such a meaning look!
So trustful, tender, and pensive,
Her soul was beautiful—but her meat!—
Was tough I 'm apprehensive.

On a pewter-plate a pig's head they brought;
And you know, in the German nation,
It 's the snouts of the pigs that they always crown
With a laurel decoration.*

* Deutschland, ein Wintermärchen..

What power of scornful utterance Heine possessed, the potentates of Germany, who persecuted him, felt to the uttermost—none more than Friedrich Wilhelm IV., of Prussia, and Ludwig II., of Bavaria. Both were monarchs possessed of intellectual gifts and with some good purposes. Each, however, was in his own way weak and sensual. Stupidly brutal were the heels that sought to crush Heine; but like a snake, writhing and rearing its crest, he strikes with fangs so full of diabolical venom, that we are almost forced to pity the oppressor.

The brilliant wit and poet must be judged with severity, however beneficial the scourging which he administered may sometimes have been. His wit was often distorted to cynicism, his frivolity to insolence and vulgarity. It is hard to believe he was in earnest about anything. In multitudes of passages, both prose and poetry, he suddenly interrupts the expression of intense emotion by a grotesque suggestion which makes the emotion or its object ridiculous. For Napoleon one would imagine that he felt the most genuine and earnest enthusiasm of his life. There is a certain passage in the "Book Le Grand" full of power, in which he denounces England for her treatment of the emperor at St. Helena; yet as if an actor, after giving the curse in Lear, should suddenly thrust his tongue into his cheek and draw his face into a grimace, Heine ends his denunciation with a laughable turn, in which he gratifies his petty spite at his old university. "Strange! a terrible fate has already overtaken the three principal opponents of the emperor: Lord Castlereagh has cut his throat, Louis XVIII. has rotted on his throne, and Prof. Saalfeld is still always professor at Göttingen!"

Among English writers, Heine has points of resemblance to Sterne, still more to Byron; but to my mind his closest English analogue in genius and character is Dean Swift. In Swift's career, it is perhaps the pleasantest incident that he could attract the love of Stella and Vanessa, and feel for them a friendship which perhaps amounted to love. In Heine's honorable affection for two women, his wife "Nonotte" and his mother, the "old lady of the Damm Thor," we see him at his best. Heine and Swift were place-hunters, who sought for advancement in questionable ways, only to be disappointed; for both there was disease at the end that was worse than death. Such gall and wormwood as they could pour upon their adversaries, what sinners elsewhere have tasted! With what whips of scorpions they smote folly and vice, but who will dare to say it was through any love of virtue? Both libelled useful and honorable men with coarse lampoons; in both there was too frequent sinking into indecency.

But there was a field in which the bitter dean had no part with the sufferer of the "mattress-grave." Heine was not altogether a scoffer; his power of touching the tenderest sensibilities is simply wonderful. In his plaintive songs the influence of Romanticism can be clearly seen, and also of the popular ballad, whose character he caught most felicitously. He assumed a certain negligence, which gave his poems an air of pure naturalness and immediateness, whereas they were the products of consummate art.* But no poet has ever been able to convey so thoroughly the impression of perfect artlessness. The "Princess Ilse," for instance, one would say could have been written by no other than the most innocent of children.

ILSE.

I am the Princess Ilse,
    To my castle come with me,—
To the Ilsenstein, my dwelling,
    And we will happy be.

Thy forehead will I moisten
    From my clear-flowing rill,
Thy griefs thou shalt leave behind thee,
    Thou soul with sorrow so ill!

Upon my bosom snowy,
    Within my white arms fold,
There shalt thou lie and dream a dream
    Of the fairy lore of old.

I'll kiss thee, and softly cherish,
    As once I cherished and kissed
The dear, dear Kaiser Heinrich,
    So long ago at rest.

The dead are dead forever;
    The living alone live still;
And I am blooming and beautiful;
    My heart doth laugh and thrill.

O come down into my castle,
    My castle crystal bright!
There dance the knights and the maidens;
    There revels each servant wight.

---

* Kurz: "Geschichte der deutschen Literatur."

There rustle the garments silken,—
There rattles the spear below.
The dwarfs drum and trumpet and fiddle,
And the bugle merrily blow.

Yet my arm shall softly enclose thee,
As it Kaiser Heinrich enclosed ;
When the trumpets' music thundered,
His ears with my hands I closed.

It is very pleasant, too, to read these lines to his wife, written on his death-bed :

I was, O lamb, as shepherd placed,
To guard thee in this earthly waste.
To thee I did refreshment bring ;
To thee brought water from the spring.
When cold the winter storm alarmed
I have thee in my bosom warmed.
I held thee folded, close embracing,
When torrent rains were rudely chasing,
And woodland brook and hungry wolf
Howled, rivals, in the darksome gulf.
Thou didst not fear—thou hast not quivered,
Even when the bolt of thunder shivered
The tallest pine ; upon my breast,
In peace and calm. thou lay'st at rest.

My arm grows weak. Lo, creeping there
Comes pallid Death ! My shepherd care,
My herdsman's office, now I leave.
Back to thy hands, O God, I give
My staff ; and now I pray thee guard
This lamb of mine, when 'neath the sward
I lie ; and suffer not, I pray,
That thorns should pierce her on the way.
From nettles harsh protect her fleece ;
From soiling marshes give release ;
And everywhere, her feet before,

> With sweet grass spread the meadows o'er ;
> And let her sleep from care as blest
> As once she slept upon my breast.

Once at a critical time in our country's history, it happened to me to visit a negro school. We went from room to room among the dusky faces, until at last one said : " Let us have them sing." Presently the voices rose and fell in a marvellous song. Out of the windows the heavens hung sombre about us ; the dark faces were before us, the children of the race whose presence among us has brought to them, in each generation, tragedy so pathetic,—the race that has brought to us so innocently such subject for controversy, such occasion for bloodshed, and on account of which we still sometimes seem to hear such fateful thunder-mutterings of approaching disaster. The news of the morning had predisposed us to gloom ; the associations now conspired to deepen it ; the strange melody which came pouring forth seemed, somehow, singularly in keeping. There was in my spirit no defined feeling, but a vague unrest, at once a foreboding of calamity and yearning after peace. It was precisely the sentiment of the song. The singers seemed to feel it ; we who listened felt it, and there were eyes whose lids trembled with the coming tears. It was the " Lorelei " of Heine :

> " I cannot tell what it forebodeth,
> That I am so sad to-day."

The words so simple—so infantile almost in sense, and yet with which is marvellously bound such tender feeling ! As one repeats the lines, they are almost nothing; yet caught within them, like some sad sweet-throated nightingale within a net, there pants such a pathos! What could have been farther away! What cared we then for the Rhine, and the sorceress who sings upon its banks, and the boatman engulfed in the whirlpool! What knew or cared the singers! But something indescribable came pulsing forth to us from out of the words, and I felt that somehow it was the appropriate utterance for the mood in which we found ourselves—the thing to hear from the dark-faced youths before us, —an undefined sorrow,—a foreshadowing of danger all unknown and vague! Mighty the poet, I thought, whose verse can come home with such power in lands and among races so far away!

The child of the Jew he was—of the race among the races of the earth possessed of the most intense passionate force—and in him his people found a voice. Now it is a sound of wailing, melancholy and sweet as that heard by the rivers of Babylon, when the harps were hung upon the willows; now a Hebrew aspiration, lofty as the peal of the silver trumpets before the Holy of Holies in the Temple service, when the gems in the high-priest's breast-plate flashed with the descending deity; now a call to strive for freedom, bold and clear as the summons of the Maccabees. But think of the cup that has been pressed to the Jew's lips for almost two thousand years! The bitterness has passed into his soul, and utters itself in scorn and poisoned mocking. He cares not what sanctities he insults, nor whether the scoff touches the innocent as well as the guilty. Persecution has brought to pass desperation, which utters itself at length in infernal laughter.

A touching story is told of Heine's last walk in the Boulevard, from which he went home to the death in life he was doomed to undergo for many years. It was in May, 1848, a day of revolution. "Masses of people rolled along the streets of Paris, driven about by their tribunes as by storms. The poet, half-blind, half-lame, dragged himself on his stick, tried to extricate himself from the deafening uproar, and fled into the Louvre close by. He stepped into the rooms of the palace, in that troubled time nearly empty, and found himself on the ground-floor, in the room in which the ancient gods and goddesses stand. Suddenly he stood before the ideal of beauty, the smiling, entrancing goddess, the miracle of an unknown master —the Venus of Milo. Overcome, agitated, stricken through, almost terrified at her aspect, the sick man staggered back till he sank on a seat, and tears, hot and bitter, streamed down his cheeks. The beautiful lips of the goddess, which appear to breathe, smiled with her wonted smile at her unhappy victim."* Heine says himself in a letter:

"Only with pain could I drag myself to the Louvre, and I was nearly exhausted when I entered the lofty hall where the blessed goddess of beauty, our dear lady of Milo, stands on her pedestal. At her feet I lay a long time, and I wept so passionately that a stone must have had compassion on me. Therefore the goddess looked down pityingly upon

* Meissner.

me, yet at the same time inconsolably, as though she would say: 'See you not that I have no arms, and that therefore I can give you no help?'"

Of the spots associated with Heine, there is none so interesting as that room in the Louvre. I stood there on a day when disturbance again raged in the streets of Paris. It was the end of August, 1870. In Alsace and Lorraine the armies of France had just been crushed; in the next week was to come Sedan. The streets were full of the tumult of war, the foot-beat of passing regiments, the clatter of drill, the Marseillaise. On the Seine, just before, a band of *ouvriers* had threatened to throw us into the river as Prussian spies. In the confusion, the shrine of the serene goddess was left vacant, as at that former time. I found it a hushed asylum, the fairest of statues, rising from its pedestal, wearing upon its lips its eternal smile. The rounded outlines swelled into their curves of perfect beauty; within the eyes lay the divine calm; on the neck a symmetry more than mortal;—all this, and, at the same time, the mutilation, the broken folds of the drapery, the dints made in the marble by barbarian blows, the absent arms. When one stands before the Venus of Milo, it is not unworthy of even so high a moment to call up the image of that suffering man of great genius, shamed from his sneer, and restored to his best self in the supernal presence. May we not see in the statue a type of Heine's genius, so shorn of strength, so stained and broken, yet in the ruin of beauty and power so unparalleled!

CHAPTER XX.

SOME HARMONIOUS LIVES.

FELIX MENDELSSOHN BARTHOLDY shall be our type of the Hebrew artist; but since he was scarcely less interesting in his character than he was as a musician, and since the household of which he was a member were in great part as fair in their lives, and almost as gifted in their genius as he, we must not take him as an isolated figure, but look at him in his relations. In this way we shall best understand the beauty of his spirit, while some idea is formed of the kindred, some of whom scarcely less than he, deserve to be celebrated.

The family of Moses Mendelssohn, the little children who walked with their father through the streets of Berlin, and could not understand why the Christian boys hooted at them and called them names, became men and women remarkable in themselves, and noteworthy also as the parents, in their turn, of children who have led, in times near our own, famous and charming lives. The noble thinker was, with all his liberal spirit, as we have seen, nevertheless, thoroughly a Jew, answering the over-zealous Lavater, with true Hebrew haughtiness, when he felt that the sanctities of his hereditary faith were too rudely touched, In minor matters of discipline he was faithful to the ancient standards, maintaining, for instance, in his family the rigid patriarchal rule which did not relax, even though the child grew gray, until the father died.

Of the three sons and three daughters of Moses Mendelssohn, Dorothea was probably in her time the most distinguished, a woman of brilliant mind and admirable qualities, whose career in spite of great eccentricities, deserves a glance from us. She was the least exemplary of the children; her irregularities, however, were due to her strange surroundings, and do not cancel her substantial worth.

According to Hebrew fashion, the sons of a family had small liberty in the choice of wives, and the daughters none at all in the choice of husbands. Moses Mendelssohn married Dorothea, with no consultation of her wishes, to the Berlin trader, Veit, a man worthy but thorougly uncongenial to the bright-minded girl. After some years of union, during which she bore to him children, she forsook her husband to form an irregular connection, similar to that between George Eliot and G. H. Lewes, with the distinguished Friedrich Schlegel. Strangely enough honest Veit remained thoroughly friendly, acquiescing in the separation, in fact, with an equanimity which seems to imply that the discomfort had not been entirely on the side of the wife. Schlegel soon rose to brilliant fame, with which Dorothea, whose literary gifts were remarkable, was closely connected. Schlegel's story " Lucinde " a memorable utterance of " Romanticism," of which literary tendency he was the founder and best type, was an outgrowth of this left-handed relation, a book not edifying, but curious as an expression from a strange world, now passed away. Schlegel and Dorothea at last were married. The latter became a Christian, and, with her husband, a Catholic. Removing to Vienna they were at last distinguished personages at the court of Austria, where the political course of Schlegel became as reactionary as his course in religion; for he used his fine powers to uphold against all revolutionary tendencies the threatened House of Hapsburg.

Another of the daughters of Moses Mendelssohn, a bright and amiable woman, also became a devout Catholic. The sons possessed characters of better balance than the daughters. They advanced from the position of their father as far as he himself had gone beyond the ancient landmarks. Joseph, the elder, became a prosperous banker, but maintained a great interest in intellectual pursuits, having especial note as an important friend and helper of Alexander von Humboldt. Abraham, however, the second son, is, of all the children of Moses, the most attractive, a sweet enlightened soul, as devoid of extravagance as of narrowness,—a most engaging figure in himself, and the parent of children whose memory the world will not willingly let die. The great composer, Felix Mendelssohn Bartholdy, was his second child. The modest father deemed himself inconspicuous and unimportant between the illustrious names that preceded and followed him. "Formerly, I was the son of my father," he used to say, "but now I am the father of my son." But he was really in himself a vigorous and independent character. With his wife, Leah Salomon, a Berlin Jewess, he was suitably mated. Her portrait, in the book of her grandson, Sebastian Hensel, which is the authority upon which this sketch of the Mendelssohn family is based, shows a face in which power and amiability are blended, the eyes in particular looking forth with a light that suggests genius.

Of the four children, Fanny, the elder, as well as Felix, early showed remarkable musical genius. Rebecca, the third, perhaps surpassed the others in intellectual power, though inferior to Fanny and Felix as regards their special gift. Though Abraham and Leah themselves preferred, until late in life, to remain Jews, they resolved that their children should be brought up as Christians, and here we reach a point which some will find it hard to approve. How can parents, without insincerity or culpable indifference, while retaining one faith, cause their children to be educated in another? What justification is possible can best be given in the words of Abraham Mendelssohn himself; whether it is sufficient the reader must judge. The perusal of the explanation, however, will satisfy all that the father was delicately conscientious, and that he himself had no scruples. In reaching his conclusion, he was much influenced by a brother of Leah, who had himself become a Christian, whose expressions all will admit to be wise and broad. Wrote the brother-in-law, when Abraham at first felt that the children must be brought up as Jews:

"You say you owe it to the memory of your father. * * * You may remain faithful to an oppressed, persecuted religion—you may leave it to your children as a prospect of life-long martyrdom, as long as you believe it to be absolute truth; but when you have ceased to believe that, it is barbarism." Abraham had ceased to believe that. He wrote to Fanny, at the time of her confirmation, a letter that might have been penned by Nathan the Wise:

"Does God exist? What is God? Is He part of ourselves, and does He continue to live after the other part has ceased to be? And where and how? All this I do not know, and, therefore, I have never taught you any thing about it. But I know that there exists in me and in you and in all human beings an everlasting inclination towards all that is good, true, and right, and a conscience which warns and guides us when we go astray. I know it, I believe it; I live in this faith, and this is my religion. Everybody has it who does not intentionally and knowingly cast it away. * * * When you look at your mother, and turn over in your thoughts all the immeasurable good she has lavished upon you by her constant, self-sacrificing devotion as long as you live, and when that reflection makes your heart and eyes overflow with gratitude, love, and veneration, then you feel God and are godly. * * * The outward form of religion your teacher has given you is historical and changeable, like all human ordinances. Some thousands of years ago, the Jewish form was the reigning one, then the heathen form, and now it is the Christian. Your mother and I were brought up by our parents as Jews, and without being obliged to change the form of our religion, have been able to follow the divine instinct in us and in our conscience. We have educated you and your brothers and sisters in the Christian faith, because it is the creed of most civilized people, and contains nothing that can lead you away from what is good, and much that guides you to love, obedience, tolerance, and resignation, even if it offered nothing but the example of its founder, understood by so few and followed by still fewer."

Felix could sing and compose almost before he could talk; he was a skilful pianist at six, and gave a public concert at nine. Compositions published when he was fifteen are regarded as classical. Before he had passed beyond boyhood he had become famous through the beautiful overture to the " Midsummer Night's Dream." Fanny was equally precocious. At thirteen she gave a proof of an uncommon musical memory, by playing without notes twenty-four preludes of Bach, as a surprise for her father, and had not passed beyond her girlhood before she had produced lovely music of her own. In her early womanhood she won the love of a young artist destined to fame, Wilhelm Hensel, whom she at length married after an interval of some years, spent by the painter in Italy. The good sense and brightness of the faithful mother, Leah, are well shown in the following letter to the young lover, in which, with the authority of a true Hebrew mother, she shields her daughter:

"Seriously, my dear Mr. Hensel, you must not be angry with me, because I cannot allow a correspondence between you and Fanny. Put yourself, in fairness for one moment in the place of a mother, and exchange your interests for mine, and my refusal will appear to you natural, just, and sensible; whereas you are probably now violently denouncing my proceeding as most barbaric. For the same reason that makes me forbid an engagement, I must declare myself averse to any correspondence. You know that I truly esteem you, that I have, indeed, a real affection for you, and entertain no objection to you personally. The reasons why I have not yet decided in your favor, are the difference of age and the uncertainty of your position. A man may not think of marrying before his prospects in life are, to a certain degree, assured. At any rate, he must not blame the girl's parents, who, having experience, sense, and cool blood, are destined by nature to judge for him and for her. An artist, as long as he is single, is a happy being; all circles open to him, court favor animates him; the small cares of life vanish before him; he steps lightly over the rocks which difference of rank has piled up in the world; he works at what he likes, the most delighted, happy being in the whole creation. As soon as domestic cares take hold of him, all this magic disappears, the lovely coloring fades, he must work to sustain his family. Indeed, I made it a point in my children's education to give them simple and unpretending habits, so that they might not be obliged to look out for rich marriages; but in the eyes of parents a competency, a moderate but fixed income, are necessary conditions for a happy life; and although my husband can afford to give to each of his children a handsome portion, he is not rich enough to secure the future prosperity of them all. You are at the commencement of your career, and under beautiful auspices; endeavor to realize them, and rest assured that we will not be against you when, at the end of your studies, you can satisfy us about your position. Fanny is very young, and, Heaven be praised, has hitherto had no concern and no passion. I will not have you, by love-letters, transport her for years into a state of consuming passion and a yearning frame of mind quite strange to her character, when I have her before me now blooming, healthy, happy, and free."

In the letters which have been quoted, father and mother have been sufficiently reflected, and now we must look at the home. "The rooms were stately, large, and lofty, built with delightful spaciousness. One room, especially, overlooking the court, and opening by means of three arches into an adjoining apartment, was beautiful and most suitable for theatrical representations. For many, many years, at Christmas, and on birthdays and festive occasions, this was the scene of interesting performances. Generally it was Leah's sitting-room. The windows opened upon a spacious court, closed by a one-storied garden-house, over which looked the tops of ancient trees. In summer the garden-house, in which Fanny and Hensel lived after their marriage, was perfectly charming. The windows were embowered in vines, and all opened on to the garden, with its blooming lilacs and avenues of stately old trees. The large court and high front building kept off every sound; you lived as in the deepest loneliness of a forest,—opposite, the magnificent trees, with merrily twittering birds, no lodger above or below, after the noise of the streets the quietest seclusion, and at your windows green leaves. The centre part of the house, and its most invaluable and beautiful portion, consisted in a very spacious hall, too large to be called a drawing-room. There was space in it for several hundred people, and it had on the garden side a movable glass wall, interrupted by pillars, so that the hall could be changed into an open portico. The hall commanded a view of a park, which, in Frederick the Great's time, had been part of the *Thier-garten*, and was therefore rich in most superb old trees. In this house and garden arose a singularly engaging, poetic life. * * * The Mendelssohn children loved Shakespeare, especially the 'Midsummer Night's Dream.' By a singular coincidence, in that very year, 1826, in their lovely garden, favored by most beautiful weather, they themselves led a fantastic, dream-like life. For them and their friends, the summer months were like one uninterrupted festival day, full of poetry, music, merry games, ingenious practical jokes, disguises, and representations. The whole life had a higher and loftier tendency, a more idyllic coloring, more poetry, than is often met with. Nature and art, wit, heart, and mind, the high flow of Felix's genius,—all this gave coloring to their doings, and on the other hand this wonderful life gave a new impulse to his creative spirit. The most brilliant result of that strangely poetic frame of mind is the overture to the 'Midsummer Night's Dream.'"

Any thing more ideal than this charming life, it is scarcely possible to conceive. The Mendelssohns, one would say, had found for themselves a paradise without the serpent. An abundant basis of wealth, the father and mother so wise, and of spirit so pleasant, the children maturing in beautiful promise,—no shadow of disease, sorrow, or anxiety. Felix was already famous, for the overture to the " Midsummer Night's Dream " caused the world to think that a successor to Beethoven was born ; Fanny, his equal in gifts and talents, but remaining modestly within the bounds which custom had set for women ; Rebecca, in her way not less remarkable and attractive than the elder brother and sister ; and Paul, the younger son, a thoroughly good and clever youth, if less highly endowed than the rest. The circle of friends about them, whom they visited, or who came to their sunbright home, were present at the sports and representations at Christmas, and who sat looking out upon the beautiful garden while the wonderful children from their instruments conquered the nightingales, as they now rendered the works of the old composers, now improvised, now gave their own compositions, which have come to be esteemed as the most precious things in music,—this circle of friends comprehended the best and brightest men of the time in art, philosophy, science, and literature,—Goethe, Hegel, Humboldt, Heinrich Heine, Encke the astronomer,

Paganini, Moscheles, Spontini, Schadow, and Devrient. No more serious ripple disturbed the even flow of the life than some such little incident as follows, narrated by Fanny. Alexander von Humboldt had arranged an observatory in the garden, on account of the silence and quiet of the place, where he and Professor Encke often met by night, as well as by day.

"I hear somebody entering our bedroom, and passing out again at the other side. I call. No answer. Wilhelm awakes, and cries out, 'Who *im Teufelsnamen* is there?' Enter, with majestic step, Louise (Hensel's sister), saying that she heard thieves rummaging about in the hall, and then going into the garden with a lantern. She had thought it her duty to wake somebody, but had only wanted to call the servant, and was very sorry for having disturbed us. Wilhelm gets up, wraps himself in a red blanket, and goes into the hall with a drawn sword, Louise in her dressing-gown and night-cap showing him a light. He opens the door just in time, for the thief with his lantern is on the point of escaping toward the garden. When he hears the noise he looks around, and seeing a red spectre with a drawn sword, runs away, Wilhelm after him. The thief makes straight for the gardener's lodge. When they both are in the gardener's room, pursuer and pursued burst into a peal of laughter. 'Professor Hensel!' 'Professor Encke! I beg you a thousand pardons, but I took you for a burglar!'"

From this home Felix went forth to become in his sphere a conqueror, the favorite of princes, and at

FELIX MENDELSSOHN.

the same time of peasants, the recipient of homage the most enthusiastic and intoxicating, in all the lands of Europe, an outpouring which he seems to have undergone without injury to his character, for to the end of his too short life he remained simple, affectionate, and dignified. The music that he wrote, like the lyrical poetry of Goethe, reflected accurately the mood for the time being of the spirit from which it proceeded. The "Scottish Symphony" and the "Isles of Fingal" suggest the wild beauty of the Highlands and Hebrides, the far North, upon whose soil they were elaborated. The reading of "Faust" brought forth the "Walpurgis Nacht," the study of Greek, the music for the "Antigone" and the "Œdipus." He found the best appreciation in England, chiefly for his sacred music, and this appreciation, reacting upon him, perhaps brought it to pass that his works in this field are his masterpieces. His great oratorios, "St. Paul" and "Elijah," must be regarded, it is said, as "the main pillars of his fame."*

It is indeed marvellous how complete a dominion Mendelssohn exercised over those who came under his spell. He was short and slight, and in his features strongly Jewish. The countenance was very mobile, the brow full, the eyes possessed of a power of expression quite extraordinary. When he was extemporizing they seemed to dilate to twice their natural size, the brown pupil becoming a vivid black. His slender hands upon the key-board of piano or organ became like living and intelligent creatures. His form bent over the instrument, heaving and

* Grove: Musical Dictionary.

swaying with the emotion which was born amid the tones. When with slender wand, at the performance of the "St. Paul" or "Elijah," he stood among the great multitude of singers and instruments, all turned to the magician with one soul, and the listening thousands beyond trembled to the music in sympathy not less intense. To illustrate this magical power, the account of a musical enthusiast, the authoress of "Charles Auchester," may here be well transcribed. Mendelssohn, described under the name of Seraphael, conducts a performance of sacred music in Westminster Abbey.

"Entering the centre of the nave, we caught sight of the transept, already crowded with hungering, thirsting faces. The vision of the choir itself, as it is still preserved to me, is as a picture of Heaven to infancy. What more like one's idea of Heaven than that height, the arches whose sun-kissed summits glowed in the distance, whose vista stretched from the light of rainbows at one end to the organ at the other, music's archetype? Below the organ stood Seraphael's desk, as yet unhaunted,—the orchestra, the chorus beneath the lofty front. Seraphael entered so quietly as to take us by surprise.

"Down the nave the welcome rolled, across the transept it overflowed the echoes; for a few moments nothing else could be felt, but there was, as it were, a tender shadow upon the very reverberating jubilance, subdued for the sake of one whose beauty lifted over us, appeared hovering, descending from some late-left heaven, ready to depart again, but not without a sign for which we waited. Immediately, and while he yet stood with his eyes of power upon the whole front of faces, the solo singers entered also and took their seats all calmly. We held our breath for the coming of the overture.

"It opened like the first dawn of lightening, but scarce yet lightened morning,—its vast subject introduced with strings alone, in that joyous key which so often served him. But soon the first trombone blazed out, the second and third responding with their stupendous tones, as the amplifications of fugue involved and spread themselves more and more. Then, like glory filling up and flooding the height of Heaven, broke in the organ, and brimmed the brain with the calm of an utter and forceful expression, realized by tone. In sympathy with each instrument, it was alike with none. The vibrating harmonies, pulse-like, clung to our pulses, then drew out each heart, deep-beating and undistracted, to adore at the throne above, from which all beauty springs. Holiness, precious as the old Hebrew psalm of all that hath life and breath, exhaled from every modulation; each dropped the freshness of everlasting spring.

"I cannot describe the hush that hung above and seemed to spiritualize the listeners; nor how, as chorus after chorus rang, our spirits sank upon the strains and songs. Faint supplications, deep acclaims of joy, all surcharged the spirit with the mysterious tenderness of the uncreate and unpronounceable Name. When at length those two hours, concentrating such an eternity in their perfection of all sensation, had reached their climax,—or, rather, when, in the final chorus, imprisoned harmonies burst down from stormy-hearted organ, from strings all shivering alike, from blasting, rending tubes,—it was as if the multitude had sunk upon their knees, so profound was the passion-cradling calm. The blue-golden lustre, dim and tremulous, still crowned the unwavering arches. So many tears are not often shed as fell in that time.

"During the last reverberations of that unimaginable Alleluiah, I had not looked up at all; now I forced myself to do so, lest I should lose my sight of *him*, his seal upon all that glory. As Seraphael had risen to depart, the applause, stifled and trembling, but not the less by heartfuls, rose for him. He turned his face a moment; the heavenly half-smile was there; then the summer sun, that falling downward in its piercing glare, glowed gorgeous against the stained windows, flung its burning bloom, its flushing gold, upon that countenance. We all saw it, we all felt it,—the seraph strength, the mortal beauty,—and that it was pale as the cheek of the quick and living changed to death. His mien was of no earthly triumph!"

While Felix grew great, the beautiful life in Berlin proceeded. Paul matured into worthy manhood; Rebecca, fulfilling her promise, becoming a woman of real intellectual power, was chosen as a wife by one of the most distinguished mathematicians of his time. The fame of Hensel grew, and under the influence of Fanny the Berlin home became the centre of a culture more than ever rich and brilliant. Hensel had a habit of sketching their guests, and in the series is contained almost every interesting man and woman known to fame, who lived in or visited the Prussian capital of that time—painters and singers, actors and sculptors, poets, statesmen, scientists, and philosophers. " The musical parties, from small beginnings, became at last regular concerts, with choral and solo-singing, trios and quartets of the best Berlin musicians, and before an audience that filled all the rooms. Fanny took the greatest pleasure in rehearsing her splendidly schooled little choir, which she generally did on the Friday afternoons. On a beautiful summer morning, nothing prettier could be seen than the *Garten-saal*, opening on to the trees, filled with a crowd of gay, elegantly-dressed people, and Fanny at her piano, surrounded by her choir, performing some ancient or modern masterpiece. When Hensel had a picture nearly finished, the doors of the studio stood open, and a grave Christ might look down upon the throng, or Miriam, leading her own people, would symbolically express upon the canvas what was in living truth passing in the music-room." " Last month," wrote Fanny June, 1834, " I gave a delightful fête—' Iphigenia in Tauris,' sung by Madame Decker, Madame Bader, and Mantius. Any thing so perfect will not soon be heard again. Bader especially was exquisite, but each rivalled the other, and the sound of these three lovely voices together had such a powerful charm that I shall never forget it. Every thing went off beautifully."

In this home the parents accomplished their days, —the mother so full of good sense and watchful affection, the father broad-minded and religious. Always they bear in their hearts their children and grandchildren. " O Sebastian!" breaks out Abraham, during a visit to London, thinking of his little grandchild; "I thank God you are not the child four and a half years old which a few days ago was advertised in thousands of placards as missing. The thought of it never leaves me, and is interwoven as a black thread with my London life. The poor child has surely not been brought back, but was most probably stolen and thrown into the street, starved and naked, to be brought up by a gang of beggars and thieves. And all this because perhaps the parents lost sight of it for half a minute!"

And yet one does not have to go far back in the generations to find the intense Jewish fierceness, such as glared in John of Giscala, in Shylock, and in the elders of the Amsterdam synagogue, who poured out malediction upon Spinoza. The mother of Leah was an unrelenting Israelite, who denounced her own son, an apostate from the ancient faith to Christianity, with blasting curses. In the grandchildren, however, we find nothing but affections of the gentlest and the sweetest. Paul, the youngest, of whom little mention has been made, thoroughly unobtrusive, but a highly successful man of business, was distinguished for his charity, and was in no way less lovable than the more conspicuous Felix and Fanny. It is of these two only that we have the full record, and we must draw from it still more to make plain their loveliness of soul, and the peace and happiness of their lives. Upon the christening-day of her boy,

Fanny writes to her father: "I cannot allow such a joyful and beautiful day to come to an end, dear father, without writing to tell you how we have missed you. An event like this will make one's past life rise vividly before one, and my heart tells me I must again thank you, dear parents (for this letter is meant for mother also), at this moment, and I hope not for the last time, for guiding me to where I now stand, for my life, my education, my husband! And thank you for being so good—for the blessing of good parents rests on their children, and I feel so happy that I have nothing left to wish for but that such happiness might last. I truly know and feel how blessed I am, and this consciousness is, I think, the foundation-stone of happiness."

At another time Fanny writes from Rome, at the end of a long sojourn, during which she and her husband had given and received much joy, in the midst of a brilliant company, many of them great men, or about to become so. Fanny's music had been a constant source of delight: "The instrument had been moved into the large hall, the twilight was rapidly deepening, and a peculiar sensation stole over the whole company. For a long time I preluded as softly as possible, for I could not have played loud, and everybody talked in whispers, and started at the slightest noise. I played the adagios from the concerto in G major, and the sonata in C sharp minor, and the beginning of the grand sonata in F sharp minor—with Charlotte, Bousquet, and Gounod sitting close beside me. It was an hour I shall never forget. After dinner we went on to the balcony, where it was lovely. The stars above, and the lights of the city below, the glowworms, and a long-trailing meteor which shot across the sky, the lighted windows of a church on a hill far away, and the delicious atmosphere in which every thing was bathed,—all combined to stir in us the deepest emotion. Afterwards we went to the end of the hall and sang the part-songs, which gave great satisfaction. I repeated, by general request, the Mozart fantasia to finish with, and the two capriccios, and then the part songs were asked for once more, and then midnight had arrived and our time was over. 'They weep they know not why!' was our last music in Rome.

"A glorious time has passed away! How can we be thankful enough for these two months of uninterrupted happiness! The purest joys the human heart can know have succeeded each other, and during all this time we have scarcely had one unpleasant quarter of an hour. The only drawback has been that the time would go so fast. Our last farewell from St. Pietro in Montorio was not easy work; but I retain in my mind an eternal, imperishable picture, which no lapse of time will affect. I thank Thee, O God!"

She describes her father as he lay in death: " So beautiful, unchanged, and calm was his face that we could remain near our loved one, not only without a sensation of fear, but felt truly elevated in looking at him. The whole expression was so calm, the forehead so pure and beautiful, the position of the hands so mild! It was the end of the righteous, a beautiful, enviable end, and I pray to God for a similar death, and will strive through all my days to deserve it as he deserved it. It was death in its most peaceful, beautiful aspect."

That Felix could receive the homage of the great without compromise of his independence of character, appears in the following: " Prince Albert had asked me to go to him at two o'clock, so that I might try his organ before I left England. I found him alone; and as we were talking away the Queen came in, also alone, in simple morning dress. She said she was obliged to leave for Claremont in an hour, and then, suddenly interrupting herself, exclaimed: ' But, goodness! what a confusion!' for the wind had littered the whole room, and even the pedals of the organ, with leaves of music from a large portfolio that lay open. As she spoke she knelt down and began picking up the music; Prince Albert helped, and I, too, was not idle. Then Prince Albert proceeded to explain the stops to me, and she said that she would meanwhile put things straight.

" I begged that the Prince would first play me something, so that, as I said, I might boast about it in Germany; and he played a choral by heart, with the pedals, so charmingly and clearly and correctly, that it would have done credit to any professional; and the Queen, having finished her work, came and sat by him and listened, and looked pleased. Then it was my turn, and I began my chorus from ' St. Paul '—' How Lovely are the Messengers!' Before I had got to the end of the first verse they had both joined in the chorus, and all the time Prince Albert managed the stops for me so cleverly; first a flute, at the *forte* the great organ, at the D major part the whole register; then he made a lovely diminuendo with the stops, and so on to the end of the piece, and all by heart, that I was really quite enchanted. The Queen asked me if I had written any new songs, and said she was very fond of singing my published ones. 'You should sing one to him,' said Prince Albert; and after a little begging she said she would try. * * * After some consultation with her husband, he said: 'She will sing you something of Gluck's.' While they were talking I had rummaged about amongst the music, and discovered my first set of songs. So, of course, I begged her rather to sing one of those than the Gluck, to which she very kindly consented; and which did she choose? '*Schöner und schöner schmückt sich*'—sang it quite charmingly, in strict time and tune, and with very good execution. * * * The last long G I have never heard better or purer or more natural from any amateur. Then I was obliged to confess that Fanny had written the song (which I found very hard, but pride must have a fall), and to beg her to sing one of my own also. If I would give her plenty of help she would gladly try, she said, and then she sang the Pilgerspruch, '*Lass dich nur*,' really quite faultlessly, and with charming feeling and expression. * * *

"After this Prince Albert sang the Aerndte-Lied, '*Es ist ein Schnitter*,' and then he said I must play him something before I went, and gave as themes the choral which he had played on the organ and the song he had just sung. * * * As if I were to keep nothing but the pleasantest, most charming recollection of it, I never improvised better. I was in the best mood for it, and played a long time, and enjoyed it myself so much that, besides the two themes, I brought in the songs that the Queen had sung, quite naturally; and it all went off so easily that I would gladly not have stopped. It was a delightful morning! If this long description makes Dirichlet set me down as a tuft-hunter, tell him that I vow and declare I am a greater radical than ever."

The following letters show touchingly his manly piety and the depth and purity of his love as a son and a brother: "The wish which of all others every night recurred to my mind was that I might not survive this loss, because I so entirely clung, or rather still cling, to my father, that I do not know how I am to pass my life; for not only have I to deplore the loss of a father, but also that of my best and most perfect friend for the last few years, and my instructor in art and life. When in later years you tell your child of those whom you invited to his baptism,* do not omit my name, but say to him that one of them, too, on that day began his life afresh, though in another sense, with new purposes and wishes, and with new prayers to God."

After the death of Fanny, in the spring of 1847, which preceded his own by a few months only, Felix

---

* The letter was written in reply to one inviting him to a christening which was to take place on the day on which he heard of his father's death.

wrote thus to her husband and son : " If you ever want a faithful brother, who loves you with his whole heart, think of me. I am sure I shall be a better man than I have been, though not such a happy one. But what shall I say to you, my dear Sebastian? There is nothing to say or do but this one thing: pray to God that He may create in us a clean heart and renew a right spirit within us, so that we may even in this world become more and more worthy of her who had the purest heart and spirit we ever knew or loved. God bless her, and point us out the way which none of us can see for ourselves ; and yet there must be one, for God himself has inflicted this blow upon us for the remainder of our lives, and may He soften the pain. Alas, my dear brother and friend ! God be with you and with Sebastian, and with us three, her brothers and sister ! "

These children and grandchildren of Moses Mendelssohn were as fortunate in their deaths as in their lives. Abraham and Leah, before the weaknesses of age had made themselves felt, sank painlessly away in the arms of their children. Felix, Fanny, and Rebecca, in like manner, without knowing long-continued suffering or any benumbment of the powers of spirit and body from advancing years, closed their eyes quickly and quietly upon the world. As one reads of their careers, it seems almost the ideal life. Where can be found more charming pictures of refinement, happiness, brilliant powers, achieving at once the best success ! Rare and beautiful as were their gifts, these are less interesting than their spiritual graces,—the unobtrusive piety, the sweet domestic affections, the tender humanity, the large-minded superiority to prejudice, which constantly appear. The trace of human infirmity is plain enough in the household, as, for instance, in the irregularities of Dorothea. According to the universal lot of mortals, we may be sure that each man and woman of them had his and her share of shortcomings. But as one reads, the drawbacks make little show, and it is a natural aspiration, would that men in general were as fortunate and as good!

CHAPTER XXI.

OUR HEBREW CONTEMPORARIES.

WE have traced the Jew from his first appearance, in the most remote antiquity, until the present time. The pride and force with which he confronted the most powerful nations of the ancient world have been portrayed; the unyielding spirit with which he defied the Roman, even while he was driven from his land to wander as an outcast; the spiritual intensity with which he subdued his very conquerors to his ideas, even at the moment when he was himself crushed; the gulf of woe through which he has passed; the new glory which he is at length seizing upon now that the chain is broken, and his imperishable energy has once more free course. It is a people of astonishing vigor, the wonderful character of whose achievements it is hardly possible to exaggerate.

In some parts of the world the idea seems to be gaining ground that we are all to be pushed to the wall by the all-conquering Israelite; that the money power is falling into his hands, and political power is following; that he is, in fact, seizing upon the best places in every direction; that the time is at hand when the Jew, with all his haughty pride of race, is to grasp the headship of the world; that, holding himself apart more arrogantly than ever, he will suffer no contact between himself and those whom he has brought under, except where his scornful foot is pressed upon the Gentile neck.

Said Dr. Stöcker, not long since, a well-known preacher of Berlin, who is a leader in the anti-Jewish movement in Germany: "At the post-mortem examination of a body lately, there were present the district physician, the lawyer, the surgeon, and a fourth official, all of whom were Jews. None but the corpse was a German. Behold a picture of the present!"

The best business men of Germany, it is declared, are Hebrews; banking they almost monopolize; the journals are largely in their hands; they have seventy professors in the universities; they have the most brilliant parliamentary leaders. Strong as the Germans are, a great party among them appears actually to feel that the one and one half per cent. of Hebrews in their population is likely to crowd on until Teutonic power and prestige, by their hands, are deftly and properly laid out and interred. The hate entertained against the Israelites by the rabble, and even by those higher in station, has uttered itself at the present day in the old mediæval cry, "Hep! Hep!" The days of proscription are scarcely passed, and men have even been tortured and murdered in times quite recent, under the old accusation of poisoning wells and crucifying children. This mingled fear and repugnance finds a half-humorous but forcible expression in certain stanzas by Franz Dingelstedt, a poet of Vienna, which may be thus translated:

> Gone are the days of bitter tribulation ;
> Changed are the times which now we see emerge.
> The cunning Jew, amid our lamentation,
> From our unskilful hands doth wrest the scourge.
>
> He crowds the farmer hard with scheming knavish,
> The trader from the mart he elbows well ;
> And half with gold and half with mocking slavish,
> Buys from the spirit of the age his spell.
>
> Where'er you turn, the thrusting Jew will meet you,—
> The chosen of the Lord in every view.
> Lock them in Juden-gassen I entreat you,
> Lest in some Christen-gasse they lock you !

Whether the apprehensions of the Germans are reasonable or not, we will not stop to inquire ; but what testimony is this to the astonishing power of the Jew, that one of the greatest of modern nations seems to shudder with the fear that this fraction of Jews in its population is about to reduce it to subjection !

While the heart of the Christian cannot be said to have thoroughly relented, can the heart of the Jew be said to have lost its scorn ? " Be on your guard when you enter a synagogue," it was once said to me. The Christian needs to take heed if he enters a temple in some parts of Europe, whether it be some ancient low-walled sanctuary, like those in little towns on the Rhine, or the superb structures that may be found in the great cities, where shrine and canopy are beautiful as frost-work,—with fringe of gold and lamp of silver,—the Oriental arches throwing back from their purple vaults the sound of the silver trumpets and the deep chant of the high-priest.

The Jew comes in his sanctuary to the most vivid sense of his race and faith; even while he reveres the sacred tables of the Law, his eye can darken, and his lip spit forth contumely upon the unwelcome Nazarene.

I well remember also going into the shop of a Jew, in an ancient city, and during our bargaining, crossing his purpose in a way that aroused his anger. The flash in his dark eye was of the hereditary wrath bequeathed to him from many generations of persecuted fathers, called out by the son of the Christian who stood before him; in the hiss with which his words came forth, I seemed to hear a serpent that had been gathering its poison for a thousand years.

Even those among the Hebrews who are leaders for intelligence, and whose minds have become broadened by contact with the Gentiles, like Moses Mendelssohn and Sir Moses Montefiore, cling tenaciously to the traditions and usages of their forefathers. If one studies the race where it has been shut off in a measure from contact with other men, many heirloom customs and prejudices from the dark old days come to light, sometimes picturesque, sometimes startling, sometimes, indeed, terrible. A strange interest attaches among them to the burial of the dead, and there is a curiously affectionate care of the sepulchres of their lost ones. As has been mentioned, the office of *lavadore*, the one who prepares the body for the grave, is one of high honor among them; their cemeteries are tended and made beautiful, even when the descendants of the sleepers have utterly disappeared, by fellow-Hebrews, who will not suffer an Israelite grave to go uncared for, even though it holds a stranger. Longfellow's stanzas upon the Jewish cemetery at Newport contain a sentiment most sweet and pensive :

>How strange it seems ! these Hebrews in their graves,
> Close by the street of this fair sea-port town,
>Silent beside the never silent waves,
> At rest in all this moving up and down !
>
>The trees are white with dust, that o'er their sleep
> Wave their broad curtains in the south wind's breath,
>While underneath such leafy tents they keep
> The long mysterious Exodus of Death.
>
>And these sepulchral stones, so old and brown,
> That pave with level flags their burial-place,
>Seem like the tablets of the Law, thrown down
> And broken by Moses at the mountain's base.
>
>The very names recorded here are strange,
> Of foreign accent and of different climes ;
>Alvarez and Rivera interchange
> With Abraham and Jacob of old times.
>
>Closed are the portals of their synagogue ;
> No psalms of David now the silence break ;
>No rabbi reads the ancient Decalogue
> In the grand dialect the Prophets spake.
>
>Gone are the living, but the dead remain,
> And not neglected ; for a hand unseen,
>Scattering its bounty like a summer rain,
> Still keeps their graves and their remembrance green.
>
>How came they here ? What burst of Christian hate,
> What persecution, merciless and blind,
>Drove o'er the sea, that desert desolate,
> These Ishmaels and Hagars of mankind ?

They lived in narrow streets and lanes obscure,
  Ghetto and Judenstrass in mirk and mire ;
Taught in the school of patience to endure
  The life of anguish and the death of fire.

All their lives long, with the unleavened bread
  And bitter herbs of exile and its fears,
The wasting famine of the heart they fed,
  And slaked its thirst with Marah of their tears.

Anathema Maranatha ! was the cry
  That rang from town to town, from street to street ;
At every gate the accursed Mordecai
  Was mocked and jeered, and spurned by Christian feet.

Pride and humiliation, hand in hand,
  Walked with them through the world where'er they went ;
Trampled and beaten were they as the sand,
  And yet unshaken as the continent.

For in the background figures vague and vast
  Of patriarchs and of prophets rose sublime,
And all the great traditions of the past,
  They saw reflected in the coming time.

And thus forever with reverted look
  The mystic volume of the world they read,
Spelling it backward like a Hebrew book,
  Till life became a legend of the dead.

But ah ! what once has been shall be no more !
  The groaning earth in travail and in pain,
Brings forth its nations, but does not restore,
  And the dead nations never rise again.

In a book* which gives many a curious picture of the Jews of Poland, an account is contained of a burial-place, a story which may well follow the plaintive lines just transcribed. Until within a few

* "Die Juden von Barnow," by Emil Franzos.

years, it was the only soil the Hebrews were allowed to own, and it was cherished until the grass was green upon every mound; elders grew by every head-stone, with purple berries among their leaves, giving forth in spring a powerful perfume, while in autumn the heather glowed with a deep red. About stretched the level landscape, to where in the distance could be seen the faint hue of the distant Carpathian mountains. On four hundred headstones was chiselled the same date. These marked the graves of the victims of a massacre. Two rival nobles had claimed a town, from both of whom the Jews had sought to buy protection. Both, however, turned upon them in wrath, slaying them for three days and nights. Other graves again had found their tenants, when a magnate of the land, because there was no other game in the neighborhood, hunted the Jews. The head-stones are all shaped alike, differing only in size, with no carved figures, for the prohibition of Moses must be obeyed. Stones which bear no name mark the graves of those held to have committed some great sin, and there are many nameless graves in this Podolian field. They are left uninscribed rather in mercy than in punishment; for at the last day, the angel of eternal life will call the sleepers, reading the names upon the stones, the good to inherit bliss, the wicked, to suffer. If the stone is without a name, the sleeper may be passed over.

As a visitor one day approached the burial-ground, he saw two old Israelites engaged in the ancient custom of "measuring the boundaries." Each carried in his right hand a short, yellow stick; a continuous thread united the two, being wound upon each stick into a close, thick ball. First, the men stood still, holding the sticks near together, and singing in unison a strange traditional chant. Then one paused, standing fixed and holding his stick vertical, while the other, walking on slowly and gravely by the side of the inclosing hedge, singing meantime in high nasal tones, unwound the thread as he went, keeping it straight and tight. At about thirty paces distance, he in turn stood fixed and silent, while his companion, singing in his turn, advanced, winding up the thread as he did so, the ball on the one stick becoming larger, as that upon the other grew less. As the measurers stood together, the chant in unison once more took place, followed, as before by the single voice, as another thirty paces was accomplished. It is said the bounds are measured by some such ceremony, wherever Jews are to be found, but never in this peculiar way except in the province of Podolia, upon the anniversaries of the deaths of near relatives. The thread is used afterwards for some pious purpose, as to form the wick of candles used in sacrifice, or to sew a prayer mantle.

The visitor had observed a nameless head-stone in a hollow alone. Its shape indicated that it marked the resting-place of a woman; to the right and left were the unmarked graves of babes. What could be the fearful crime which had condemned the mother to a nameless grave in such isolation? At length, from one of the old measurers of the bounds, he obtained the story. Leah Rendar had been marked, as a girl, among her companions for a wealth of shining, golden hair. She had been very beautiful, of a German rather than Jewish type, and her chief charm had been her sunny locks, of which she was very vain. They wrapped her like a veil, so that she was called "Leah with the long hair." It is prescribed among the Jews of Poland, that no married woman shall wear her own hair, which must be cut short, perhaps even shaved, before the wedding. A high head-dress of wool or silk must crown the head in its place. To neglect this rule is a terrible sin.

In due time came to Leah the day of betrothal, then of marriage. At the latter she appeared without the golden hair, and with the great head-dress. All went merrily, and for a year to come happiness attended bridegroom and bride. Leah's first child, however, came dead into the world. When a year or two more had rolled by, a second child came, but lived only six days, and the rabbi of the synagogue suspected that some law had been broken by the mother. At length, on the Day of Atonement, husband and wife spent the hours with the people in the crowded synagogue. The odor of the candles, and the close air, caused Leah to fall fainting from her prayer-stool. In the effort of the women to restore her, her head-dress became displaced, when lo! the iniquity was revealed: the golden locks fell as of old about her form. Her vanity had induced her to violate the law, and leave her hair uncut. Both husband and wife were straightway excommunicated. Neither they nor their belongings could be touched except in enmity. They were outcasts.

In course of time another son was born to Leah. Said the rabbi : "The parents are outcasts; the father is under the ban, the mother wears her own hair. The child is innocent, but if it remains with its parents, it must share their fate." When the child was six days old, masked men broke into the house, dragged the mother from her bed, and cut off her hair. She died two days after, her child following her, and the poor mother was placed apart from her fellows in the lonely dell. So she lies under her head-stone which is uninscribed, that the recording angel may, perhaps, at the great day of judgment, pass her by, and her soul, with its sin, not be cast forth into the outer darkness.

An ancient custom, not yet forgotten in some parts of Germany, is that daughters who apostatize, are counted as dead, mourned as such by their parents, and that graves even are prepared for them. The poet Meissner has described this usage in verses which have been translated as follows : *

> The anthems for the dead are sung ;
> The old Jew's garb in grief is rent ;
> And yet no corpse is sunk to earth,
> For she still lives whom they lament.
> The grave awaits her.

> From oldest days and earliest times,
> The Jews such saddening custom have,
> That she who leaves their Father's God,
> They count as dead and dig her grave.
> The grave awaits her.

* Translated by Henry Phillips.

In Venice city, bright and gay,
  Upon the purple flood there flies,
In swift gondol, a soldier fair,
  And on his breast a Jewess lies.
    Her grave awaits her.

He kisses tresses, lips, and cheek ;
  He calls her his own darling bride ;
She nestles in his golden hair ;
  She gazes on her love with pride.
    Her grave awaits her.

In noble halls, at banquets rare,
  She strikes the zither's golden chords,
Till wearied deep by pleasure's sway,
  Refreshing sleep its joy affords.
    Her grave awaits her.

But once, as sped a dream of bliss,
  When daydawn broke she was alone.
With traitorous flight beyond the seas,
  Her faithless love for aye was gone !
    Her grave awaits her.

She tears her silky curling locks ;
  She wanders on the sea-beat shore ;
When lo, her father's words return !
  " Be thou accursed forevermore !
    Thy grave awaits thee."

A beggar-wench on Alpine road
  Wanders toward home through night-wind wild.
Unwept, within a deep ravine,
  Unblest, lies tombed her ill-starred child.
    Her grave awaits her.

The ancestral graves mourn sad and lone ;
  Their silent, solemn rest, who breaks ?

A shadow falls on church-yard walls,
The moonbeam shows a form that seeks
    The grave that waits her.

She rolls the slab from off the grave,
With wearied limbs and failing breath.
In silent prayer she lays her form
Within the tomb, and welcomes death.
    The grave had waited.

But dismissing these melancholy pictures, let us inquire for a moment what we need to fear from the Hebrews. Some one has defined the type of shrewdness to be: "A Jewish Yorkshireman of Scottish extraction with a Yankee education." Such a combination would indeed be likely to bring to pass a very sharp result. We are to notice that if the Jew is to be taken as the Alpha of shrewdness, the American is at the same time the Omega. The two ends balance each other, and I for one have too much faith in my compatriots to expect ever to hear it said that the American end of the tilting board has gone up. In the competitions of American life it is diamond cut diamond; it is hard to say whether Jew or Yankee will show most nicks as marks of the grinding power of the other. Take your real down-Easter that has been honed for a few generations on the New England granite. Can Abraham or Jacob or Moses show a finer edge? We may hope that in any competition upon this lowest plane the American will be able to hold his own. Would that we might be as sure that we shall match them in those higher spheres in which Hebrew genius, wherever the Jesses have been thrown off, has soared with such imperial sweep!

Do we like our Hebrew neighbors and rivals?* Says Felix Adler, the scholar and teacher of ancient Jewish blood, but who has cast off all narrow Judaism to stand upon a platform of the broadest : " The Jews have certain peculiarities of disposition ; they have Asiatic blood in their veins. Among the highbred members of the race the traces of their Oriental origin are revealed in noble qualities, in versatility of thought, brilliancy of imagination, flashing humor, in what the French call *esprit;* these, too, in powerful lyrical outpourings, in impassioned eloquence, in the power of experiencing and uttering profound emotions. The same tendencies among the uneducated and illiterate give rise to unlovely and unpleasing idiosyncrasies, a certain restlessness, loudness of manner, fondness of display, a lack of dignity, reserve, repose. And since one loud person attracts greater attention than twenty who are modest and refined, it has come about that the whole race is often condemned because of the follies of some of

*In " Imperfect Sympathies," Charles Lamb frankly writes : " I have, in the abstract, no disrespect for Jews. They are a piece of stubborn antiquity compared with which Stonehenge is in its nonage. They date beyond the pyramids. But I should not care to be in habits of familiar intercourse with any of that nation. Centuries of injury, contempt, and hate on the one side,—of cloaked revenge, dissimulation, and hate on the other, between our and their fathers, must and ought to effect the blood of the children. I cannot believe it can run clear and kindly yet ; or that a few fine words, such as candor, liberality, the light of the nineteenth century, can close up the breaches of so deadly a disunion. A Hebrew is no where congenial to me."

the coarsest and least representative of its members."

The characteristics which Felix Adler thus describes as belonging to a portion of his countrymen, have no doubt sometimes repelled. It is, however, great narrowness to allow our estimation of the race to be determined in this way. In the popular play, "Sam'l of Posen," the hearty young Jew, of blood quite unadulterated, just from the frontiers of Poland, where we are told the Jew is at his worst, is no more remarkable for his love of money and hard business push than he is for his good nature, his gratitude, and kindness of heart. The voice of the people declares it a portrait faithful to the life.

This Semitic flotsam and jetsam thrown upon the Aryan current, after that current had wrecked so cruelly ancient Israel—always upon it and in it, yet never of it,—soluble by no saturation, not to be pulverized or ground away by the heaviest smitings, unabsorbed, unoverwhelmed, though the current has been rolling for so many ages ever westward, until at length the West is becoming East, is it to subsist forever apart, or will it some time melt into the stream that bears it? Whatever Judaism may have lost through abjurations of its creed, there has so far always remained a compact nucleus firmly clinging to the old Judaic standards. From the immemorial rites and traditions, they say, there shall be abatement of neither jot nor tittle. Circumcision and Passover, Talmud and Torah,—be these to us as they were to our fathers. They are no more a proselyting body, it has been said, than the House of Lords; they are the aristocracy of the human race, though for the time they may be pawnbrokers, or sell old clothes. "Intermarriage with the Gentile is a thing abhorrent. Let the chosen people hold itself aloof until a time shall come when Jehovah shall give to it the headship of the nations." Such a nucleus there is to-day. Meantime, however, there are Hebrews of a spirit quite different. Moses Mendelssohn looked not so much toward any headship for his race, as toward a brotherly coming together of men, a recognizing in the spirit of charity of the necessity of differences between creeds,—an era of tolerance and mutual forbearance.

When in the eye of the Hebrew there beams thus a gentle and conciliatory light, what can the Gentile better do than hail it with gladness and meet it with cordiality? The path into which Moses Mendelssohn struck has been followed by his disciples farther, sometimes, than he would have approved. His own children and grandchildren proceeded to lengths from which he, with all his noble breadth of soul, would have recoiled, holding as he did to various Israelite limitations. In laying his foundations he builded more wisely than he knew, for the superstructure was to be a beautiful and all-embracing charity. How hopeful is the influence proceeding from this gentle teacher! The world in these latter days has seen few men and women more richly adorned with gifts and graces than his descendants. As from a bed of repulsive refuse will sometimes spring blossoms of perfect loveliness, so out from the *askenazim*, that degraded German Judaism, with its foul Juden-strassen, from among the people despised even by those

of their own faith, have come those who in beneficent
genius, in gentle virtues, in all forms of sweetness
and light, present a most delightful picture. It is a
very fair flowering of humanity. Our story has had
many a page of horror; it has been pleasant at last
to turn to things so tranquil and lovely. One cannot
but wish that the lot of the Mendelssohns were the
universal lot, and that the world in general deserved
as thoroughly as they, to have so much happiness
given them for a portion. Would that the children
of Israel, following their new Moses, the son of Mendel, might all come out into such a Canaan of kindliness, wisdom, and breadth of soul; and would that the
Gentile world, leaving behind their thousand forms of
cruel narrowness, might meet them through gaining
a similar loveliness of spirit! Through all the ages
no gulf has seemed so deep and wide as that which
severed the Jew from the world which he would not
have and which would not have him. Even to-day
it seems almost utopian to imagine that the chasm
can be filled. As, however, in the slow evolution of
man his heart gradually refines and softens, it is not
a vain hope that there will some time be such a
coming together of those as yet unreconciled, each
advancing from his shadows into a space made beautiful with the radiance of charity.

INDEX.

A

Aaron and the oral law, 77
Abarbanel at the court of Spain, 158
Abraham, Rabbi, story of, 168, etc.
Abram goes southward from Haran, 12
Adler, Felix, on the Jews, 367
Ælia Capitolina, Roman city on site of Jerusalem, 133
Ahasuerus, see Wandering Jew
Alexander the Great at Jerusalem, 60
Alexandria, its library destroyed, 55 ; its large Jewish population, 64, 133
Alliance Israélite Universelle, 282
America, number of Jews in, 235
American rapacity, 274, 275
Ammonites subdued by the Hebrews, 12
Ananus, high-priest, slain, 111
Antiochus Epiphanes oppresses the Jews, 64
Antiochus of Commagene at the siege of Jerusalem, 120
Antonia, fortress of, described, 104 ; destroyed, 117
Apelles slain by Mattathias, 65
Apocrypha, how composed, 76
Apollonius defeated by Judas Maccabæus, 66
Aramaic, spoken in Palestine, 75
Ark, of the Covenant, described, 16

Arnold, Matthew, on Spinoza, 230
Artorius, Roman soldier at Jerusalem, 120
Aryans, first contact with Jews, 61 ; origin and spread of, 62 ; spiritually conquered by the Jews, 126
Askenazim, name for the German Jews, 239 ; give birth to Moses Mendelssohn, 240 ; beautiful outgrowth from, 369
Asmonæus, ancestor of the Maccabees, 64
Assyrians, threaten Palestine, 26 ; their prominence in Hebrew annals, 27 ; relics of, in British Museum, 29, 30 ; sources of information concerning, 32 ; how they told their own story, 34 ; discoveries of Botta and Layard, 35 ; the cuneiform, 36 ; nature of the dominion of, 37 ; conquests in Palestine, 38 ; splendor of, under Sennacherib, 39 ; progress in arts, 40 ; commerce of, 42 ; magnificence of the kings, 43 ; palaces of, 44 ; decadence of, 54 ; their imperishable records, 55 ; their cruelty, 56
Atonement, fast of, 56
"Atta Troll," satire of Heine, 318
Auerbach, and Spinoza, 229 ; first German novelist, 238
Auto-da-fe in Spain, 161, etc.
Averroes and Avicenna, Moorish philosophers, 138

371

B

Babylon, captivity at, 57
Bacchides defeats Judas Maccabæus, 69
Badges worn by mediæval Jews, 201
Bamberger, Jewish statesman in Germany, 296
Barak defeats Sisera, 18
Bar Cocheba, rebels against Rome, 133 ; a false Messiah, 216
Beaconsfield, see Disraeli
Beautiful, gate of the Temple, 104
Benfey, Sanscrit scholar, 238
Ben Hadad, of Syria, conquered by the Assyrians, 38
Bernays, Jewish scholar, 238
Bernhardt, Sarah, Jewish artist, 238
Bismarck and Lasker, 296
Black Death in the 14th century, 167, 198
"Book Le Grand," work of Heine, quoted, 318, etc.
Börne, Ludwig, with Heine in the Frankfort Juden-gasse, 230
Botta, Assyrian explorer, 36
British Museum, Assyrian collection at, 29
Buckle, harsh toward Jews, 202

C

Cabala described, 222
Cahorsin, money-lenders, 193
Caleb, ancient Hebrew champion, 18
Canaanites, their civilization, their conquest by the Israelites, 18
Canon, of the Old Testament, formation of, 76
Canute banishes the Jews from England, 189
Cartaphilus, see Wandering Jew
Castelar, Spanish statesman of Jewish origin, 295

Cerealis leads Romans to the final attack on Jerusalem, 117
Chaldeans, their ancient empire, 37
Charlemagne and the Jews, 139
"Charles Auchester," description of Felix Mendelssohn from, 343, etc.
Chasidim, a division among the Hebrews, 77
Christian idea of the Jews, 2
Cicero, depreciates trade, 254 ; the corn-ships at Rhodes, 273
Cobbett taunts the Jews, 283
Coleridge introduces Spinoza to English thinkers, 229
Commerce, how the Jews came to follow it, 136 ; skilful pursuit of, in modern times, 237
"Conqueror," battering-ram of Titus, 114
Crémieux, French statesman of Hebrew birth, 282, 298
Cromwell brings Jews back to England, 192, 201
Cuneiform inscriptions, 36
Curse pronounced upon Spinoza, 224
Cyrus, the Mede, conquers Assyria, 54 ; restores Jews to Palestine, 57

D

Damascus, seat of a Syrian kingdom, 25 ; conquered by Assyria, 38 ; Jews persecuted at, in 1840, 281
David, conquests of, 20 ; the most popular poet in England, 311
Deborah inspires the Hebrews, 18
Dingelstedt, Franz, his anti-Semitic poem, 357
Dispersion of the Jews, 133
Disraeli, Benjamin, Earl of Beaconsfield, his assertion of Hebrew superiority, 2 ; his origin, a typical Jew, 305 ; his

INDEX. 373

entrance into Parliament, 306; his public career, devotion of his wife, 308; enthusiasm of, for his race, 310, 311
Disraeli, Isaac, father of Lord Beaconsfield, 305
Dominicans prominent in persecuting the Jews, 162
Domitius Sabinus, the centurion, at the siege of Jotapata, 99

E

Edomites subdued by Hebrews, 12
Edward I. banishes Jews from England, 192
Eleazar, brother of Judas Maccabæus, death of, 69
Elijah and Elisha protest against idolatries, 26
"Elijah," oratorio of Mendelssohn, 342
England, Jews in, 189, etc.
Essenes, a Jewish sect, 80
Ezra, restores the power of Israel, 58; establishes the canon, 75

F

False Messiahs, 216
Fasts and feasts, 84
Ferdinand, King of Spain, persecutes the Jews, 140; expatriates them, 158
Fichte influenced by Spinoza, 229
Finance, skill of Jews in, 237; not exceptionally sordid and harsh, 255, etc.
Fine Arts, Jews as cultivators of, 237
Flagellants destroy the Jews, 167
Florence, Jews at, 193
Fould, Achille, French statesman and financier of Hebrew birth, 298
France, Jews in, 197, etc.
Franke, famous in medicine, 238
Frankfort, Juden-gasse in, 166, 259

Friedrich Wilhelm IV. and Heine, 322
Froude and Spinoza, 230

G

Galilee, Romans attempt to conquer, 95, etc.
Gambetta, descended from Genoese Jews, 298; puts out an eye in his boyhood, 300; steps into fame in 1868, 300; in the Corps Législatif in 1870, 301; his astonishing energy, 302; his oratory, 303, 304
Gemara, combined with the Mischna to form the Talmud, 143
Germany, Jews in, in mediæval times, 165, etc.; in modern times, 239, 240; ridiculed by Heine, 321.
Gessius Florus, Roman procurator, attacks Jerusalem, 94; is defeated, 95
Gibbon sneers at the Jews, 202
Gideon, ancient Hebrew champion, 18
Goethe, his "Faust" quoted, 216; admirer of Spinoza, 229; friend of the Mendelssohns, 339
Goldwin Smith unjust to the Jews, 253
Göttingen, Heine's hatred for, 314
Grace Aguilar quoted, 154, 158
Graetz, Jewish historian, quoted, 161
Grimm, Jacob, studies of, in folklore, 210
Gugenheim, father-in-law of Moses Mendelssohn, 249

H

Halévy, Jewish musician, 237
Handicrafts, Jews restrained from, at the dispersion, 136; followed in Sicily, 195; Hebrew dislike of, in modern times, 236

Hanoukhah, feast of, its origin, 68, 84; celebrated by the Rothschilds, 260
Hazael, of Syria, conquered by Assyrians, 38
Hebrews, see Jews.
Hegel, admirer of Spinoza, 229
Heine, Heinrich, his "Rabbi of Bacharach," 167; admirer of Spinoza, 229; called by Matthew Arnold first German poet since Goethe, 238; with Börne in the Frankfort Juden-gasse, 260; with James Rothschild at Paris, 271; his origin and career, 312–317; his inconsistency, his descriptive power, 318; his wit and bitterness, 320; his frivolity, 32 2 ; analogues in English literature, 323; his poetic power and sweetness, 324, etc.; as voicing the Jewish heart, 327; before the Venus of Milo, 328, 329
Heine, Solomon, uncle of the poet, 313
Heliodorus tries to rob the Temple, 72
Hensel, Wilhelm, brother-in-law of Felix Mendelssohn, 335, 340, 346
"Hep! hep!" cry of the persecutors, 200, 356
Heptarchy, Jews under the, 189
Herod, rules Judea, 73; slays the children, 88
Herodians, Jewish sect, 79
Hesse Cassel, Landgrave of, and Rothschild, 259
Hezekiah, King of Judah, 39; his good reign, throws off the yoke of Assyria, 48
Hillel, Jewish teacher, 81
Hiram of Tyre and Solomon, 23
Holland, the refuge of the oppressed, 219

I

Idumæans, subdued by Judas Maccabæus, 68; come to defend Jerusalem against Titus, 110
"Ilse," poem of Heine, 324
Inquisition and the Jews, 155, etc.
"Iron Maiden," apparatus for torture, 156
Isaac the patriarch, 12
Isaac, ambassador of Charlemagne, 139
Isaac Arama, Jewish poet, quoted, 161
Isabella, queen of Spain, a persecutor, 140; assents to exile of the Jews, 158
Isaiah, the prophet, counsels Hezekiah, 52
Israel, kingdom of, 25; conquered by Assyria, 39
Israelites, see Jews.
Italy, Jews in, 193, etc.

J

Jacob the patriarch, 12
Jaddua, high-priest, meets Alexander the Great, 58
Jael slays Sisera, 18
Jehovah, Hebrew name for God, 16
Jephthah, ancient champion of Israel, 18
Jerusalem, founded, 22; embellished by Solomon, 23; sacked in time of Jeroboam by the Egyptians, 26; described, 102, etc.; besieged by Titus, 109, etc.; its capture and destruction, 119; visits of Sir Moses Montefiore to, 284, 289; the new town near the Jaffagate, 292
"Jerusalem," work of Moses Mendelssohn, 244
Jesus, of Nazareth, his birth, 86; in the Temple, baptism, 88; his temptation, gospel, passion, death, and resurrection, 89; his character the beauty of holiness, 92; in the legend of the Wandering Jew, 209

Jews, their assertion of superiority, 1; character of their literature, 3; tenacity as a race, 4, 5; their force and passion, 6; religious nature, 7; at their origin, 12; valor under David, 20; vigor declines, 22; the kingdoms of Judah and Israel, 25; force of, as shown in the struggle with Assyria, 32; at Nineveh, 41; their defiance of Sennacherib, 52; captives at Babylon, 57; restoration to Palestine, 58; contact with Aryans, 61; dispersion, 64; civilization in time of the Maccabees, 74; parties and sects, 75, etc.; oppressed and at last crushed by Rome, 94, etc.; their spiritual conquest of the Aryans, 126, etc.; dispersion 133; temper rarely conciliatory, 134; how they became traders, 136; their services in commerce, 137; contact with the Moslems, 138; enter Spain, 138; at the Renaissance, 139; favored by the Saracens, and by Charlemagne, 139; persecuted in later times, 140; in Spain, 152; insincere converts, 153; a Hebrew shrine, 154; before the Inquisition, 155, etc.; driven out of Spain, 158, etc.; in other lands, 160; lamentations over Spain, 161; an auto-da-fé, 162, etc.; in Germany, 165, etc.; lightly touched by the Black Death, 167; picture of their mediæval life, 168, etc; in England, protected by early Plantagenets, 189; Richard Cœur de Lion persecutes, massacre at York, 190, etc.; driven out by Edward I., 192; restored by Cromwell, 192; drowning of, near London Bridge, 192; in Venice, Florence, Genoa, and Papal states, 193; at Rome, 194; in Southern Italy and Sicily, 195, 196; in France, under Philip Augustus and St. Louis, 197; sufferings from the "Pastoureaux," in time of the "Black Death," 198; become chattels, 200; badges, narrowness of Protestants, 201; of unbelievers, 202; sometimes retaliate, 203; as typified in Shylock, 204, etc.; in the Wandering Jew, 208, etc.; intolerance and unamiability of, 215; false Messiahs, 216; enthusiasm for Sabbatäi Zevi, 217; they seek refuge in Holland, 219; respect for the Cabala, 222; the persecution of Spinoza, 223, etc.; total number and distribution, of at present, their eminence, 235; seldom soldiers, farmers, or artisans, 236; as financiers, as artists, 237; as philosophers and scholars, 238; their degradation in Germany, 239; influence of Moses Mendelssohn, 240, etc.; their distrust of him, 245; as business men; 254; their ill-repute undeserved, 255, etc.; their genius for affairs, 276; persecuted in the Levant in 1840, 281; helped in Palestine and elsewhere by Montefiore, 283; in Morocco, 288; incited to work in Palestine by Montefiore, 290, 291; as statesmen, 295; Disraeli's enthusiasm for, 310, 311; find a voice in Heine, 312, 327; dreaded for their energy and power, 355, etc.; their inveterate scorn, 357; curious customs of, 358, etc.; cemetery at Newport, 359, 360; in Poland, 360, etc.; "measuring the boundaries," 361; treatment of apostates, 364; compared with Yankees, 366; described by F. Adler, 367; orthodox nucleus,

368; reformers, 368, 369; promise of a better day, 369
Joachim, Jewish musician, 237
John the Baptist and Jesus of Nazareth, 88
John of Giscala defends Jerusalem against Titus, 110, etc.; dies in prison, 119
John Hyrcanus, descendant of the Maccabees, 71
Jonathan, son of Saul, 20
Jonathan, brother of Judas Maccabæus, 70
Joseph, son of Jacob, 12
Joseph, husband of Mary, 86
Josephus, commands in Galilee, 45; the prisoner of Vespasian, 100; counsels the defenders of Jerusalem to yield, 115; value of his history, he follows Titus to Rome, 121
Joshua, an ancient champion, 18
Joshua, the priest, surrenders the Temple treasures to Titus, 118
Jotapata, defended by Josephus against Vespasian, 95, etc.
Judah, kingdom of, 25; invaded by Sennacherib, 49
Judas Maccabæus, defeats Apollonius, Seron, and Lysias, 65, 66; his later career, 67, 68; his death, 69; his burial at Modin, 70
Juden-gasse, at Frankfort, 166; birthplace of the Rothschilds, 258; Heine's account of, 260; his association with, 313

K

Kant, Immanuel, his tribute to the "Jerusalem" of Moses Mendelssohn, 245
Karaites, Jewish sect rejecting the Talmud, 148

L

Lamego, Portuguese ancestor of Sir Moses Montefiore, 280
Lasker, German statesman of Hebrew birth, 296

Lavater, his connection with Moses Mendelssohn, 245; his description of Mendelssohn, 249
Law given on Sinai, 14; written, included in the canon, 76; origin of, 76; scrolls of, 155, 184, 194
Layard, his Assyrian discoveries, 36
Leah Rendar, story of, 363
Leibnitz, his treatment of Spinoza, 229
Lessing admires Spinoza and spreads his fame, 229; friend of Moses Mendelssohn, 243; his "Nathan the Wise," 251, etc.
Libraries, cities as, 33; destruction at Alexandria, 55
Literature, Jews in, 238
Lombard traders, 193
London Bridge, Jews drowned near, 192
Longfellow, his "Sandalphon," 146; "Jewish Cemetery at Newport," 359, 360
"Lorelei," poem of Heine, 326
Lost tribes of Israel, 39, 133
Louis IX. (St. Louis) persecutes the Hebrews, 140, 197
Louis XVIII. helped by Rothschild, 269
Louis Philippe helped to the throne by Rothschilds, 270
Lucius, Roman soldier at the siege of Jerusalem, 120
Ludwig II., of Bavaria, and Heine, 322
Luther intolerant toward Jews, 140, 201
Lysias defeated by Judas Maccabæus, 67

M

Maccabees, their origin, 64; their career, 65, etc.; the power of the successors of Judas, 70
Macedonians, contact of, with the Jews, 63

Maria Theresa, unfriendly to Hebrews, 140
Mary, the mother of Jesus, 86
Massena, Marshal, his Jewish origin, 236
Mattathias, founder of the line of the Maccabees, 64; slays Appeles, 65; death and burial at Modin, 66
Matterhorn in the legend of the Wandering Jew, 213
Maurice, F. D., admirer of Spinoza, 230
Maximilian, Emperor, at Niegesehenburg, 180
"Measuring the bounds," picturesque custom, 361, etc.
Meissner, German poet, friend of Heine, quoted, 328, 364
Menasseh ben Israel obtains from Cromwell the restoration of Jews to England, 192
Mendelssohn, Abraham, son of Moses and father of Felix, 332; his letter as to the religious education of his children, 334; his death, 349
Mendelssohn, Dorothea, daughter of Moses, marries Veit, her connection with Friedrich Schlegel, 331, 332
Mendelssohn, Fanny, daughter of Abraham, 333; marries Wilhelm Hensel, 335; her home in Berlin, 337, 345; letters, 348, 349; death, 352
Mendelssohn - Bartholdy, Felix, his birth, 332; his precocity, 335; his boyhood in Berlin, 339; his early success, 340; character of his music, his fame in England, appearance, 342; described in "Charles Auchester," 343; with Victoria and Prince Albert, 350, etc.; letters on death of his father and sister Fanny, 352, 353; his death, 352
Mendelssohn, Joseph, son of Moses, 332

Mendelssohn, Leah Salomon, wife of Abraham, 333; her letter to her daughter's lover, 336
Mendelssohn, Moses, his birth and education, 242; his literary work, 243; his breadth of spirit, 244; his attachment to Judaism, 245; his letter to Lavater, 246, etc.; his death, 248; his wooing, 249, 250; portrayed in "Nathan the Wise," 251; his fine spirit and beautiful influence, 368, 369
Mendelssohn, Paul, 339, 347
Mendelssohn, Rebecca, 345
Mesopotamia under the Assyrians, 40
Messiah expected, 85
Meyerbeer, Jewish composer, 237
"Midsummer Night's Dream," overture to, by Mendelssohn, 338
Mischna, combined with the Gemara to form the Talmud, 81, 142
Moabites subdued by Israel, 12
Modin, home of the Maccabees, 64
Montefiore, Judith, wife of Sir Moses, her diary, 283, etc.
Montefiore, Sir Moses, a typical Jew, 278; his ancestry and early career, 280; his philanthropic journeys, 281; at Damascus, 282; in Palestine and Russia, 283; enters Jerusalem, 286; his strength in age, 288; at Morocco, 289; incites the Jews to industry and thrift, 290; his breadth of mind, 292; his widespread fame, personal appearance, orthodoxy, 293; belief in the restoration of the Jews to the Holy Land, 294
Moors, see Saracens
Moriah, Mount, site of the Temple, 103
Morocco, Montefiore visits, 288
Moscheles, Jewish composer, 237

Moses, the ancient lawgiver and leader, 14
Moslem contact with Hebrews, 138

N

Napoleon I. frees Jews temporarily, 313; admired and described by Heine, 319
Napoleon III. and Gambetta, 300, 301
"Nathan the Wise," drama of Lessing, 251, etc.
"New Christians," insincere converts from Judaism, 153
Niegesebenburg, a mediæval German city, 179
Nineveh, see Assyria
Nonotte, wife of Heine, 323; lines to, 325
Novalis on Spinoza, 229
Nuremberg, torture-chamber at, 155

O

O'Connell, Daniel, and Disraeli, 306
Odin, connection with the legend of the Wild Huntsman, 210
"Old Lady of the Damm Thor," mother of Heine, 323
Old Testament, origin of, 76
Oppenheim, German statesman of Jewish birth, 296
Oxford, insult to the cross at, 203

P

Palestine, physical description of, 9, 10, 12; conquered by Assyria, 38; Montefiore's work in, 290
Passover, the feast of, 84; its celebration in mediæval times, 169
Pastoureaux in France persecute Jews, 198
Paul, conversion of, 90
Pedanius, Roman horseman at Jerusalem, 120

Pentecost, feast of, 84
Pereire, Isaac and Émile, railroad kings of France, 276, etc.
"Phædo," work of Moses Mendelssohn, 243
Pharisees, 78; their tenets, 79
Philip Augustus, of France, persecutes the Jews, 197
Philip the Fair, of France, persecutes the Jews, 198
Philistines as conquerors, 18; as conquered, 20
Philosophy, eminence of Jews in, 238
Phœnicians, contact with Jews, 23; subjected by Assyria, 47
"Pilgrimage to Kevlaar," poem of Heine, 317
Poland, Jews in, 360
Pompey takes Jerusalem, 73
Popes, their changing policy toward the Jews, 194
Portugal, cruelties in, 160
Prince Albert and Felix Mendelssohn, 350, etc.
Prophets, account of, 22
Protestants intolerant of Jews, 201
Punch on the conversion of the Jews, 155
Puritans intolerant of Jews, 201

R

Rabbi Abraham, story of, 168, etc.
Rachel, Jewish actress, 238
Rahel, wife of Varnhagen von Ense, her salon at Berlin, 313
Rationalist idea of the Jews, 3, etc.
Renan, admirer of Spinoza, 230
Rhodes, Jews persecuted at, in 1840, 281
Ricardo, political economist of Hebrew birth, 254
Richard Cœur de Lion persecutes the Jews, 140, 190
Romans, first contact of, with the Jews in time of Judas

/ *N D E X.*

Maccabæus, 70; their coming to Palestine, 73; their oppression of the Jews, 94; under Vespasian and Titus, they crush Palestine, 95, etc.
Rome, Jews in, 193
Rothschild, Baron Alphonse, and Napoleon III., 272
Rothschild, Baron James, at Paris, 268; helps Louis XVIII., 269; helps Louis Philippe, his brusqueness, 270; his fear of Heine, 271
Rothschild, Baron Lionel, London, 268
Rothschild, Meyer Anselm, founder of the house, in Frankfort Juden-gasse, 258; the Landgrave of Hesse Cassel, 260; wife of, 261; her attachment to the Juden-gasse, 262; their five sons, 262
Rothschild, Nathan Meyer, goes to London, 262; at Waterloo, 263; his great speculation, 264; his death, 267
Rubenstein, Jewish musician, 237
Russia, large Jewish population of, 235; testimony to their ability, 283; diplomacy of, guided by Jews, 295

S

Sabbatäi Zevi, a false Messiah, 216, etc.
Sadducees, origin of, 77; their tenets, 78
Samaria, capital of Israel, 26; conquered by Assyria, 38; people of, 82; cursed by the Jews, 83
"Sam'l of Posen," popular play, 367
Samson, ancient champion, 18
Samuel, the prophet, 20
"Sandalphon," the legend versified from the Talmud by Longfellow, 146
Saracens and Jews, 138, 203

Sarah, wife of Rabbi Abraham, story of, 169, etc.
Saul, king of Israel, 20
Savonarola unfriendly to the Jews, 140
Schlegel, Friedrich, and Dorothea Mendelssohn, 331
Schleiermacher, his tribute to Spinoza, 230
Science, distinction of Jews in, 238
Seleucidæ oppress the Jews, 64
Semiramis, legend of, 29
Semites, origin of, 12
Sennacherib, his accession, 39; his palace at Nineveh, 46; attacks Judah, 48; his magnificent array, 49, etc.; destruction of, 53
Sephardim, a name for the Spanish Israelites, 152; give birth to Spinoza, 220; to Disraeli, 305
Septuagint, how prepared, 76
Seraphael, a name for Felix Mendelssohn, 343
Seron defeated by Judas Maccabæus, 66
Shelley inspired by Spinoza, 230
Shylock, what he might have heard on the Rialto, 204, 205; palliation for his cruelty, 206; Heine's portrayal of, 206, etc.
Sicily, Jews in, 195
Simon, son of Gioras, defends Jerusalem against Titus, 111, etc; slain at Rome, 123
Sisebut, Visigothic king of Spain, 152; Jews rise against, 203.
Sisera slain by Jaël, 18
Solomon, his splendor and wisdom, 22; his folly, 25
Spain, Jews in, 152, etc.
Spinoza, his high and pure spirit, 219; falsely accused of atheism, 220; his origin and childhood at Amsterdam, 220; his precocity, revolts at the Cabala, 222; escapes assassination, but is excommunicated, 223; the

curse pronounced upon him, 224, 225; his magnanimity, polishes crystals for a livelihood, 225; his catholicity, his death, 226; his philosophy outlined, his humanity, 227, 228; history of his fame, 229; his present supremacy, 230; tribute to his worth, 231

Standing Men in the ancient Temple service, 83

Stephen, Paul at the stoning of, 90

Stöcker, German anti-Semitic leader, 356

"St. Paul," oratorio of Mendelssohn, 342

T

Tabernacle, description of, 18
Tabernacles, feast of, 84
Taine, admirer of Spinoza, 230
Talmud, its origin, 141; the Mischna and Gemara, 142, 143; subtleties of the rabbis, value of, 143; its incoherency, 144; its wisdom and beauty, 145, 146; its hygienic value, 148
Targums, Aremaic paraphrases of Scripture, 76
Temple of Solomon, building and consecration of, 23, 24; rebuilding of, after captivity at Babylon, 57; in the time of Titus, 103; destruction of, by the Romans, 118
Tenth legion at the siege of Jerusalem, 112
Titus storms Jotapata, 99; advances upon Jerusalem, 108; his army, 109; his narrow escape, 111; besieges the city, 112, etc.; his victory, 119; his triumph, 121, etc.; the arch of, 124
Torah, see Law
Torquemada, as grand inquisitor, persecutes the Jews, 159

Tribes of Israel, their position on the march, 16
Turks, their comparative humanity to the Jews, 159; their treatment of Sabbatäi Zevi, 218

V

Varnhagen von Ense and Heine, 313
Venus of Milo, Heine in presence of, 328, 329
Vespasian, besieges Jotapata, 95, etc.; becomes emperor, 100; at the triumph of Titus, 121
Victoria, Queen, and Felix Mendelssohn, 350, etc.
Visigoths and Jews, 152
Voltaire harsh toward Jews, 202

W

Wagner, his futile effort to bring the Jews to confusion, 238
Wandering Jew, different versions of the legend, Cartaphilus or Ahasuerus, 208; his pilgrimage, 209; becomes blended with the Wild Huntsman, 210, etc.; before the Matterhorn, 213
Wellington, his dislike of the Rothschilds, 266
Werner, Saint, his shrine on the Rhine, 168
Wild Huntsman becomes blended with the Wandering Jew, 210, etc.
William the Conqueror protects the Jews, 189.
William Rufus befriends the Jews, 189
Woistes, mediæval German town, Jews at, 168, etc.

Y

Yankee and Jew, 366
York, tragedy at, 190, etc.

Z

Zadikim, division among the Jews, 77

Zealots, a Jewish sect, 79; at the siege of Jerusalem, 110

Zion, symbol of Hebrew nation, 1; the ark finds a sanctuary there in the time of David; at the time of the siege by the Romans, 102

www.ingramcontent.com/pod-product-compliance
Lightning Source LLC
Chambersburg PA
CBHW051245300426
44114CB00011B/897